1E674

INDUSTRIAL GEOGRAPHY

INDUSTRIAL GEOGRAPHY

By

R. C. RILEY
Portsmouth Polytechnic

1973

CHATTO & WINDUS

LONDON

Published by
Chatto & Windus Ltd
42 William IV Street
London WC2N 4DF

★

Clarke, Irwin & Co. Ltd
Toronto

ISBN 0 7011 1955 1

© R. C. Riley 1973

Printed in Great Britain by
Butler and Tanner Ltd
Frome & London

CONTENTS

MAPS AND DIAGRAMS

FOREWORD

Simply defined, industrial geography is the study of the distribution of manufacturing industry. One approach is to account for differences in the development of particular industries as between nations. This is useful in the case of an activity such as shipbuilding where the leading nation, Japan, lies outside the world's industrial core of the U.S.A. and Western Europe. An alternative and more profitable approach is to analyse the distribution of industries within a smaller area, for example, a nation or region. Industrial geography then becomes the relatively precise study of the distribution of factories that collectively make up an industry. By considering the distribution of many plants in several industrial areas or nations, it becomes possible to formulate general principles of location. Technological and economic considerations cause the iron and steel and brewing industries, for instance, to take up the same pattern of location in the U.S.A., Great Britain and West Germany, and the nation in which a plant is found is a less important consideration than the factors governing the location of the industry of which the plant is part.

Industry is made up of many individual industries, each with their own locational characteristics. This sometimes results in industries being treated in isolation from each other, when in fact they can all be fitted into a general framework or hierarchy. The hierarchy adopted in this book has five components. The first and second consist of those industries which are orientated to their source of materials or power. Others cannot so readily be classified, for some of their constituent plants exhibit material or power orientation, while others are at markets or break of bulk sites. Such industries—iron and steel is an example—are termed multi-locational. The fourth component is the market-oriented industries, and the footloose industries, capable of locating anywhere within manufacturing areas, complete the hierarchy. A complete chapter is devoted to each category of industry, and the method is to examine a few industries in considerable detail so that the reader is better able to grasp the principles of location than would be possible were a more superficial approach adopted. An introductory chapter considers the models of industrial location which have been advanced as theoretical explanations of reality, and where they are relevant these models are used in the

analysis of the different categories of industry considered in the subsequent chapters.

Such have been the changes in the content of geographical teaching
in schools over the past decade that what was formerly regarded as
university work is now being introduced for 'A' Level study. This applies
in particular to the first chapter of this book, but in any case the theoretical material presented has been simplified, and if the diagrams and text
are followed closely there is no reason why it should not be understood
by those who are not yet undergraduates. For those following College of
Education and degree courses the book should provide a useful background
and act as an introduction to the more detailed studies referred to in the
references at the end of each chapter.

The production of a book necessarily involves a large number of people
and this one is no exception. I am most grateful to the many in industry
who have provided information and offered advice, and to colleagues with
whom so many issues have been discussed. Two people above all have
been of inestimable assistance. Both John Bradbeer and Robert Jackson
have not only produced large quantities of data, but by exercising their
critical faculties and suggesting approaches they have made the task of
composition both speedier and easier. I hope the finished work meets their
own high standards. The project has proceeded with the constant en-
couragement of the Editor of the series, Professor Emrys Jones, to whom
I owe a special debt of gratitude. Finally, but by no means least, I would
like to acknowledge the services of the staff of the Cartographic Unit of
the Department of Geography, Portsmouth Polytechnic in general, and
Jack Render in particular, for their ability to transform the roughest of
sketches into the most polished of maps and diagrams.

Chapter 1

THE THEORY OF THE LOCATION
OF INDUSTRY

The distribution of manufacturing industry does not at first glance appear to follow any simple and readily applicable law as is the case with the provision of shops and services such as schools and hospitals. Here there is a very strong link with population size, so that large towns have a much wider range of goods and services than smaller centres. Indeed we expect to find shops with a very large range of goods in a metropolis as much as we anticipate their absence in rural villages. Large cities do have a wider range of industrial activities than small towns, but the largest city seldom if ever includes all industries among its activities, because many industries seem to grow up in certain towns, giving rise to specialization. The existence of highly specialized industrial centres, such as the Lancashire cotton and Yorkshire woollen and worsted towns, undermine the application of the size–function relationships, as it is known, to manufacturing, because towns of their size 'ought' to exhibit much greater diversification. Equally, the presence of specialist towns prevents the largest city from possessing the wide range of industrial activity that theory would predict.

Specific data on the size–function relationship for manufacturing industry has been provided by Alexandersson.[1] He investigated 864 United States cities of more than 10 000 inhabitants, and recognised 20 service industry groups and 16 manufacturing industry groups. He found that the service industries were present in all towns, but that only three manufacturing industries—construction, printing and publishing, and food processing—were similarly ubiquitous. Even though these three industries were to be found in all cities, they were nevertheless unevenly developed as between cities. The remaining 13 industries occurred in very few cities and no correlation with the size of settlement was evident. Since collectively these 13 sporadically distributed industries account for most manufacturing, attempts to relate the distribution of industry to the size of settlement are not especially fruitful. The United States motor vehicle industry represents an extreme case of sporadic manufacturing industry. Vehicle production is absent from more than half the cities but important in very few. Some of the latter are small towns, for example, Flint, Michigan, the headquarters of the Buick Motor Corporation.

1.1 LOCATION FACTORS IN MANUFACTURING INDUSTRY

The problems involved in accounting for the distribution of industry have not prevented a number of theories of location from being advanced. However, before considering the main theoretical aspects of location, it is useful to summarise briefly the principal influences, or location factors, at work, since these are central to most theoretical considerations.

MATERIALS INCLUDING SOURCES OF ENERGY

The essential function of industrial activity is the transformation of material or materials into a product which is of greater value than the original material(s). In the capitalist world the profit deriving from the transforming process provides the incentive for the existence of the activity. It is important to recognise that the great bulk of manufacturing is concerned with the processing of materials that have already been transformed earlier in the production process, and that the significance of industries that actually use the raw materials of the extractive industries —mining, agriculture and forestry—is diminishing. The products of the extractive industries do not occur uniformly over the surface of the earth, but are sporadically distributed, while their quality, quantity and cost are variable. So too is the cost of moving them to industry. It is these raw materials rather than the semi-finished producer goods that exercise a real influence on industrial location. Firstly, they have a low value in relation to their weight (unit value), so that transport costs are high. Secondly, there is frequently considerable weight-loss in processing, and manufacturers will save on transport costs by locating close to the resource. Thirdly, they normally make up a relatively high proportion of the cost of the product; for example materials, including coke, make up 78% of the value of the pig iron produced in the blast furnaces in Great Britain. Not surprisingly industries using these materials must keep their transport costs to a minimum, and as a result are said to be transport-oriented. Since more than one material is normally employed, a location where transport costs on all materials are at a minimum, such as a port or other break-of-bulk point, is a frequent solution.

MARKETS

The term 'market' does not only imply the final consumption point of a manufactuered good, but also the consumer of semi-finished goods. The population of London represents an important market for motor cars, but the vehicle industry itself is a market for components from the engineering and other industries. Two of the three points made in respect of materials are relevant to products to explain much of the attraction of markets. Thus low unit-value products will cause the manufacturer to keep transport costs to a minimum. Secondly, an increase in weight or bulk during processing, as in brewing and furniture manufacture on the latter count, is conducive to a market location. Put another way, where the cost of moving the product represents a high proportion of the value of that product, there are advantages in a market location. Other benefits include the possibility of delivering perishable goods rapidly, the opportunity of consultation where items are made to the consumer's specification, the speed with which servicing can be carried out, the presence of a large pool of labour (mechanisation has reduced the immobility of labour as between different industries), and the availability of materials such as scrap iron for steel production or waste paper for paper mills.

TRANSPORT COSTS

From what has been said, it might be thought that location at material sources or markets is a function of the relationship between transport costs on materials and products; higher unit transport costs on materials than on products will result in material-orientation and vice versa. To a large extent this is true of the transport-oriented industries, which have to face transport costs of up to 30% of total costs, but the principle has rather less relevance for most manufacturing because transport costs are usually less than 4% of total costs. Industries employing advanced technologies, for example electronic products manufacture, which is able to assemble its materials for 0·25% of its total costs, are virtually unrestricted by transport cost considerations. Improvements in transport techniques, investigated more fully in Chapter 2, have also helped to diminish the importance of transport as a location factor.

Transport costs are subject to various distorting influences which make particular regions or sites more than normally attractive to manufacturers. Perhaps the most obvious is the relative cheapness of water transport for the movement of bulky low unit-value goods, thereby favouring the growth of industry at ports, riverine and canal-side sites. Where water transport competes with rail transport, the latter is obliged to retaliate by lowering its charges to the benefit of plants along the route; an example is the New York State Barge Canal, New York City in particular benefiting from the competition. An interesting case is that of steel deliveries by rail from Hamilton, Ontario, to Regina, Saskatchewan, and Vancouver, British Columbia; the freight rate to Regina is 243 cents per 45 kg/100 lb, but the charge to Vancouver is only 110 cents—a result of competition at Vancouver from ocean freighters using the Panama Canal.[2] Where there is a preponderance of traffic in one direction on a transport route, freight rates on the underutilised return haul are often very low indeed. The rate for moving coal from Toledo on Lake Erie to Duluth is half that charged for iron ore moving in the reverse direction, and was a major factor in the establishment of an iron and steel plant at Duluth. Low unit-value commodities are charged very low freight rates while valuable cargoes are rated above the ordinary level; the effect here is to encourage manufacture at markets. Governments sometimes use freight rates as a means of regional development; examples are legion, but we may note the 10 to 50% reduction in freight charges on machinery moving into the Italian problem area, the South, from other areas of Italy.

LABOUR

A major characteristic of labour is that it is immobile in the short run, thus allowing areal differentiation in quality or skill, numerical availability and in cost (wages). Since labour accounts for up to 60% of total costs in some industries, for example, textiles, it is to be expected that it provides an important locational influence. Although mechanisation is rapidly reducing the need for a high degree of skill, there are some sectors of manufacturing characterised by small capital investment, short production runs, and by a small size of firm—cutlery, furniture and clothing, for instance—where craftsmanship is still a vital requirement. The existing production centres thus exercise an attraction for new entrants to these industries. The best labour supply areas in numerical terms are normally important markets, reinforcing the significance of the latter. It has been a notable feature of the last half century that old-established declining industrial areas with high unemployment rates have proved to be of little interest to manufacturers until government policies have made them additionally attractive. It would seem that labour availability, on its own, is not a powerful locational influence. National wage rates have reduced areal cost differences, although an outstanding example of change largely caused by labour cost differentials is presented by the United States cotton textile industry, which has almost entirely vacated its original New England location in favour of the South.

ECONOMIES OF LARGE-SCALE PRODUCTION

In any industry, large plants have advantages over small plants by virtue of their ability, firstly, to carry a larger supply of materials needed to ensure a steady flow of output, secondly, to even out more easily imbalances between processes, and thirdly, to benefit more from bulk purchases of materials, energy and services. Technological considerations in production processes dictate the most efficient size of plant for each industry. These economies of scale determine whether an industry will be characterised by small, medium or large plants; hence the most efficient steel plant is very much larger than the most efficient furniture plant. It follows that large plants will have a large share of national output, and small plants the reverse. Indeed, theoretically, only three or four typewriter plants are required to meet the entire United States' demand, while 500 meat-packing plants are needed to supply the same country. Small plants exhibit a dispersed pattern of distribution, but large plants must concentrate in the major market areas. Technological change is gradually allowing plants to become larger, thereby increasing the degree of concentration in most favoured areas such as the manufacturing belt of the U.S.A.

EXTERNAL ECONOMIES OF SCALE

Having achieved its most efficient size in terms of its internal technological structure, a plant may be able to enjoy cost savings from sources external to itself in the vicinity. The presence of specialised suppliers, specialist servicing agencies, organised markets and brokers, the possibility of joint research, the availability of particular labour and management skills, and technical education facilities, coupled with superior transport services following the size of the agglomeration, all make a valuable cost contribution. Existing industrial areas are able to offer useful external economies to new plants which may rely heavily on outside specialists in their early stages, while these new plants themselves improve the external economies available to older firms. External economies help to explain the survival of old-established industrial areas which are then said to exhibit geographical inertia. This may be regarded as the ability of an area to retain its industrial activity after the disappearance of the original locating factors. The locational effect of external economies is to strengthen the tendencies to market orientation, thus providing a further explanation for the growth of large cities.

External economies provide a powerful reason for the existence of highly specialised industrial areas which partly invalidate the size–function relationship for industry. Plants in the same industry, but performing different operations and exhibiting a high degree of interdependence, will sometimes cluster like a swarm of bees, with little reference to the economic environment. The cluster possesses great external economies for the industry concerned and thus great attraction for new plants. The Birmingham-Black Country is an excellent example of swarming in the metal industries, illustrating the five types of linkage between plants: (a) vertical, where different plants carry out different processes in the production of an item, (b) convergent, where different plants produce components which are later assembled to form the finished product, (c) diagonal, where a plant provides a service for others, (d) indirect, where plants not necessarily in the metal trades benefit from the existence of the swarm, and (e) information linkage, or the exchange of new techniques and production methods and of information concerning suppliers and consumers. It has to be observed that external economies are not the original cause of industrial agglomerations, they only account for their continued existence.

OTHER FACTORS

(a) Government activity, in the form of financial subsidies for industrial development in declining areas, coupled with restrictions on growth in prospering regions, is perhaps the most important of the remaining influences on industrial location. Regional development has become an accepted part of governmental policy in the countries of Western Europe and elsewhere. If direct intervention, as in the control of major industries like coal, steel, gas and electricity, is included, political influence on the distribution of industry can be seen to be considerable. (b) Site costs are instrumental in causing the 'suburbanisation' of industry since manufacturing can seldom afford the rents of near city-centre sites. (c) Capital from private sources has always shown a marked preference for growth areas, hence the need for governmental finance for declining areas. (d) Entrepreneurial ability, enshrined in the 'Ford-Detroit' or 'Morris-Oxford' problem, has been responsible for the creation of industrial complexes at one of half a dozen apparently similar locations. Decision-making and entrepreneurship are now studied under the heading of 'behaviour'.

Not only is there a large number of locational influences at work, but their strength can vary through time. These influences can also have a different impact upon different plants in the same industry, and there is support for the argument that there is a unique set of forces influencing the location of each individual plant. Location theorists take the opposite view, however, and endeavour to isolate general principles to account for the distribution of manufacturing. General principles do not seek to explain all occurrences, indeed they may only relate to particular areas of economic activity, but it is preferable to have a theory that will explain a large proportion of occurrences rather than a complete absence of theory. Without generalisations industrial geography would become an exercise in the compilation of pointless inventories, and would hardly constitute a thorough-going academic discipline. Location theorists fall into five main groups: the least cost school, the transport cost school, the market area school, the marginal location school and the behavioural school.

1.2 THE LEAST COST SCHOOL

ALFRED WEBER

The first major attempt at the formulation of a general theory of the location of manufacturing was made by Alfred Weber, whose work, *Theory of the Location of Industries*, was published in 1909. In essence Weber's theory is based on the assumption that the need to minimise costs, above all transport costs, is the most important locational consideration; if this can be achieved there will automatically follow a demand for the product. Even though Weber wrote about 19th-century industry in which low unit-value materials and products were more important than today, the assumption that price and demand are not significant in themselves is not something we can easily accept. Nevertheless Weber introduced many new ideas and much subsequent work has been based, at least in part, on his model. For this reason it is justifiable to look at his work in some detail.

In endeavouring to build a general 'pure theory' of location, that is one that is applicable to any industry in any economic or political system, Weber accepts only those influences that seem to have universal application irrespective of economic and political circumstances. Consequently, both local and central governmental activity are excluded from consideration. The cost of capital is disregarded because variations in interest rates are the result of institutional factors which vary between nations, for example, as between socialist and capital countries. Climate and entrepreneurship are discounted on the grounds that they affect too few industrial locations to warrant their inclusion. Weber concludes that there are only three general factors of location: transport costs, labour costs and agglomerating forces. Transport and labour costs he regards as general regional factors, which influence location over broad areas. Transport costs represent the most powerful determinant, providing the basic orientation of industry. Labour costs are what he terms the 'first distortion' of the transport-oriented system of industrial location. Agglomeration is classed as a general local factor which causes concentration at particular points as a result of external economies; it represents the second distortion. 'Deglomeration'—those set of forces causing dispersal from a manufacturing concentration, for example, high site cost—is considered with agglomeration. Weber accepts that there may be variation in material and energy costs at different locations, but in order to simplify the analysis, these are included with transport cost.

Thus, when material or energy costs are higher at one point than another, this situation is treated as though the location is more remote than the others. We see that, with the exception of the economies of large-scale production, Weber considers all the location factors discussed in the earlier part of the chapter. Whether he assigns to them what we would now consider to be adequate weight is, however, another matter.

(i) *The assumptions of Weber's model*

Acknowledging that reality is complex, Weber makes certain 'simplifying assumptions' in order to understand the operation of the basic causal factors. By this method the latter factors are isolated from factors that Weber considers to be of secondary importance. The less significant issues, initially held constant, are than reintroduced into the model to engender realism. His preliminary assumptions are:

(a) Uniformity of cultural, economic (technological) and political systems in a given area which has a uniform climate.

(b) Predetermined distribution of materials including energy sources. He comments that this has validity in the case of minerals, for example, but not of manufactured goods which are producer goods.

(c) Predetermined points of consumption. Here the assumption is that each plant sells to one given market. He does concede that in practice the distribution of manufacturing influences the pattern of consumption.

(d) Predetermined distribution of labour whose wages are fixed, but not necessarily at the same level, at each location, while the supply of labour at this fixed cost is unlimited. Complete immobility of labour is implied.

(e) Transport costs are a function of weight and distance, increasing in direct proportion to the length of the haul and the weight of the load. Considerations such as the size of the shipment, the nature of the goods, characteristics of the terrain and the intensity of usage of the track are handled by adjustments to transport costs. This was in fact the method employed by German railways at the time.

Having made these assumptions, Weber then sets out to discover the least transport cost location for the manufacture of one product at one plant. Products of different quality, though similar in nature, are treated as different products. The influence of labour, the 'first distortion', is then introduced into the model, and finally adjustment is made to allow for the 'second distortion', agglomeration.

(ii) *The search for the point of minimum transport cost*

The solution Weber adopts is principally to use geometric shapes. By constructing straight lines between the sources of the materials, including energy, required to manufacture the product, and the market at which it is sold, a 'locational figure' is created. A 3-point case of one raw material, one energy source and one market results in a locational triangle, within which the plant will be sited. A simple 2-point case of one material and one market causes the locational figure to shrink to a straight line, somewhere along which the plant will take up a position. Whether the factory will be at a material source, at the market, or at an intermediary point will depend on two factors. Firstly, the distribution pattern of the materials, which either are to be found everywhere and are termed 'ubiquities' (for example, water and wood), or are 'localised' (for example mineral deposits). Secondly, the extent to which the materials employed lose weight in processing. 'Pure' materials such as yarn woven into cloth experience no weight-loss, but 'gross' materials lose at least some of their weight: coal and low-grade copper ore are excellent

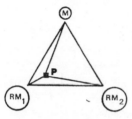

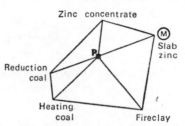

Fig. 1 The locational
triangle

Fig. 2 A locational polygon: the
example of zinc smelting

examples. Weight-loss is significant because in a model where location is a function of transport costs, these costs will be minimised by manufacturing as close as possible to the localised weight-losing material. When more than one such material is employed, the point of minimum transport cost may be at an intermediate point, but closest to that material exhibiting greatest weight-loss.

Fig. 1 is a locational triangle comprising two localised weight-losing materials and one market. The plant P is at its point of least transport cost, and the length of the lines drawn from the three apices to P is inversely proportional to the attraction exercised by the materials, RM_1 and RM_2, and the market, M. In other words, the short line between RM_1 and P indicates that RM_1 is a strongly weight-losing material, and because of the need to keep transport costs down it has a powerful pull on P. It is unusual for a plant to possess only two material sources and one market. However, the Weberian system can easily be expanded to deal with any number of points (the n-point case). Fig. 2, a locational figure representing a typical U.S. zinc-smelting plant with one market, is an example of a 5-point case. Here again the length of the lines drawn to

P is inversely proportional to the cost of movement. For more complex locational problems, Weber would use the Varignon frame shown in Fig. 3. Weights equivalent to the unit transport cost of each component are suspended by threads which run over rollers at the edge of the frame. The threads are tied together at their other end, representing the plant P. Wherever P comes to rest, this is equilibrium, and the point of least production cost. The Varignon frame is known as a mechanical or force table analogue model.

An indication of the degree to which a plant will be oriented towards its materials or towards its market can be obtained by the calculation of a 'material index'. The material index (MI) is the ratio of the weight of localised materials to the weight of one unit of output. Thus for every ton of pig iron produced at a blast furnace, approximately 4 tons of localised materials are used, giving a MI of 4 (inputs/outputs $= 4/1 = 4$),

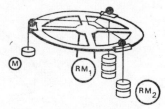

Fig. 3 The Varignon frame

and indicating the degree of material-orientation exhibited by blast furnaces. Where the MI is greater than 1 there is material-orientation, where it is less than 1 market-orientation ensues, and when it is equal to 1 location at the material source, the market or an intermediate site is possible. A plant using pure materials will always have a MI of 1.

Weber illustrates his argument with a number of cases using different combinations of materials in respect of their distribution and weight-loss characteristics. (a) The use of ubiquities only will cause the locational figure to be reduced to a single point, the market, because the selection of this point will make transport unnecessary. (b) The use of localised pure materials alone or with ubiquities. A single pure material allows the plant to locate at the source, the market or at a point between the two, since transport charges will be identical in each case. If an ubiquitous gross material is used in conjunction with the pure material, production will be effected at the market. Two pure localised materials will be processed at the market, while the addition of ubiquities will merely strengthen the attraction of the market. (c) The use of a single localised weight-losing material will cause manufacture to take place at its source. The addition of an ubiquitous gross material may cause a shift to the market; whether this will occur depends on the relative importance of weight-loss and the quantities of each material used. The case of several weight-losing materials has been previously mentioned.

(iii) *The influence of labour on the transport-oriented model*

Not only do wages paid for a particular job vary from place to place, but the productivity of labour also varies spatially. It is possible, therefore, for effective labour costs, that is, wages in relation to productivity,

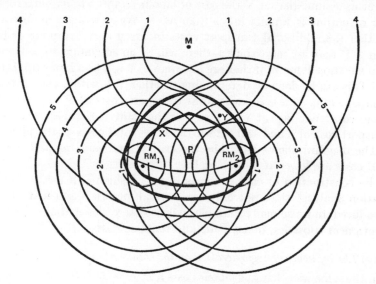

Fig. 4 The construction of isodapanes

at a particular location to be so favourable that a plant will vacate its least transport cost site and move to the source of cheap labour. It will do this because the additional transport costs are less than the savings in labour costs. The plant is said to substitute between inputs, in this case between transport and labour costs. Weber introduced the effect of labour, his first distortion, into the model by the use of cost contours, perhaps his greatest contribution to location theory.

In Fig. 4 lines joining points of equal transport costs—Weber calls them isotims—are drawn round the two material sources, RM_1 and RM_2, and the market, M. Two assumptions are made. First that RM_1 and RM_2 are gross materials and lose 50% of their weight in processing. Second, that the freight rates per ton on both materials and product are equal. The isotims round RM_1 and RM_2 therefore represent the cost of obtaining sufficient materials to produce a unit, say 1 ton, of the product.

The isotims concentric to M measure the cost of distributing a unit of the product. Because both raw materials are weight-losing and the product is pure, the isotim 'contour interval' about RM_1 and RM_2 is more frequent than that around M. P is the point of least transport cost. The thick lines, termed isodapanes by Weber, join points of equal total transport cost; they are the sum of the value of isotims at particular points on the transport cost surface. Thus X lies on the 8 isodapane (2 transport cost units from RM_1 + 4 from RM_2 + the delivery charge to M of 2 = 8).

Let us assume that at Y the cost of labour required to manufacture a unit of output is 2 units lower than at P. We now need to discover whether the additional transport costs incurred at Y are more or less than 2. If they are more than 2, there will be no advantage to be gained from vacating P for Y; if they are less than 2, Y will be a lower total cost site. This can be done by determining whether Y is within the 'critical' isodapane of 9. This is because total transport costs at P = 7, but the labour cost advantage at Y = 2, so that the plant at Y can afford a total transport cost of 9 and still return the same total costs as the plant at P. The diagram shows Y within the critical isodapane, implying that total costs are lower at Y than at P.

The construction of cost contours in this fashion is a useful tool in location analysis, since not only can several materials and markets be introduced, but also many variables whose cost varies spatially, such as government subsidies, taxes, rents and building costs

(iv) *The influence of agglomeration on the transport labour-oriented model*

In the same way that low labour costs may overcome the attraction of least transport cost locations, so agglomeration economies may cause a deviation from both transport- and labour-oriented locations. Weber argues that agglomeration economies may be caused firstly, by increases in the size of plant, bringing economies of large-scale production; secondly, by the association of several plants in the same industry; thirdly, by the growth of external economies. 'Accidental' agglomeration, that is the advantages gained from a site in a large city, port or transport node, is not considered to be 'pure' agglomeration, which is the concentration of industry for the purpose of agglomeration economies only.

A plant will be agglomeration-oriented if the savings in so doing are greater than the additional costs incurred by the vacation of the least transport cost or least labour cost site. Cost contour analysis is again employed to establish the point of least cost. Fig. 5 shows three locational triangles, around the optimum point, in which isodapanes are constructed. The critical isodapanes are those contours along which the savings from agglomeration equal the additional transport/labour costs incurred by shifting from the least transport/labour cost points P_1, P_2 and P_3. If the advantage to be gained from agglomeration is 3, the contour whose value is 3 becomes the critical isodapane. Providing transport/labour cost increases are less than 3, agglomeration of plants will then take

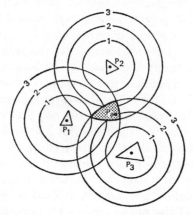

Fig. 5 The development of an area of agglomeration

place within the critical isodapane in the 'common segment' (shaded) formed by the intersection of the three critical isodapanes. The new plant site, P_a, will depend on the influence exerted by the largest plant, in this case P_3. It follows that agglomeration cannot obtain unless two or more plants are involved.

(v) *Criticisms of the Weberian model*

Technological change and the evolution of location theory since 1909 not surprisingly make it possible to criticise Weber's model. We may also question some of his assumptions.

(a) The importance he attaches to the various location factors. Although Weber could not have anticipated the role of the state in communist, socialist and even capitalist countries, his deliberate disregard of institutional factors now represents a serious shortcoming in a theory purporting to be of general application. His rejection of the significance of entrepreneurial decisions can also be attacked, especially since the neotechnic revolution of the 1920s and after has endowed a large part of industry with considerable locational mobility.

(b) Transport. The structure of freight rates is much more complex, and its effect on the location of industry more important, than Weber allowed for. Many plants sell their products at one price, irrespective of the point of consumption and this disrupts Weber's assumptions about transport costs. In reality, because of the advantage of locating at break of bulk points, the least transport cost site is frequently determined by transport networks and nodes, rather than by pure geometry. As we shall see, the point of minimum transport cost is often at the raw material source or at the market, rather than at some point between the two. Improvements in transport technology are forcing down the cost of transport relative to the cost of other inputs, thus undermining the relevance of a transport-oriented model. At the same time, the growth of late-stage manufacturing is taking place at markets, and transport is not an important consideration for this type of industry.

(c) Agglomeration. Weber's use of isodapanes grossly oversimplifies the forces at work. It is unrealistic to suppose that plants will combine to move to a common segment; indeed it is much more likely that large plants will remain immobile and that smaller units will cluster round them.

(d) Demand. Weber presupposes the existence of perfect competition, that is, large numbers of equally well-informed suppliers and consumers operating in one market, no single individual or plant being able to influence the state of the market, in which price is fixed. Demand is therefore limitless. He further assumes an absence of variation in production costs between plants. By ignoring the possibility of fluctuations in price, and the associated changes in demand, Weber implies that market areas are static. In the real world plants are aware of competitors' market areas, and evolve a location strategy to control the largest possible market area.

WILFRED SMITH

Writing in 1955 and admitting that 'industrial location is too rich and too varied to fit into Weber's formalised economic box', Smith builds on one of Weber's propositions, the material index, by testing its validity for 65 British industries. He finds that some industries with a high MI, such as beet sugar refining (MI = 8), and butter, cheese and milk production (MI = 6) are raw material-located, but others, such as pig iron production (MI = 3 to 4), are not always so to be found. Some industries with a MI of up to 5 are market-located, while others where the MI = 1 are sited at their raw material source. Smith concludes that within the range of MI = 1 to 5, the weight-loss criterion is of little use. He therefore excludes coal from the computation of the MI, thereby improving the validity of the weight-loss theory, but within the range of MI = 1 to 2, which includes half of the sample, there is still much overlapping. Smith therefore proposes an index based on the weight of materials handled per operative. An index above 40 tons is indicative of a material location; a figure of less than 30 tons implies a location other than at the material source. The index is useful in that it is accurate in cases where the MI is insensitive. Thus the engineering industry has considerable weight-loss but a small weight of materials handled per operative, and is by no means tied to materials.

1.3 THE TRANSPORT COST SCHOOL

EDGAR M. HOOVER

In his two books, *Location Theory and the Shoe and Leather Industries*, 1937, and *The Location of Economic Activity*, 1948, Hoover develops many of the concepts advanced by Weber, at the same time analysing the spatial aspects of supply and demand and the effect of governmental activity. However, his work is heavily influenced by Weber, and there is much emphasis on the need to minimise costs. Perhaps his greatest contribution is his close investigation of the locational effect of the structure of transport costs, and it is for this reason that he is dealt with in this section.

(i) *The structure of transport costs**

Transport costs are made up of two components, terminal costs and line and haul costs. The former include the cost of warehouses, docks, offices and maintenance, the latter include fuel and wages incurred by drivers and crew. Terminal costs are fixed regardless of the length of the haul, and can be spread over a larger number of miles on longer than shorter hauls. Thus the cost per mile is less on long hauls than on short hauls, with the consequence that the transport cost curve tapers off with distance, as illustrated in Fig. 6. Transport costs are not proportional to distance, as Weber assumed, and the problem or 'friction' of distance diminishes with increasing length of haul. All transport media exhibit tapering, but each medium has a different curve, depending on the relationship of terminal and line haul costs. Fig. 7, where tapering is not shown for the sake of simplicity, shows this relationship for road, rail and water transport. Road transport has low terminal charges and high running costs, while water transport is the reverse of this. The former is best suited to short hauls and the latter to long hauls. Hoover found that point A, where rail becomes cheaper than road, was 56 km/35 miles, and point B, where water becomes cheaper than rail, 608 km/380 miles from the origin.

* Sometimes the term transfer cost is used when costs such as insurance, duties and brokers' fees are included, while the term transport cost is reserved for the cost of moving goods. Here the term transport cost is employed to denote all costs incurred.

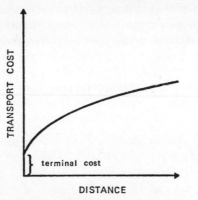

Fig. 6 Transport cost and the length of haul

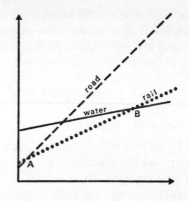

Fig. 7 The relationship between transport media according to the length of haul

Since transport media compete for business outside their most advantageous distances, the freight rates charged depend in part on those charged by other media. Thus short-distance railway rates are kept down by road transport, and long-distance railway rates are lowered by water transport. However, these losses are recovered by raising the rates

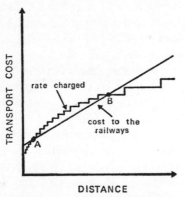

Fig. 8 The relationship between transport costs and the rates charged

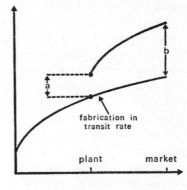

Fig. 9 The fabrication-in-transit rate

in rail's most efficient sector, between points A and B in Fig. 8. An excellent example of lowering freight rates because of media competition is afforded by the case, quoted above, of steel moving from Hamilton to Regina and Vancouver. Despite downbending by rail on short hauls, road haulage can still offer lower freight rates over these distances, thereby encouraging short road hauls and a general market orientation. Fig. 8 shows the curve of the rate charged proceeding in a series of steps or zones, which increase in size proportionate to distance. This method is adopted to save administrative costs, since it avoids the need to calculate the rate for every haul. It also implies that plants receiving materials over long distances have greater locational flexibility than plants relying on short-haul deliveries.

Competition for traffic among U.S. railroads has resulted in 'fabrication-in-transit' rates. We know that a break in the journey between origin and destination will cause the loss of the advantage of long hauls and tapering freight rates. (Weber seems not to have been aware of this.) The fabrication-in-transit rate allows materials to be processed at intermediate locations without an additional terminal charge and without loss of tapering. The railroad absorbs the terminal charges equal to height *a* in Fig. 9, while the total cost absorption is equal to height *b* in the diagram. Other factors which distort freight rates considered by Hoover include the availability of return cargoes, the size and volume of shipment, and the ease with which the goods can be carried.

(ii) *Transport costs and the plant*

Using the principles developed above, Hoover presents a least transport cost model which owes much to Weber. He postulates a single manufacturer using one material to produce a commodity sold at one market. Costs are divided into three: procurement costs, production

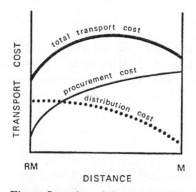
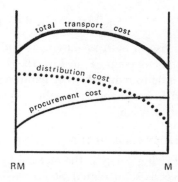

Fig. 10 Location of the plant at the source of raw materials

Fig. 11 Location of the plant at the market

costs and distribution costs, of which the first and last are influenced by transport costs. In Fig. 10 procurement costs show a steeper curve than distribution costs because the material is weight-losing, with the consequence that the total transport cost curve is lowest at RM, the raw material source. The plant will be established at RM rather than at M, the market. Where the production process results in appreciable weight-gain, as with brewing, the reverse situation obtains. Thus in Fig. 11, total transport costs are lowest at M, which will be the optimum location for the plant. Both diagrams illustrate the humped nature of the total transport cost curve, giving substance to Hoover's argument that terminal locations are preferable to intermediate ones. This represents a modification of Weber's opinion. Hoover contributes a useful diagrammatic solution to the growth of manufacturing at break of bulk points, especially ports. The costs of transferring goods from one transport medium to another, coupled with the loss of tapering freight rates, cause a sharp increase in transport charges at break of bulk points. This can be seen in

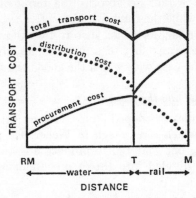

Fig. 12 Location of the plant at a break of bulk point

the rise in both procurement and distribution cost curves at the trans-shipment point, T, in Fig. 12. By setting up at such a point, a plant will be able to reduce further handling and will be able to reduce the weight, and increase the unit value, of raw materials. T is the least transport cost location.

PRICING POLICIES

Pricing policy is the method by which transport costs on the delivery of goods is calculated. So far we have assumed that the delivered price of a commodity is the factory price plus the freight rate, which, although not precisely proportionate to distance, nevertheless is heavily influenced by distance. This is not always the case. Hoover was aware of the existence of other, discriminatory, pricing policies, but paid them scant attention since he regarded them as exceptional. The opportunity is therefore taken of extending Hoover's comments. There are three main types of pricing policy: free-on-board (f.o.b.) works, basing-point pricing and uniform delivered pricing.

(i) *F.o.b. works*

This is the policy already referred to under which delivered prices are equal to production costs plus transport charges which are influenced by distance. Consumers close to a plant, or a plant close to materials, will

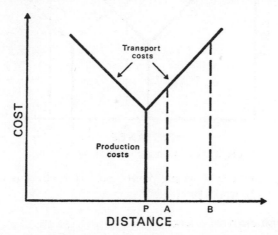

Fig. 13 The f.o.b. works pricing system

be able to enjoy lower delivered prices than consumers more distant from plants and plants more remote from materials. Thus in Fig. 13, consumer A would be able to purchase the product of plant P at a lower delivered price than would consumer B.

(ii) *Basing-point pricing*

In the extreme case, this pricing policy regards all production as emanating from one point, the basing-point, irrespective of the actual location of production. Delivered prices are calculated by adding production costs, which are fixed at a predetermined level, to the freight charges from the basing-point. Such a system benefits consumers, and plants, close to the basing-point, as can be seen in Fig. 14. Here plant P is also the basing-point, so that all deliveries, irrespective of their origin, are subject to P's transport cost curve. P_1 is a second plant whose consumers are A and B. Although B is closer to P_1 than A, it must pay more for its goods than A, because it is distance from the basing-point, not the plant, that is the crucial consideration. The pecked lines represent P_1's transport cost curve had f.o.b. works pricing obtained. The classic example of basing-point pricing is the U.S. steel industry between 1900 and 1924 when Pittsburgh was the basing-point, to its great benefit. This highly discriminatory system was known as the Pittsburgh Plus.

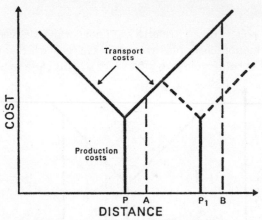

Fig. 14 The basing-point pricing system

When a large number of basing-points exist, the effect is not too dis-similar from f.o.b. works pricing.

(iii) *Uniform delivered pricing*

It is now being realised that the practice of setting prices at a uniform level either in zones or in entire countries is not the aberration that Hoover thought it to be. Most consumer goods and many producer goods are now subject to this form of pricing, which is practised to cut administrative

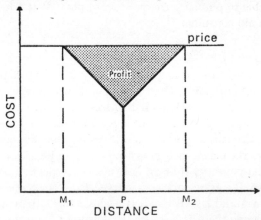

Fig. 15 Uniform delivered pricing: optimum plant location

costs. Since prices are everywhere equal, the consumer is not influenced by his distance from his supplier. However, the plant will want to be located as centrally as possible in respect of its market in order to avoid the necessity of absorbing transport costs on deliveries. Compare Figs 15 and 16. In both price does not vary through space and is shown as a straight line. In each case M_1M_2 is the market area—either a zone or a country—of plant P. In Fig. 15 the plant is centrally sited and the transport cost curve does not cut the uniform delivered price 'curve'

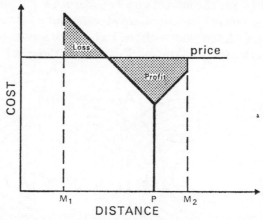

Fig. 16 Uniform delivered pricing: non-optimum plant location

within the market area. The plant thus has no need to absorb any transport charges. In Fig. 16, however, the plant is peripherally sited and is obliged to make some deliveries at a cost higher than the price. It must absorb these losses and accept reduced profitability.

1.4 THE MARKET AREA SCHOOL

We have seen how Weber treats consumption unrealistically by assuming that all output is sold in one market in which there is no limit to demand. Later scholars, reacting to this, introduce the concept of competition, and argue that plants will locate in respect of scattered consumers, or markets, and will as far as possible endeavour to monopolise as many consumers as they can. This approach is a rejection of the least cost model and its substitution by the market area or profit-maximising model.

FRANK A. FETTER

Writing in 1924, Fetter investigates the size of market areas under varying assumptions. Since the success of a plant is directly related to the volume of its sales, each manufacturer evolves a strategy to undercut the price of his competitors' products, thereby increasing the size of his market area, and therefore profits. Many strategies are possible, but Fetter sees them all as variations in production costs and transport costs.

In his limiting case, Fetter envisages two plants, P and P_1, with identical production and transport costs, selling to evenly distributed

C

consumers. Each producer monopolises the market on his side of the boundary, AA, in Fig. 17. The concentric circles are isotims drawn round each plant. Let us now assume that production costs at P_1 are 2 units higher than at P, and that transport costs are identical at both, as illustrated in Fig. 18. The market area boundary AA will join the points at which the two sets of isotims of equal value intersect. AA is closer to, and bends round, the plant with the higher production costs. Finally, let us assume that transport costs at P_1 are twice those at P, production

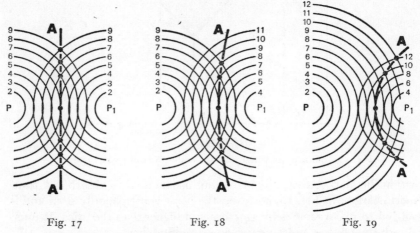

Fig. 17   Fig. 18   Fig. 19

Fig. 17 Market areas with identical production and transport costs

Fig. 18 Market areas with identical transport and dissimilar production costs

Fig. 19 Market areas with identical production and dissimilar transport costs

costs being equal. The 'contour interval' of the isotims round P_1 is thus twice that of those round P, as can be seen in Fig. 19. The market area boundary AA bends even more closely round P_1 than in the previous example, because here there is not merely a single addition to costs, but an additional increase with each unit of distance travelled from the plant.

THE BREAKING POINT THEORY

Schaffle in 1878 pointed out that industries are attracted to markets in direct proportion to the size of the markets, as measured, say, by their population, and in inverse proportion to the square of the distance between the markets. This can be expressed by the formula:

$$M_{ij} = \frac{P_i P_j}{d^2}$$

where i and j are the two markets, M_{ij} is the interaction between the markets, P_i and P_j are the populations of the two markets, and d is the distance between them. An extension of this model is the breaking point theory. This predicts the position of the market area boundary between towns of unequal size by the use of the formula:

$$M = \frac{d_{ij}}{1 + \sqrt{\dfrac{P_i}{P_j}}}$$

where M is the distance of the breaking point from the smaller town, d_{ij} is the distance between the towns, P_i is the population of the larger town and P_j the population of the smaller town. Using the data in Fig. 20, $M = 16 \cdot 6$. By employing the formula to compute the breaking points

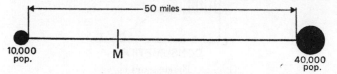

10,000
pop.

M

40,000
pop.

50 miles

Fig. 20 The breaking point

in respect of surrounding towns, it is possible to construct the market area for a plant in the central town, providing that the towns peripheral to it possess similar plants. It is purely a geometric approach, and factors such as those introduced by Fetter must also be taken into consideration in the establishment of the size of a market area. However, it provides an indication of the expected breaking point between market areas. Like the Schaffle model, its use is most effective in respect of market-oriented industries such as baking.

AUGUST LOSCH

August Losch, whose penetrating book *The Economics of Location* appeared in 1940, has done more than anyone else to develop the understanding of market areas. Weber's fundamental error, he argues, is to seek the lowest cost location. 'This is as absurd as to consider the point of largest sales as the proper location. Only search for the place of greatest profit is right.'[3] This greatest profit can be achieved by ascertaining what production costs will be at various locations, and establishing the size of market area which can be controlled at those various locations. Although Losch accepts the importance of production costs, he does not incorporate spatial variation in production costs into his model, and his basic model assumes a homogeneous land surface.

(i) *The demand cone*

We have seen how Weber considered demand as being limitless, but it is clear that the demand for a good will depend essentially on the price of that good. We would expect that a reduction in price of a product will lead to an increase in its consumption, and *vice versa*. Losch relates this simple proposition to market areas by means of his demand cone. Assuming, for the sake of simplicity, a uniformly distributed population

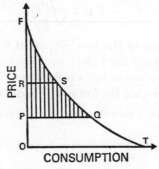

Fig. 21 The demand curve

in which all people have like tastes, and a uniform transport surface, the demand curve for beer will be as shown in Fig. 21. OP is the price of beer at the brewery, which is at P, where quantity PQ will be consumed. Further away from P, say at R, rather less (RS) will be consumed because the price of beer will have risen by the amount of transport costs from P to R. At F the transport charges are so onerous that no beer at all

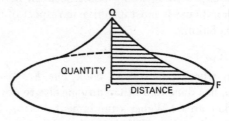

Fig. 22 The demand cone

can be sold. FT is thus the demand curve for beer. The quantity of beer sold will be equal to the volume of the cone produced by rotating the area PFQ about PQ to form a demand cone and a market area, as in Fig. 22. PF, the transport cost in Fig. 21, becomes distance, and is equal to the radius of the market area.

(ii) *The shape of market areas*

The shape of the market area derived from the demand cone is circular. In reality, there are many breweries, each monopolising a market area, but competing with each other at the edges of their market areas—a situation known as monopolistic competition. While brewing is profitable new plants are set up, causing the circular market areas eventually to shrink to form hexagons. The hexagon, Losch argues, is the ideal market area shape because it is closest in shape to the circle, yet ensuring that there are no empty corners, thus tapping all consumers, and at the same time minimising transport costs compared with shapes such as the triangle and the square. Evidence that the hexagon is a highly efficient shape is suggested by such forms as the honeycomb of the bee.

(iii) *A network of hexagonal market areas*

With a uniformly distributed population, each industry has its characteristic size of hexagon, and space is divided by a honeycomb of such hexagons. If three nets representing, say, baking, brewing and gasmaking,

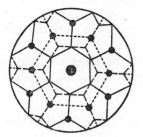 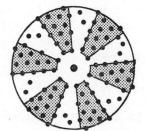

Fig. 23 A three-tier system of nets

Fig. 24 Cogwheel without nets

all with different sized hexagonal market areas, are thrown at random on a table, the relationship of the centres (manufacturing plants) to each other can be seen. Occasionally a bakery and a brewery will bunch together, or a gasworks and a bakery. More rarely all three activities will be found in the same locality, suggesting that industrial centres emerge even where the population is continuous. In practice, and in theory, there are as many nets as there are manufactured products, making up a complicated network of hexagonal market areas superimposed one upon the other.

Losch's next step is to arrange the nets so that they have at least one point in common which because of the size of local demand becomes the metropolis, as in Fig. 23, which illustrates three nets as they appear immediately about the metropolis. These nets are rotated about the metropolis to produce a cogwheel pattern of six sectors containing many production centres and six sectors with few production centres. The result of the concentration of plants in six sectors is the development of population, the minimisation of transport costs, and the expansion of demand by enabling diverse purchases to be made from the multiplicity of local plants. In contributing to market area analysis, Losch thus explains the tendency for industry to agglomerate. This system of rich zones (shaded) and poor zones surrounding the metropolis is shown in Fig. 24. With the accompanying nets, which are not shown in the diagram, the system is known as the Loschian landscape.

Losch can be criticised for his failure to consider cost differentials, other than those stemming from agglomeration and transport advantages, and for failing to develop the benefits of agglomeration, for example in terms of the size of plants. The reality of his economic landscape has been attacked by Walter Isard on the grounds that concentration of population at the metropolis would result in a parallel concentration of market areas. The size of the market area needed to generate sufficient demand to justify the production of a good is very much smaller in cities than in rural areas. Assuming the same size of plant, rural market areas are thus very much larger than those in cities, with the consequence that Losch's hexagons become grossly distorted. Isard also points out that the Loschian system does not take localised raw materials into account, and observes that rich and poor zones may also take the form of concentric rings round cities.

1.5 THE MARGINAL LOCATION SCHOOL

This small school of thought, comprising geographers rather than economists interested in the spatial aspect of economic activity, regards the work of Hoover and Losch as lacking in reality and as being concerned with ideal locations. Entrepreneurs establish factories at particular points for a great many different reasons, many of which may conflict with least cost and maximum profit theories. It is an unusual entrepreneur who is actually aware that he is at the point either of least cost or maximum profit; for most there are only areas within which it is possible to make a profit, and other areas within which losses are incurred. It is therefore possible only to identify the margin, that is, the zone in which profits change to losses and *vice versa*.

E. M. RAWSTRON

Rawstron believes that the examination of the structure of costs and their variation through space is a more realistic initial approach than principles based on weight-loss, weight-gain, or quantity of materials handled per worker. The plant will be more restricted in its choice of location when the cost of at least one of the components in the cost structure varies appreciably from place to place, if this variation forms a large proportion of total costs. Only those component parts of the cost structure that are likely to vary from place to place need be examined; these include labour, materials, marketing, land and capital. Power is considered with materials and transport with each component, where relevant.

Fig. 25(a) represents an industry in which the cost of materials accounts for 60% of the total locational costs. (Management and the efficiency of production processes, for example, are excluded from locational costs, since they are held to be everywhere constant.) A large variation in the cost of materials from place to place, as in the cement industry, will cause great economic restriction and the margin will be

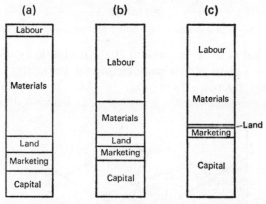

Fig. 25 Locational cost structures in three industries

close to the plant. Example (b) shows labour accounting for 45% and materials for 20% of locational costs. Materials are a localised mineral, rising sharply in cost away from the source, while labour shows very little variation. In this case it is not the component with the largest share of the total locational cost that causes restriction. Example (c) shows marketing costs accounting for 5% of locational costs. However, marketing costs vary spatially to a greater extent than labour and materials, so that this industry would comprise market-oriented plants.

D. M. SMITH

Smith develops Rawstron's ideas on the existence of margins of profitability with the construction of what he calls a space cost curve. In Fig. 26, demand and price are held constant while average costs vary from place to place. The average cost curve is the space cost curve. Profits can be obtained when the space cost curve is below price, but beyond Ma and Mb, the margins of profitability, losses are incurred.

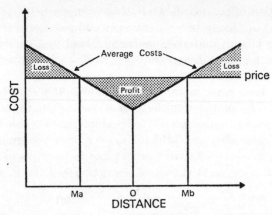

Fig. 26 Optimum location and profitability margins with price held constant

The greatest profit can be obtained at O, the optimum location, although the presence of a plant at O is quite fortuitous. In reality, both cost and price (demand) fluctuate from place to place, a situtation shown in Fig. 27. Here price falls on each side of B as demand diminishes with

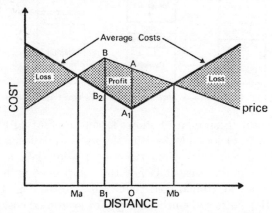

Fig. 27 Optimum location and profitability margins with variable price and average costs

distance from the plant. The diagram is especially useful since it illustrates not only the margins of profitability, Ma and Mb, but also the least cost location, O, and the location of the greatest demand, B_1. AA_1 is greater than BB_2, so the maximum profit location is also the least cost location, O. Once again, the presence of a manufacturing plant at either of these points is purely accidental. It follows from Fig. 27 that if the cost and price curves are steeper than shown, the distance between Ma and Mb will be smaller, indicating that where there is great spatial variation in price and cost the area within which profits are possible is considerably restricted. With shallow curves, characteristic of industries adding greatly to the value of materials during processing, for example, computer production, it is possible for an entire country to lie within the margins of profitability.

The model can easily accommodate change, whether this be in terms of price, costs, managerial skill or taxation. In Fig. 28 a plant is able to

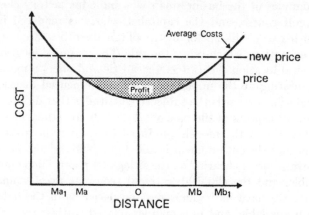

Fig. 28 Change in price and profitability margins

increase its price with the result that its margins of profitability widen from $MaMb$ to Ma_1Mb_1. A decrease in average costs caused, for instance, by improved management efficiency, or a reduction in material costs or a favourable tax or subsidy, would have a similar effect on economic margins, as is depicted in Fig. 29. Changes in the reverse direction, such

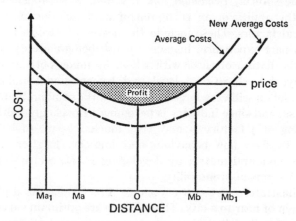

Fig. 29 Change in average cost and profitability margins

as a decrease in price or an increase in average costs, would result in a contraction of the area within which production could profitably occur.

1.6 THE BEHAVIOURAL SCHOOL

Until quite recently most geographers, and economists, have disregarded the possibility that decisions made by individuals might be a significant factor in the understanding of the distribution of industry. The oft-quoted examples of the businessman who built his factory close to his favourite golf course, and the capitalist who was rendered immobile because of his wife's liking for metropolitan amenities, are regarded as irrational exceptions which prove the rule. The marginal location school reject classical location theories as unrealistic and offers a more flexible approach, hinting at the importance of entrepreneurial decisions. The behavioural school regards the subjective attitudes that different people have about all aspects of life as a vital part of the study of industrial location. Central to the models produced by earlier theorists was the assumption that the entrepreneur is able to understand and finely assess all the relevant factors bearing on the siting of a plant. Such omniscience is impossible, and the classical 'rational economic man' cannot exist. In his place we have individuals making decisions in the light of the information available, and in a manner related to their own ability to use that information. There may be no great desire to maximise profits, but merely to produce a reasonable return. The behavioural school sees economic man as a 'satisficer' rather than an 'optimiser'.

Allan Pred

The leading exponent of this school is Allan Pred, whose first major work on the subject, *Behaviour and Location*, was published in 1967. Pred sees the ability of an entrepreneur as a function of a range of psychological factors. These include the degree of success to which he aspires, his past experience, his age — youth being more dynamic than old age — the nature of those with whom he mixes both economically and socially, his educational level and his emotional stability. The location of a plant will very largely depend on the combination of factors such as these, and since industry is becoming increasingly footloose, the precise siting of a factory is now very much a result of behavioural influences. To show how behaviour may influence location, Pred constructs a behavioural matrix by developing D. M. Smith's space cost curve and margins of profitability.

Fig. 30 illustrates space cost curves for three similar-sized plants, O_1, O_2, and O_3, in or near to a city. These curves are optimum curves, and it does not necessarily follow that the plants are at the optimum location.

There are three space cost curves because it is not possible to supply the whole city from a single plant owing to the high incidence of transport costs. The areas within which each plant could economically operate,

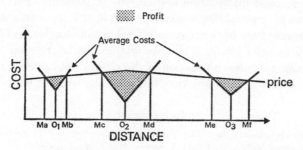

Fig. 30 Three optimum locations and profitability margins

MaMb, McMd and MeMf, are different in each case because costs differ as between plants. The three margins of profitability are then mapped by rotating the radii about the optimum points, that is, Ma or Mb about O_1, Mc or Md about O_2 and Me or Mf about O_3. The circular result is

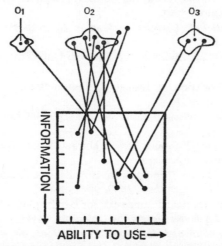

Fig. 31 A map of profitability margins and manufacturing plants linked to a behavioural matrix

distorted to take into account transport facilities and the distribution of population, as indicated in Fig. 31. Thirteen plants are then inserted on the maps; none is at an optimum location, and three are shown as loss-making. The plants are then linked to cells in a behavioural matrix best characterising the quality of information possessed by plants, and

their ability to use that information. Plants close to the optimum locations, O_1, O_2 and O_3, on the maps are to be found linked to cells in the
bottom right hand of the matrix, since it is reasonable to assume that
they possess good information and employ it shrewdly. Plants outside
the margins of profitability appear in cells in the top left hand of the
matrix, because they have access only to poor information and have only
low ability to act upon it. The unprofitable plants are seen as having
been marooned by the contraction of the profitability margin round O_2.
They are continuing in production, but will eventually be forced to close.

References

1. Gunner Alexandersson, *The Industrial Structure of American Cities*,
   University of Nebraska Press, Lincoln, Nebraska, 1956.
2. D. Kerr, 'The Geography of the Canadian Iron and Steel Industry',
   Economic Geography, 1959, pp. 151–63.
3. A. Losch, *The Economics of Location*, Yale University Press, New Haven,
   1954, p. 29.

Further Reading

R. C. Estall and R. O. Buchanan, *Industrial Activity and Economic Geography*,
Hutchinson, London, 1961.

P. Haggett, *Locational Analysis in Human Geography*, Arnold, London,
1965, pp. 114–52.

A. Weber, *Theory of the Location of Industries*, University of Chicago Press,
Chicago, 1929.

W. Smith, 'The Location of Industry', *Transactions, Institute of British
Geographers*, 1955, pp. 1–18.

E. M. Hoover, *The Location of Economic Activity*, McGraw-Hill, New York,
1948.

Frank A. Fetter, 'The Economic Law of Market Areas', *Quarterly Journal of
Economics*, 39, 1924, pp. 520–9.

E. R. Rawstron, 'Three Principles of Industrial Location', *Transactions,
Institute of British Geographers*, 1958, pp. 135–45.

D. M. Smith, 'A theoretical Framework for Geographical Studies of Industrial Location', *Economic Geography*, 1966, pp. 95–113.

Allan Pred, *Behaviour and Location: Foundations for a Geographic and
Dynamic Location Theory, Part I*, Lund Studies in Geography, Series B,
1967.

D. M. Smith, *Industrial Location: An Economic Geographical Analysis*, John
Wiley, New York, 1971.

Chapter 2

RAW MATERIAL-ORIENTED INDUSTRIES

We have seen how it is theoretically possible for a raw material which loses a great deal of weight in the manufacturing process, to exercise a powerful influence on the location of a factory. When this influence is such that the factory is constructed at the site of the raw material, then that factory is said to be material-oriented. A great many manufacturing processes result in some weight-loss; metal is wasted when it is cut or bored into particular shapes, chemicals are used up in the production of new substances, while some of the cloth from the textile mill becomes tailors' clippings. However, in these examples the industries are not necessarily material-oriented because the materials have a high value and the manufacturer is not especially concerned that he has to meet transport charges on materials which are subsequently wasted. For weight-losing materials to draw plants to their source, then, the materials must also be of low value.

Industries using low-value raw materials which lose weight during processing will endeavour to keep their transport costs to a minimum because these costs account for a significant proportion of total costs. Such industries can be termed not only material-oriented but also transport-oriented. They will seek locations at which movement is minimised and at which costs are lowest, in accordance with Weberian analysis. Put another way, variations in transport costs at different locations are much greater than variations in other costs. A location where transport costs are not minimised would probably result in total costs being excessive, and the plant would eventually go out of business. It is important to note that not all transport-oriented industries are material-oriented. Transport orientation simply implies that transport cost considerations are of crucial importance in the siting of a plant. The plant could equally well be located at a market, as in the case of brewing which has to face high distribution costs on beer, or where many materials are used at a point convenient for the assembly of materials and the distribution of products, such as at a port or other break of bulk point.

The classic example of a transport- and material-oriented industry was iron smelting which, in the early stages of its growth, was located on coalfields because of the very large quantities of coal used for fuel and power per ton of pig iron produced. When low-grade iron ore came to be used, for example in Lorraine, iron smelting took place on the ironfield since the weight of iron ore lost in processing was greater than the loss in weight of coal per ton of pig iron. Continuing progress in fuel technology has resulted in very few new iron and steelworks being built on coalfields since the Second World War. Iron and steel manufacture now belongs to the growing number of industries that exhibit several locational tendencies and are best described as multi-locational industries. In these cases the constituent plants show no clear orientation to materials, to markets, to intermediate locations or to break of bulk points, but are to be found at each type of site. Some plants, especially in the older established industries, give the impression of being material-oriented, but frequently the reason for the location is to be found in historic advantages such as skilled labour, or by the presence of many similar activities, rather than the proximity of materials, which may well be exhausted. Thus the Stoke-on-Trent pottery industry, although on a coalfield, uses gas- and oil-fired kilns and imports clay from elsewhere. Many blast furnaces, such as those in South Belgium, fall into this category.

2.1 THE REDUCTION IN THE LOCATIONAL IMPORTANCE OF MATERIALS

The declining significance of materials has affected the distribution pattern of so many industries that it can be regarded as a major theme in industrial geography. There are four principal reasons for the change.

IMPROVED PRODUCTION TECHNIQUES

These have resulted in a reduction in weight-loss, so decreasing the proportion of freight cost to be paid on the movement of potential waste material. The subjection of ores to a preliminary treatment, known as beneficiation, at the mine, to remove some of the sterile material before shipment is a good example of this. Thus the low-grade iron ore, taconite, mined in Minnesota is improved from 25% to 60% iron prior to transport to the Chicago steel mills. Developments in oil refinery processes, coupled with the growth of demand for an increasingly wide range of petroleum products, have caused the proportion of crude oil wastage to fall from 50% to 2%; oil refineries now enjoy great locational flexibility and are no longer primarily found on oilfields. A third example is the introduction of the by-product oven which replaced the traditional beehive oven for the production of metallurgical coke. The use of the beehive oven did not allow the collection of the valuable by-products of the carbonisation process, and such was the weight-loss and the relatively low value of the coal that the beehive ovens were strongly oriented to coalfields. The best example was the Connellsville coking coal district in Pennsylvania. By-product ovens are now to be found at integrated iron and steel plants, at coastal and inland waterway sites, and on coalfields.

CHANGES IN TRANSPORT

There has been a gradual improvement in the efficiency of transport and of bulk handling, making it possible to move materials greater distances for the same cost. The canal was very much more efficient than the horse and cart and was conducive to the movement of low-value materials which hitherto had been processed *in situ*. The trend was emphasised by the railway by virtue of its greater flexibility, lower construction costs and lower maintenance costs. Thus there was an increase in the average length of rail haul in the U.S.A. from 177 km/110 miles per ton of material carried in 1882, to 402 km/250 miles per ton of material carried in 1910.[1] The introduction of block trains, sometimes on charter for years at a time, automatic marshalling yards and larger hopper wagons have helped to reduce transport costs still further. Indeed, it has become easier to handle low-value materials rather than high-value goods because of the care the latter need. The result has been that freight rates on materials are often lower than freight rates on more valuable goods. In the U.S.A. over the period 1928–1957, the average revenue per ton of minerals hauled by rail increased by 63%, but there was a rise of 122% in average revenue per ton of manufactured products hauled.[2] Again, it is not possible to employ large-scale methods in the case of diversified products owing to the assorted sizes of shipments and the multiplicity of destinations involved. Consequently the improvement in the movement of products has not been nearly as striking as that of materials. The use of road transport is normally restricted to short hauls, since, as we have seen, railways are better suited to medium distance hauls. Expressways and motorways have made inter-urban road transport very attractive, and at the same time vehicles have been developed capable of moving materials such as heavy chemicals, oil and cement in bulk. The result has been a loosening of the ties between plants and their material sources.

Perhaps the most startling developments have been in ocean transport. The standard oil tanker in the immediate post-war period was the T2 Liberty ship with a capacity of 16 500 tons. In 1953 the first supertanker of 45 000 tons came into service, to be followed in 1956 by 80 000-ton vessels which were able to reduce by half the freight rates of the tankers built only three years earlier. 300 000-ton tankers are now afloat and 500 000 tonners are planned. Although freight rates do not decline proportionately with increases in the size of ship, the larger the vessel the lower are the transport costs and the greater the incentive to move materials to existing markets. Dry bulk carriers have not increased in size at such a speed, vessels in excess of 100 000 tons being rare, but nevertheless the attractiveness of material locations has been considerably eroded. Oil and natural gas pipelines have had the same effect, while coal and chalk for cement are now being pumped through pipes in suspension. Developments in transport have therefore eased the movement of materials rather than products, thereby diminishing the pull of material locations.

NEW SOURCES OF ENERGY

Weber regarded coal as a material, and therefore many of the industries of what W. Smith called the era of classical steam industrialism can be regarded as material-oriented. Boiler and furnace efficiency was very low so that huge tonnages of coal were needed. Coal is entirely used up in the production process, and such was the inefficiency of the transport system that a coalfield location was virtually obligatory. Innovators such as Watt and Stephenson improved the design of boilers while Nielson, Siemens and Martin reduced the quantities of coal needed in furnaces. Even so, it was not until the closing years of the 19th century, when other sources of energy began to intrude into coal's position of near monopoly, that its attraction for manufacturing was seriously undermined. Oil has been coal's major competitor. Thus in 1960 in Britain, a traditionally coal-based economy, coal and oil accounted for 74% and 25% of total energy consumption respectively. A decade later, however, the respective figures were 47% and 44%. Coal was conducive to material-orientation, but oil is conducive to industrialisation other than on oilfields, for its prime characteristic is its transportability. Since it is a fluid it can be pumped easily, it will entirely fill a storage space and it is not damaged by movement. It also has a higher heat content, or calorific value, per ton than coal, so that the cost of moving oil in calorific terms is very much lower. For example, in 1961, taking into account the calorific difference, the cost of pumping 1 ton of oil 160 km/100 miles along a 76 cm/3 inch pipe was between 9 and 13·5 cents, compared with 70 to 80 cents for hauling 1 ton of coal 160 km/100 miles by rail. It is now not uncommon to find industries such as pottery, glass, steelmaking and ironfounding still located on coalfields, but burning oil in their ovens, kilns and furnaces.

Of equal significance to industrial location has been the generation of electric power, principally from coal but also from water, oil, natural gas, lignite and atomic fuels. Since electric power can be economically transmitted up to about 1000 km/600 miles, and since most advanced countries possess a grid system, electricity is merely a particularly mobile form of primary energy. In the U.K. 75% of electricity is derived from coal, and we might therefore regard electric power as mobile coal. The locational effect has been to allow industry to shed its coalfield ties and to become market-oriented, a tendency borne out by the great growth of manufacturing plants along main roads in the suburbs of London and other cities from the 1930s onward.

Not only have oil and electric power reduced the influence of coal, thereby reducing material orientation, but also new industries in which energy accounts for a small proportion of total costs have arisen. For example, energy accounts for 1·7% of the value of the product in the rubber tyre industry, for 1·4% in the vehicle industry, for 1% in pharmaceuticals, and for 0·8% in the machine tool industry. It is therefore not merely coal that is of decreasing importance in location decisions, but energy in all its forms.

THE INCREASING COMPLEXITY OF INDUSTRY

Technological progress has caused manufacturing processes to become increasingly complex and the number of materials used to increase, thus reducing the significance of any one. Substitution between materials is frequent, perhaps the most common is the use of plastics in place of metals. Increasingly large increments of labour and capital equipment are employed in the production of one unit of output, that is, a car or a radio. Thus the value of the original materials is increased enormously during manufacturing. These industries are said to be high value-adding, and they are typified by engineering, electronic products, plastics and pharmaceuticals. The materials of these industries are semi-finished, medium value manufactured goods themselves, so that transport costs are a very small proportion of total costs—normally not more than 5%. Clearly materials can exert little influence on the location of these new industries.

The modern entrepreneur or board of directors are presented with an increasingly wide freedom of choice of location as a result of these four main influences. This freedom has given rise to marginal location theory and to the study of behaviour as we have seen in Chapter 1. There are, however, some industries that still exhibit material-orientation. They are very largely concerned with mineral, forest product and food processing. In some cases, the cement industry for example, production takes place at one site and it is possible to be unequivocal about its material orientation. On the other hand an industry may comprise several divisible processes, each with a different orientation. Examples of this are the copper and paper and pulp industries, the former having three and the latter

D

two divisible processes. However in both cases the initial process is at the site of the raw material, and it is therefore justifiable to regard these industries as material-oriented.

2.2 THE COPPER INDUSTRY

The copper industry has three production stages, concentration, smelting and refining, each of the stages being subject to different locational pulls. Concentration invariably takes place at the mine, and in this respect the industry is clearly material-oriented. Smelting is frequently, but by no means invariably, carried out close to concentrators, while refining has the greatest degree of locational flexibility, allowing the process frequently to take place at markets. There are considerable deviations from this model as a result of changing technological, economic, political and behavioural circumstances, but concentration is always a mine activity. Paradoxically, technological developments have only succeeded in increasing the attractions of mine locations for concentrators, since modern equipment makes it possible to mine copper ores containing less than 1% copper.

The demand for copper in the pre-electrical age was small and could be met from relatively rich native copper ores in which the metal occurred in pure form. English copper ores of the late 18th century contained up to 13% copper, although they had declined to 8% by 1840. Similarly Upper Michigan 'Lake' ores averaged only 2·96% between 1887 and 1905. The demand for electricity at the end of the 19th century and afterwards outstripped the production of the native copper mines; in the absence of a substitute, prices rose and increasingly lower-grade ores were exploited, especially in the U.S.A. These ores, in which copper is mixed with other elements, principally sulphur and oxygen, would not justify shaft mining methods, and their exploitation coincided with the use of steam shovels and mass mining methods. The invention of the froth flotation process in 1941 greatly helped to overcome the problems associated with the concentration of these ores. The process involves the passing of bubbles of air through a mixture of water, chemicals, oil and crushed ore, causing particles of the metal to attach themselves to the bubbles and so rise to the surface to form a froth, which can then be creamed off. Owing to the combination of copper with other materials in the low-grade ores, it was no longer possible to produce commercial copper by separating the metal from its ore by means of a single heat treatment as with native ores. It became necessary to smelt the concentrate first in a reverberatory furnace to remove the slag, and then to charge the resulting matter into a Bessemer converter where the sulphur and iron were driven off by oxidisation. The product of the converter, blister copper, was then sent to electrolytic refineries, plants which had been neither necessary nor technically possible when native copper was exploited.

CONCENTRATION

Between 1906 and 1963 the average grade of copper mined in the U.S.A. fell from 2·5 to 0·8%, but since 0·1–0·2% is lost in processing, the actual figure is about 0·6% at present.[3] This great weight-loss suggests a Weberian model. Electric power is used to drive jigs, ball mills and other machinery in the concentrator, but such is the ease with which this form of energy can be transmitted that it can be ignored as a locational influence. Effectively energy becomes an ubiquitous factor. We are left with a weight-losing localised raw material which, because the material index is greater than 1, should draw the plant to its source since entrepreneurs will always strive to minimise movement. U.S. concentrators have a material index of 66, leaving no doubt as to their

Christmas Mine (RM) P   Miami
(Arizona) (M) (Arizona)
(E) smelter

Fig. 32 Weberian locational figure of copper concentrator location

theoretical location. At alternative sites transport charges would be enormous, and Alexander found a very strong positive correlation of 0·98 between mines and concentrating plants in the U.S.A.[4] Zambia, the second world copper producer, is able to use richer ores, the average for 1967 being 3%, giving a concentrators' material index of 13, lower than the U.S. figure, but still very high in locational terms. Copper concentrating is a good example of the Weberian case of a single material source and a single market, where the locational figure shrinks to a line as in Fig. 32.

SMELTING

The smelting of copper concentrate is also a weight-losing operation. All the oil, natural gas or coal consumed is used up and impurities in the concentrate are removed in the form of slag, giving a material index of about 2·8. Smelters using coal, as in Zambia and West Germany, have higher indices than oil- and natural gas-fired smelters because of the higher calorific value of both oil and natural gas. Consequently the greater transportability of oil compared with coal and natural gas, coupled with its high calorific value, have caused many smelters to switch from coal to oil with the result that the quantity of fuel consumed for each ton of product has fallen. Thus the pull exercised by the concentrator has increased. However, their low material index suggests that smelters do possess considerable locational flexibility, and this is the case in reality. Indeed, Alexander reports a low positive correlation of 0·35 between concentrators and smelters in the U.S.A.[5]

In Weberian terms copper smelting represents a three-point case of two weight-losing localised materials and a single market. In respect of weight-loss, concentrate is about eight times more significant than energy. It therefore follows that concentrators will exercise a very much more powerful influence over smelters than energy sources. Since blister copper is 99% pure, the very small weight-loss involved in refining implies that the smelter's market exercises virtually no pull at all. The precise location of the smelter will be determined by the shape of transport networks, especially if the networks pre-date the smelter, so that the

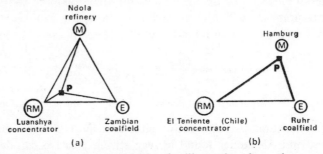

Fig. 33 Weberian locational triangles illustrating alternative copper-smelting locations

plant may not be at the theoretical least cost location. In reality the locational figure is more complex than that in Fig. 33, since smelters frequently receive concentrate from several sources and ship blister to more than one refinery. As we have seen, Weber would use the Varignon frame to illustrate such a *n*-point case.

In order to establish the relationship between concentrators and smelters on a global scale with some degree of precision, smelter production in leading copper-producing countries can be divided by copper mined in those countries. Where the quotient is equal to 1, all copper mined is smelted within the country; where it is less than 1, some concentrate is exported; where it is more than 1, concentrate is imported. The results appear in Fig. 34, which shows that the leading mining nations, with two exceptions, Canada and Mexico, return scores very close to parity, suggesting a high correlation between smelters and concentrators on a national level. Japan deviates most strongly from this pattern since her demand for copper is greater than indigenous supply, and she is reacting to this by importing concentrate from, for

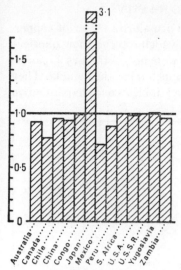

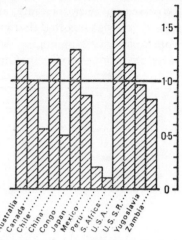

Fig. 34 Smelter-concentrator quotients in leading copper-mining nations, 1967

Fig. 35 Refinery-smelter quotients in leading copper-mining nations, 1967

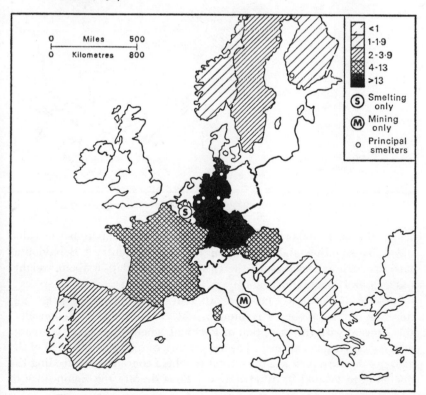

Fig. 36 Smelter-concentrator quotients, Western Europe, 1967

example, the Philippines, which, although a major producer of copper, possesses concentrators only, and Canada, which returns a low quotient of 0·777. It was reported that in 1967 there were no less than 15 Japanese companies either mining or developing copper mines in Canada. They were investing heavily in Canadian-owned mines conditionally upon

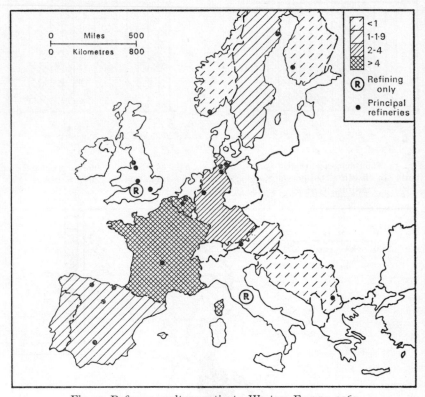

Fig. 37 Refinery-smelter quotients, Western Europe, 1967

being allowed to export concentrate to Japan to gain from the value added by smelting and refining in their own country.[6] Behavioural patterns such as this disturb the theoretical postulation about weight-loss as a locational influence.

Looking at Western Europe a different pattern emerges (Fig. 36). Here the mining of copper is unimportant yet consumption is considerable, so that with the exception of Portugal, smelting capacity is greater than concentrating capacity. The importance of smelting, reflected in the high quotients, represents the extent to which concentrators feeding the smelters are located in other nations. Thus despite the significance of weight-loss in smelting, nearly all the West European countries import concentrate for processing in what are market located smelters, contrary to what Weberian analysis would lead one to expect. West German smelters exhibit an exceptionally low correlation with their concentrating plants, most of which are in South America and Africa. The quotient in this case is 100·0. It is to be expected that West German smelters are adjacent to water transport facilities since the proportion of transport charges to total costs must be very high compared with smelters adjacent to concentrators. This example, which appears as a locational

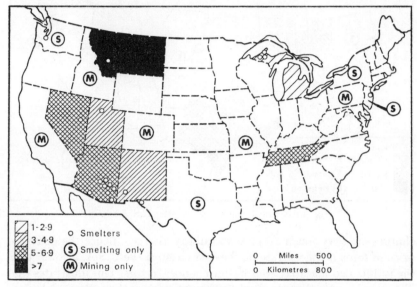

Fig. 38 Smelter-concentrator quotients, U.S.A., 1967

figure in Fig. 33(b), and the situation in most West European countries, suggests limitations in the universal application of the weight-loss concept. Indeed, Smith has observed that it is only when the material index is in excess of 5 does the theory have general application.[7] It is worthy of note that the U.K., once the world's leading smelting nation, now has no smelter.

The U.S.A. illustrates both the proximity of concentrators and smelters typical of major copper-mining nations, and the separation of these production stages as in important consuming areas. Fig. 38 emphasises the concentration of smelters in mining states; in fact, if El Paso is included in New Mexico (it is only just in Texas) the mining states have 90% of U.S. smelting capacity. The two smelters on the eastern seaboard at Carteret, New Jersey, and Laurel Hill, Long Island, and the one at

Tacoma, Washington, use imported concentrate largely from South America. Since there is no mine production in these states, no quotient is possible; among West European countries, Belgium is in a similar position. Coastal smelters are served by bulk carriers whose freight

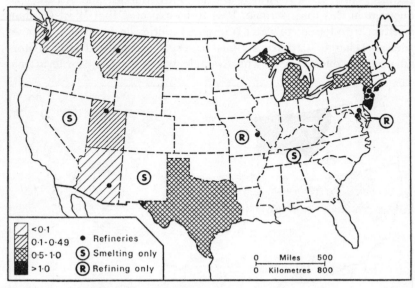

Fig. 39 Refinery-smelter quotients, U.S.A., 1967

charges are very much lower than railway charges; hence the delivered price of foreign concentrate on the east coast of the U.S.A. is lower than the rail-hauled material from western concentrators. This illustrates that distance is sometimes a less significant factor than the method of transport.

REFINING

Blister, the raw material of the refinery, is in the Weberian sense very nearly pure in that the process of refining creates only a small weight-loss of between 1 to 0·2%. Effectively there is no weight-loss at all since the impurities are very valuable metals such as gold, silver, lead, zinc manganese and molybdenum. In 1967 Zambian refineries produced 0·01% of the total South African gold output that year, and that from a refining weight-loss of only 0·2%. The material index is therefore effectively equal to 1.

Copper electrolysis is moderately energy intensive, power costs accounting for 0·8% of the value of the product, although not so intensive as zinc at 4·3%. Therefore electric power cannot be regarded as ubiquitous as in the case of concentrators. In spite of the absence of weight-loss, electric power transmission costs exercise a pull in the same way as transport costs do on both blister and refined copper. Where hydro-electric power is employed, the refinery will be drawn to the generating plant, for example, at Great Falls, Montana, representing a Weberian three-point case of two localised pure materials and one market. Transport charges on one of the materials (energy) are thus sufficiently high to determine location. Where thermal electric power is generated by the refinery company, the latter has to decide whether to locate at the source of, say, the coal, or to ship the coal to a power plant adjacent to the refinery, as in Zambia. In this case the weight-losing material, coal, exerts a less powerful pull than the pure material, a situation that Weber did not allow for. To be fair, however, it was not the pull of the blister so much as the operational and infrastructural

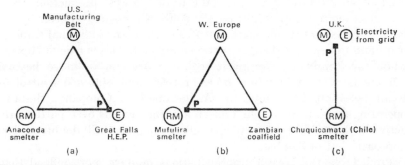

Fig. 40 Weberian locational figures showing alternative copper refinery locations

advantages conferred by the proximity of refinery and smelter that were uppermost in the location decision. In industrial areas with well-developed electricity supply systems, there is a much greater degree of locational flexibility. Here the siting may be at a break of bulk point on the coast, as Hamburg, or in old-established metalworking areas such as Prescott, Lancashire. In this case the locational figure shrinks to a straight line. Fig. 40 shows the three situations discussed.

Fig. 35 indicates that there is considerable variation in the scores achieved by the major copper-mining nations in their smelting–refining relationships. South Africa, Peru, the Congo and Chile have much greater smelting than refining capacity, in part because domestic consumption is small, so that many of the refineries which their smelters feed are some distance away, for example in Western Europe and the U.S.A. While smelting is often tied to concentrators, with refining there exists the possibility of locating the plant either in the vicinity of the smelter, or at some distance away from it. There is thus an important element of choice open to the directors of a firm so that, unlike concentrators, refinery location is subject to behavioural considerations. Hence U.S. firms such as Kennecott and Phelps Dodge carry out mining and smelting in Peru and Chile, but refine some of the blister produced at coastal plants in the U.S.A. Both Peru and Chile have high concentrator-smelter quotients, 0·887 and 0·954 respectively, but low smelter-refinery quotients, 0·216 and 0·560 respectively. At the other extreme are those nations with greater refining than smelting output, the industrialised copper mining countries led by the U.S.A. and Japan. Mexico and Zambia do not fit into either of these categories; they have small domestic consumption and yet return high quotients. There are sound economic reasons for establishing refineries in non-industrialised mining countries, such as low labour costs, low energy costs, especially where coal is used to generate electricity, low land values, and the advantages of integrated production. Zambia, in fact, has the world's lowest production costs. Perhaps even more important are the political pressures on firms by the host countries to expand operations *in situ* to create additional employment and to augment the gross national product. This is true of Mexico, while the Zambian government took the decision to move beyond refining into the fabrication stage in 1966, and obtained control of Roan Selection Trust and the Anglo-American Company, the two operating firms, in 1969. The Chilean government has been particularly active in this field, and her smelter-refinery quotient will doubtless soon approach that of Zambia.

Predictably the West European nations produce more refined than smelted copper, with three exceptions, Norway, Finland and Jugoslavia. Belgium has the highest quotient and yet mines no copper at all, a reflection of her former colonial ties with the Congo and formerly cheap coal from the Kempen coalfield. Surprisingly, in view of her low cost hydro-electric power supplies, Norway has more smelter than refinery output. The United Kingdom is restricted to refining and therefore returns no quotient. (See Fig. 37.)

The situation in the U.S.A. serves to emphasise the small extent of locational restriction placed upon refineries when companies are freed from political influences. Arizona, which mined 66% of U.S. copper in 1966, has but one small refinery and a quotient of 0·014, while the next largest mine producers, Utah and Montana, also have low scores. New Mexico and Nevada have no refineries at all. Only in Texas, New York and Michigan is there a relatively strong correlation between smelters and refineries, as can be seen in Fig. 39. Indeed, Alexander obtained a negative correlation of −0·72 for U.S. smelters and refineries.[8] Despite the lengthy rail haul from the mine-oriented smelters, it would seem that the locational advantage lies with the eastern market-oriented refineries, which now account for 60% of U.S. capacity. The three eastern states involved, New York, New Jersey and Maryland, ought to possess quotients in excess of 1; in fact only New Jersey does this since New York's Laurel Hill refinery is smaller than the nearby smelter, while Maryland has no smelter. The advantages of refining at markets are (a) proximity to fabricating plants, (b) the availability of copper scrap, which accounts for between 20 and 25% of refined copper production in the U.S.A., (c) the benefits of scale economies in electricity supply, (d) where the refineries can be sited on tidewater, as are the U.S. plants, there is the possibility of using foreign blister at minimum transport cost; this is especially useful for companies owning foreign smelters, (e) the presence of considerable external economies largely absent in mining areas where the firm is often obliged to provide the entire social and economic infrastructure.

Technological considerations involving weight-loss become less significant as a locational guide, and decisions made by firms and political factors become more important at each production stage. Weberian analysis with its stress on movement minimisation has validity for concentrating and to some extent for smelting; in postulating locational flexibility for refineries in the absence of weight-loss, Weberian theory is correct, but it does not provide the reasons for particular location decisions.

2.3 THE PULP AND PAPER INDUSTRY

As its name implies, the pulp and paper industry comprises two major processes, pulp making and paper production from that pulp. Each stage is subject to different locational determinants which cause pulp mills to be material-oriented and paper mills to be close to consumption points. Economic factors have created the integrated mill in which both products are made, at the same time ensuring that such plants be material-oriented. This apparently clear case of the locational significance of materials does not always obtain, however, in Western Europe, after Anglo-America the world's most important pulp and paper producing area, because of the influence of protectionist policies. Weberian analysis has some relevance to the understanding of distribution patterns, but perhaps more important, the industry provides a useful example of the significance of technological change and behaviour on location.

The basic material for papermaking is cellulose, which is present in most plants. Paper can thus be made from materials such as straw, bamboo or from sugar cane after the juice has been extracted, but because cellulose accounts for 56% of total weight in wood, this is employed as the principal raw material. Papermaking originated in China where rags were used as the raw material, and it was not until the invention of the mechanical wood grinder in Germany in 1840 that wood pulp was used. This method was first used in the U.S.A. at Cortisville, Massachusetts, in 1866. The advantage of wood over straw, with which experiments had been made, was the greater cellulose yield per unit of land. Between one and two tons of cellulose could be produced from an acre of straw derived from wheat, compared with three to four tons of cellulose per acre in the case of wood.[9] Initially wood pulp was inferior to rag pulp, and the two were used together for some time, thus barely disturbing the distinct market-orientation of the industry. Urban areas were both the source of raw materials and the market. Wood pulp was not used in significant quantities until, for example in the U.S.A., the 1880s, and in any case was to be had locally. Further, waste paper, which could be reused, was also a product of towns.

The problem facing the papermaker using wood was to isolate the cellulose from lignin, resin and other impurities which remained after the mechanical pulping operation. Mechanical pulp, being high in impurities, was restricted to the production of low quality papers such as newsprint, so that rags continued to be employed for medium and good quality paper. A satisfactory solution was not forthcoming until the invention of the sulphite process in 1867 in the U.S.A. Separation was achieved by boiling non-resinous wood chips in a solution of sulphur dioxide and calcium bisulphate, and its adoption first in Europe, and then in the U.S.A. in 1882, had considerable locational repercussions. For the first time entrepreneurs were faced with a locational problem, since the forces influencing wood-pulp production were different from those bearing on papermaking. The result was that the industry came to have two production stages. It was clearly preferable to move pulp made in forest areas to market-located paper mills. Subsequently technical innovations did nothing to change pulp mill location in principle. These innovations will be mentioned below, but first it is convenient to analyse pulp mill location factors.

PULP MILL LOCATION

Perhaps the most important factor in pulp mill location is the weight-loss involved in processing. This is less in the case of mechanical pulp than for chemical pulp owing to the removal of a larger proportion of impurities in chemical pulp production. Hence mechanical pulp has a weight-loss of 7% giving a material index of 1·1 compared with 45% and 2·2 for chemical pulp.[10] This gives a mean of slightly less than 2·0 in the U.S.A. where more chemical than mechanical pulp is made.

Following Weber, this would suggest material-orientation in order to minimise movement.

Secondly, a resource location has in addition considerable transport economies. Not only can pulp stand freight charges more readily than pulp wood, because of its lower bulk and greater unit value, but freight costs on logs delivered to the pulp mill can be very low indeed where the mill has a riverine location, which is frequently the case. Even where it is impossible to use this method of pulp wood delivery, improvements in forest roads and in transport vehicles keep freight charges down. That materials account for 51% of total costs emphasises the significance of both weight-loss and transport considerations.[11]

Thirdly, electric power for machinery can normally be produced at low cost in forest regions by harnessing the water power which is so abundant in the great forest belts of Anglo-America and northern Europe. Until recently, with the introduction of very large generators with efficiency levels of up to 40%, thermally produced electric power was very much more expensive than hydro-electric power generated in the forest areas referred to. In some regions, for example, Fennoscandia, hydroelectric power is still cheaper than thermal electricity. Norwegian hydro-electricity is produced for 0·08p per kwh, while the newest oil-fired thermal plant in the U.K. can achieve only 0·21p per kwh, although this would fall to 0·16p without fuel tax. Thus rural forest regions have an advantage over urban areas, although this is declining. Electricity is not normally used for heat raising in pulp production, and primary energy, that is, coal, oil, or natural gas, is employed. Approximately 0·5 ton of coal equivalent is required for every ton of pulp produced. Here the advantage is less clear since many population concentrations in the advanced countries have grown either on coalfields or at sites having access to coal at low cost. Additionally, the availability of oil and natural gas is relatively good in urban areas, so the use by pulp mills of wood waste from associated saw mills is not an outstanding advantage.

Fourthly, mechanical pulp production consumes 68 000 litres/15 000 gallons of fresh water per ton, while sulphite pulp is very much more water intensive, requiring 450 000 litres/100 000 gallons per ton. Water is needed for log washing, steam raising, and for use in the cooking process in chemical pulp production. Pulp is moved about the mill in water in suspension at a solid consistency of about 5%, implying that twenty times as much water as pulp is required for this purpose.[12] Water costs are a small proportion of total costs, but there is no question that these costs would be at a higher level in populated areas where the competition for water is very much greater, and where water would have to be cleaned before use, unless costly mains water is bought. A related cost advantage was at one time the freedom on the part of pulp mills to dump their effluent into the rural rivers on which they were sited. They are now normally required to pre-treat their waste material.

In the simple Weberian three-point case of two material sources (wood and chemicals) and one market, assuming (a) electricity to be ubiquitous in an area of high hydro-electric power potential, (b) energy in the form of wood waste to be supplied by an associated saw mill and (c) water to be ubiquitous, then the locational figure would be similar to that shown in Fig. 41. It is evident that when RM_2 is weighted according to the distance times unit freight charges times the tonnage required to produce one ton of pulp, and M similarly weighted in respect of the tonnage of pulp produced, that the plant should theoretically be located close to the apex of the triangle at RM_1. (Chemical inputs per ton

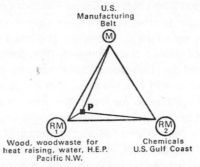

Fig. 41 Weberian locational triangle illustrating pulp mill location, Pacific Northwest, U.S.A.

of pulp are very small indeed.) In reality the plant would be more likely to be sited at the source of the wood than some distance from it, especially since the precise location will be determined by the presence of a river which itself can be used as a means of transport. The subsequent need to make use of pulp wood supplies from one or more alternative sources would disturb the theoretical locational equilibrium. However, the plant itself has a locational pull in the form of capital investment, labour supplies and other agglomeration economies. Weber's solution was isodapane analysis, referred to in Chapter 1. In practice pulp mills can normally obtain the additional pulp wood from relatively proximate sources, or are able to take delivery of wood at relatively low cost by reason of their riverine or tidewater location. In this case the sum of the forces of inertia is greater than the pull of distant material sites. Put another way, the entrepreneur prefers to substitute agglomeration economies for higher transport costs.

It can be argued that since the pulp industry is a harvesting industry, assembling pulp wood from an area, the limits of which are continually changing, the Weberian concept of the plant locating at a point of least cost is not entirely relevant.[13] Thus the mill will make use of an ubiquitous (at least within the forest area) raw material, and the precise location will be determined, for example, by the presence of a suitable riverine site. Considerations such as these have caused many Swedish mills to be established on the coast, since an important consideration is the ability to export finished products. Here, then, there is a modification of material-orientation.

INTEGRATED PULP AND PAPER MILL LOCATION

In spite of the factors conducive to complete division of pulp and papermaking, the specialised pulp mill is a rarity, especially in Anglo-America where political influences have been weaker than in Europe. There are only 12 pulp mills in the U.S.A., nearly all pulp being made in integrated pulp and paper mills. The strength of raw material pull is usually sufficient to overcome the attractions of markets for papermaking, causing integrated mills to take up locations identical to those of pulp mills. Market-oriented integrated mills are viable only when pulpwood can be shipped by water transport.

There are obvious advantages in despatching paper rather than pulp because of its higher unit value, and there are important process economies stemming from integration, for example, the cost of drying pulp for shipment is avoided since liquid pulp can be poured directly on to the screens of the Fourdrinier paper machine. However, the most significant reason for the widespread establishment of integrated mills is the economies of large-scale production. Because of the high proportion of fixed to total costs, it is desirable to achieve a high volume of production since unit costs decline as output is expanded. Large mills are able to use equipment more fully, and as a large electricity generating plant must be built, the unit cost of electric energy is lower than for smaller plants. Large mills enjoy the preferential freight rates offered by railways to shipments taking up a complete wagon or wagons. Daggett observes that for consignments of 10 tons on short hauls in the U.S.A. the 'less than carload' freight rate is four times higher than the carload rate.[14] Unit labour costs also fall with increases in the size of plants; a mill making 200 tons of paper per day has only half the labour cost per ton of paper of a mill producing 50 tons per day. Labour costs account for 15% of total costs for the industry as a whole, so these economies are important.[15] In Western Europe, where there is much international trade in pulp in particular, national governments in pulp producing countries have been supporting the development of integrated mills to add to employment and wealth. In mills producing newsprint, a low-value paper, scale economies are even more important since profits per ton of output are very small indeed. Thus plants are large; the minimum annual output for a viable integrated mill making newsprint is 150 000 tons.

The result on location is that the larger the size of plant the greater is

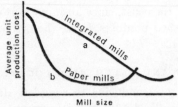

Fig. 42 Size-cost relationships between integrated mills and paper mills

the material-orientation. Fig. 42 illustrates the way in which small specialised paper mills achieve relatively low average costs following the high unit value of their product, while the less specialised integrated mills must be very large to achieve such low average costs. It is worthy of note in the case of the integrated mills that the closer curve a approaches the x-axis, the stronger is the pull of the pulp wood source.

The precise siting of both pulp and integrated mills is partly dictated

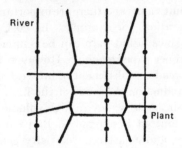

Fig. 43 Theoretical pulp wood supply areas

by the size of plant in relation to wood supplies. Because of the heavy capital investment, such costs must be written off over a long period and a location must be selected where wood supplies are sufficient to cover this time span. Once a balance is achieved between felling and planting in the supply area, then it becomes possible to amortise capital costs over long periods. Forests are frequently owned by pulp and paper companies, giving rise, theoretically, to hexagonal supply areas. In the same way as Isard has modified Losch's hexagonal market areas to take account of the fall in population density at distances away from city centres, so these supply areas will be distorted owing to the advantages of locating plants on rivers. A model of the situation is shown in Fig. 43.

Behavioural factors can distort this pattern. In the southern states of the U.S.A. mills have become particularly sensitive to criticism of their position as very large landowners. One firm, for example, owns 12% of the forested area of the state.[16] Consequently firms are tending to support local small-farm pulp wood producers rather than increase the size of their holdings. Alternatively some firms have obtained control of land as much as 160 km/100 miles from the mill,[17] thus creating a segmented company-owned supply area superimposed on a privately owned supply area. Distortion will also occur since it is unlikely that all plants will be established at precisely the same time, and further, the relative size of the various plants will create differential demand for land.

In spite of the advantages of producing paper in integrated mills, the existence of independent paper mills causes the forested countries that are sufficiently industrialised to provide the capital and technology required, to produce surpluses of pulp. The most important of these countries, the U.S.A., Canada, Sweden, Finland and Japan, therefore exhibit a relatively low correlation between pulp and paper production capacity. Division of paper output by pulp output gives quotients of 0·557, 0·619, 0·481, 0·592 and 0·826 for the five countries mentioned, suggesting that in all but Japan about half the market for pulp lies outside the boundaries of each nation. Thus in Sweden, 51% of production was exported in 1969, paper mills in Europe taking 44% of the output. Leading consumers were the U.K., West Germany, France, Italy and the Netherlands, absorbing 12, 8, 6, 5, and 2% of output respectively. Canadian pulp exports largely (21% of total production but 68% of exports) go to the U.S.A. as a result of the shortage of newsprint there, the absence of U.S. duties on pulp, the ownership of some Canadian pulp capacity by American interests, and the particularly suitable Canadian conditions for the production of mechanical pulp.

Fig. 44, a quotient map, shows that apart from Sweden and Finland, there are only two countries in Western Europe with significant surpluses of pulp (that is, countries returning quotients of less than 1): Portugal and Norway. In absolute tonnage, however, they are very much less important than Sweden and Finland. Norway has a surplus of pulp of 686 000 tons, and Portugal 75 000 tons compared with 3 553 000 tons and 2 330 000 tons for Sweden and Finland respectively. Even with distortions caused by nationalism, the map clearly indicates the significance of the forested countries of Norden for pulp production. This clear distinction between the forested pulp-producing regions and the industrialised paper-producing areas is also true of the U.S.A. Fig. 45 indicates that the five southern, forested states of Mississippi, Florida, Georgia, South Carolina and Alabama (quotients of 0·727, 0·741, 0·833,

E

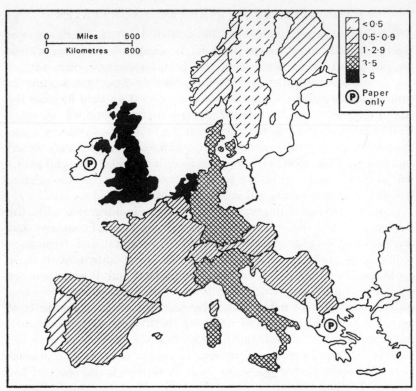

Fig. 44 Paper-pulp quotients, Western Europe, 1967

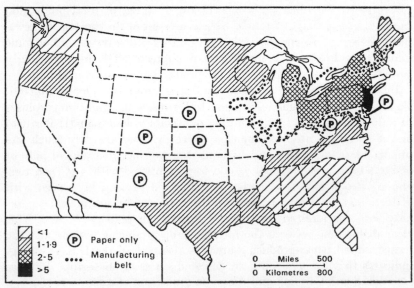

Fig. 45 Paper-pulp quotients, U.S.A., 1966

0·900 and 0·956 respectively), and Washington (0·675) have surpluses of pulp, illustrating the importance of integrated and specialist pulp mills in these areas. Data for 17 states are not published to avoid disclosing figures for individual firms, and this accounts for most of the states left blank on the map.

PAPER MILL LOCATION

We have seen how the traditional paper mill was market-located because of the availability of materials and labour. Although the main material changed to wood pulp, the market still provided a material pull since one-third of the paper in the industrialised countries comes from waste. In the U.S.A., for example, where integrated mills produce considerable tonnages of paper but do not use waste owing to their distance from urban areas, markets still provide nearly half material inputs. The process of beating the waste paper back into pulp weakens the fibres, but there is a weight-loss of only 10%,[18] an interesting case of a weight-

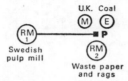

Fig. 46 Weberian locational figure of paper mill location in Lancashire

losing process being both material- and market-oriented. There are some poor quality papers such as paperboard that are made entirely from waste, while at the other end of the range high-grade writing and book-paper is produced from cotton and linen. While in a broad manner such mills may be regarded as a Weberian one-point case, more typical is the two-point case where the locational figure becomes a straight line, as in Fig. 46.

In Western Europe, just as the governments of forested countries encourage the establishment of integrated mills, so governments of the industrialised poorly forested countries, where demand for pulp cannot be met from indigenous sources, support the retention of papermaking. This is achieved by protective duties on paper imports, which not only engenders the movement of pulp rather than the more logical shipment of paper from the forest-oriented integrated mills in Norden, but also favours the specialist pulp mill in the latter area. The best example of specialist paper mills is the U.K. with its quotient of 14·082 dwarfing the other industrialised importers. It is to be expected that a port or riverine location would be crucial to British paper mills as it is to many of the older paper mills in New England. Fig. 47 suggests that this does not appear to be universally the case. The concentrations in the vicinity of the Clyde, Forth, the Manchester Ship Canal, Thames and Medway indicate possible transport-orientation, but the number of mills in industrial Lancashire and the West Riding of Yorkshire suggest that the high value of many papers, the importance of waste paper and geographical inertia are further significant locational considerations. Although the distribution pattern has evolved slowly, dynamic elements

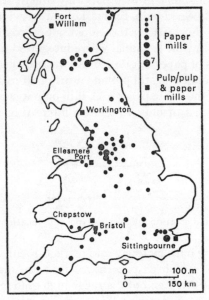

Fig. 47 Pulp and paper mills in England, Scotland and Wales, 1968

are always at work. Thus British mills badly located in respect of coal were either forced out of business or into the production of a higher grade of paper between 1800 and 1860. Similarly the removal of tariff protection from Sweden and Finland consequent upon British participation in E.F.T.A. was responsible for at least some of 23 paper mill closures in Britain between 1959 and 1971. Already smaller mills, for example those on the Medway, remain in operation by producing very high-grade papers such as art paper, banknotes, cheques and filter papers for petroleum refineries.[19] In such cases proximity to consumer is a great advantage since the need for consultation, or information linkage, is likely to be considerable.

Predictably the great concentration of U.S. paper mills is in the manufacturing belt which is marked on Fig. 45. All six states scoring more than 1·9 lie within the belt, including New Jersey with the highest quotient of 18·571. In two states, Delaware and West Virginia, partly within the manufacturing belt, the domination of papermaking is absolute, pulp making being entirely absent. The industry is represented entirely by pulp mills in four states, but here the number of mills is small. The provinces of Canada are somewhat large to use as a basis for comparisons; in this case it is enough to comment that of the 35 Canadian paper mills, 27 are located in metropolitan Canada on the linear axis between the Lakes Peninsula and Quebec, while two of the remainder are at Winnipeg.

CHANGES IN THE LOCATION OF THE INDUSTRY IN THE U.S.A.

It is doubtful whether a plant can ever be said to be in locational equilibrium since the forces at work are constantly changing. Some of these influences, especially technology and entrepreneurial behaviour, can be examined by considering the locational changes that have taken place in the industry in the U.S.A.

It has been seen how the invention of mechanical and chemical (sulphite) pulping in the 19th century caused these processes to become material-oriented. The term 'material-oriented' is not, however, sufficiently precise, since technological restrictions obliged the pulp makers to establish their plants at locations at or close to particular types of wood, namely spruce, balsam and hemlock. These varieties were to be found in northern New England, New York, Pennsylvania and the Lake States, but not in anything like adequate quantities in Connecticut, Massachusetts, New Jersey, Ohio, Indiana and Illinois. While entrepreneurs were forced to accept the technical limitations on the type of wood they could process, they appear only to have considered the short-term supply position, for many pulp mills were built in Connecticut, Massachusetts and other inadequately supplied states. Even after 1900 when wood shortages were causing prices to rise steeply and wood was imported from Canada, more new pulp mills were built in the next decade in the poorly endowed areas than in the states such as Maine and Wisconsin where the supply situation was good. The process did not cease until the 1920s, and was later repeated in Michigan and Wisconsin, where pulp wood supplies began to run down in the 1920s, but where pulp mill construction did not cease until the 1930s.[20]

Several issues are raised by these events. The influence of technology in forcing pulp mills to develop in regions where specific types of trees were available is obvious. Equally obvious is the way in which entrepreneurs acted as boundedly rational satisficers rather than as the rational economic men of the classical economic theorists. (See Chapter 1.)

Hagerstrand and others have shown that the diffusion of innovation is a gradual process, and it would be unreasonable to have expected new pulp mills immediately to have developed at great distances, in unfamiliar territory, away from the old-established districts. Psychological as well as economic spatial inertia had to be overcome. Equipped with hindsight it is possible for us to see what action the industry should have taken, but the situation was by no means so evident to new investors at the time. The consequence was that 'safe' location decisions were made, and construction in existing areas took place. Plant location is indeed dynamic, but even the most rational entrepreneur cannot perceive overnight what might be regarded as the optimum location. In the case of the early American pulp industry the period of delayed response to the new locational situation lasted for thirty years.

When the sum of the forces of change began to outweigh the advantages of inertia, that is at the end of the period of what is sometimes called 'cultural lag', entrepreneurs were obliged to adapt to the new situation or decline. Faced with severe competition from better placed mills, the poorly located small-sized pulp mills went out of business. The badly located large-sized pulp and paper mills reorganised to make the best use of their heavy fixed costs, and accepted reduced profit margins. Many badly located paper mills adapted by moving into a higher grade of papermaking, the higher value added in processing offsetting the locational cost disadvantages. Newsprint, in which Canada had a distinct advantage, was dropped, and writing papers, for example, which could use waste paper supplied locally, were produced instead. This upward shift was made easier by the nature of the papermaking machinery which not only has a long life, but which also can be made to produce different grades of paper without difficulty. Finally, some paper mills, especially those in Pennsylvania, New York and New England, were relatively well placed to receive imported pulp from Norden, long after local pulp mills had shut. The same was true of Wisconsin and Michigan after 1935, by making use of the Great Lakes' transport system.[21] The optimum location for the use of imported pulp is the east coast. Therefore it cannot be said that mills elsewhere using imported pulp are either minimising their costs or, in many cases, maximising their profits. Such mills occupy what Simon has termed satisficer locations; these are locations which exist when the owner of a plant accepts that his profit would be greater at an alternative location, but is nevertheless satisfied with the existing situation.

The final stages of locational change in the U.S.A. can be viewed as a function of comparative cost as between the newer districts of the Pacific Northwest and the South and the older regions already discussed.

Such an analysis has especial validity in the Pacific Northwest. Locational change can also be seen as a function of technological change, and this is particularly valid in the case of the South. There were five major innovations, which are listed in chronological order: (a) The sulphite process restricted the industry to non-resinous woods so that the resinous pine forests of the southern states from Texas to Virginia could not be exploited. (b) The sulphate process, first introduced at Roanoke Rapids in North Carolina in 1909, could handle resinous wood, and once the (c) sulphate bleaching process had been developed in the early 1930s, enabling sulphate pulp to compete on a cost basis with sulphite pulp, the way was open for what was an extremely rapid growth in the South. These developments had a backwash effect on the Midwestern and Northeastern mills which had specialised in wrapping paper, for the sulphate kraft wrapping paper was much more competitive. The result was an upward shift to higher grade material, further emphasising the concentration of these mills in the manufacturing belt. (d) The semi-chemical process was introduced in the 1930s following collaboration between the industry and the Federal government, and provided a means of pulping hardwoods which make up 45%of Southern forests, thereby adding to the attractions of the region. The South is now responsible for 60% of U.S. pulp. (e) The magnefite process, introduced in 1958, permits sulphite mills to pulp both pine and hardwood, thus reducing the advantage hitherto enjoyed by the South in respect of the latter wood.

2.4 THE CEMENT INDUSTRY

The cement industry differs from both the copper and the paper and pulp industries in that it is a single process activity. Its raw material sources are quarries and its markets the construction industries. Perhaps more significantly, however, the industry is an example of one that is tied to the source of a raw material which is very nearly ubiquitous, thereby allowing plants a high degree of market-orientation. The latter is an important consideration since cement is a low-value commodity, delivery costs accounting for 16·5% of selling prices in the U.S.A.,[22] and for one-third of manufacturing costs in the U.K.[23] Limitations upon the entrepreneur's freedom to select a market-oriented site do exist. Firstly, as will be obvious from Fig. 48, there are many population concentrations distant from rock suitable for cement production. Secondly, the chemical composition of the rock is very critical, so that some limestone areas are unsuitable for the purpose. Thirdly, the costs of exploitation are lowest where the rock outcrops, a site factor well exemplified by the string of plants on the northern edge of the Chiltern Hills.

Cement sells for about £7·50 per ton ex works in the U.K. and will clearly not stand long distance transport, hence the importance of proximity to markets. Copper, on the other hand, sells for about £500 per ton, although there are wide fluctuations about this point. Long hauls are very much more feasible, and as we have seen not only refined but also blister copper is shipped many thousands of miles. The two activities support the hypothesis that in the extractive industries the extent of either material- or market-orientation is a function of market

Fig. 48 Cement plants in England, Scotland and Wales, 1968

prices. The higher the latter, the less significant are delivery costs in the determination of the location of exploitation.

Cement is made by mixing finely ground calcareous minerals, such as chalk and limestone, with others containing silica and alumina, and heating the mixture to about 1500°C/1750°F. On cooling a clinker is formed and this is ground to a fine powder, a small quantity of gypsum being added to control the setting time. When mixed with gravel, sand and water, concrete results. There are two processes that may be used, the dry and the wet process, the latter being more fuel intensive. A particularly wet charge containing, say, 42% moisture, requires 0·20 tons of oil per ton of cement produced, against 0·09 tons of oil for a dry charge. The weight-loss on dry limestone is 37%, giving a Weberian material index of 1·7. Wet limestone or chalk will score greater weight-losses since water is included in the weight of the material, and coupled with higher fuel consumption returns a material index varying between 2·0 and 2·5 depending on moisture content. Gypsum is added after the roasting process and undergoes no weight-loss. The material index and the low unit value of the major raw material would suggest a resource location, and on a micro-scale this is normally the case.

As with integrated pulp and paper mills, average unit costs vary inversely with output, with the consequence that the cement industry is characterised by large plants. This receives further emphasis since cement is a standard homogeneous product, so that it is impossible for additional sales to be effected by virtue of specialization, thereby offsetting a small-sized plant. For example, the Aberthaw works, the most westerly of the three South Wales plants, has an annual capacity of 678 000 tons. The result is that one plant will serve its market area in a monopolistic fashion owing to the homogeneous nature of cement and the high incidence of transport costs. On a macro-scale, then, the industry is market-oriented. The shape of the market area will be a function of the size of the plant, the demand for cement about the plant, the distances separating the plant from competing plants and differences between production costs between plants. Market areas may also be distorted by ownership patterns. Several plants in juxtaposition, not unusual owing to the material-orientation exhibited, may well belong to one company, and the resulting market area will be that of the firm rather than that of an individual plant. Many firms have established depots at strategic points within market areas in order to reduce the incidence of delivery charges. Cement is shipped by rail from the production unit to the depot, whence delivery is effected by road, thus supporting Hoover's observations referred to in Chapter 1 on the suitability of transport media for particular lengths of haul.

The transport-oriented industries are very sensitive to shifts in freight rates, and they are very quick to make use of new developments in transport. In the cement industry the economies obtainable from the use of pipelines carrying chalk/limestone slurry are beginning to change the relationship between raw material and delivery costs. Such a slurry pipe was opened in 1967 to convey material from the Chiltern Hills to Rugby, a distance of 91 km/57 miles. Unit transport costs on raw material moved by pipe to the plant are sometimes (depending largely on the size of the pipe, the load factor and the distance involved) lower than delivery charges on cement from a plant adjacent to a quarry some distance from a major market. Total transport charges are minimised by a market location, whereas before the use of pipelines the point of minimum movement was a material location. The use of chalk slurry implies that the wet process must be employed, and it is this process that returns the higher material index. Changes in transport technology thus increasingly undermine the value of the Weberian material index and the concept of weight-loss in location analysis.

References

1. A. Pred, 'Industrialization, initial advantage and American metropolitan growth', *Geographical Review*, 1965, p. 174.
2. B. Chinitz, 'The effect of transportation forms on regional economic growth', *Traffic Quarterly*, 14, No. 2, April 1960, p. 137.
3. H. I. Schiller, 'Current Problems in Raw Material Supply', *Land Economics*, 1964, p. 362.
4. J. W. Alexander, *Economic Geography*, Prentice Hall, 1964, p. 337.
5. *Ibid.*
6. U.S. Department of the Interior, *Minerals Yearbook*, IV, 1967, Washington, 1969, p. 425.
7. W. Smith, 'The Location of Industry', *Transactions and Papers, Institute of British Geographers*, 21, 1955, p. 7.
8. J. W. Alexander, *loc. cit.*
9. J. A. Guthrie, *The Economics of Pulp and Paper*, Pullman, State College of Washington, 1950, p. 32.
10. J. B. Calkin, The Paper and Pulp Industry, in A. S. Carlson (Ed), *Economic Geography of Industrial Materials*, Rheinhold, New York, 1956, p. 312.
11. R. S. Thoman, E. C. Conkling and M. H. Yeates, *The Geography of Economic Activity*, 2nd Ed., McGraw-Hill, 1968, p. 479.
12. J. B. Calkin, *op. cit.*, p. 320.
13. O. Lindberg, 'An Economic-Geographical Study of the Localization of the Swedish Paper Industry', *Geografiska Annaler*, 35, 1953, p. 40.
14. S. Daggett, *Principles of Inland Transportation*, 4th Ed., New York, 1955.
15. E. B. Alderfer and H. E. Michl, *Economics of American Industry*, 3rd Ed., McGraw-Hill, 1957, p. 229.
16. J. B. Calkin, *op. cit.*, p. 320.
17. M. Prunty, 'Recent Expansion in the Southern Pulp-Paper Industries', *Economic Geography*, 32, 1956, pp. 52–3.
18. E. B. Alderfer and H. E. Michl, *op. cit.*, p. 287.
19. P. W. Lewis, 'Changing Factors of Location in the Paper-Making Industry as Illustrated by the Maidstone Area', *Geography*, 52, 1967, p. 292.
20. H. Hunter, 'Innovation, Competition and Locational Change in the Pulp and Paper Industry, 1880–1950', *Land Economics*, 31, 1955, pp. 315–18.
21. *Ibid.*
22. E. B. Alderfer and H. E. Michl, *op. cit.*, p. 184.
23. P. N. Grimshaw, 'The U.K. Portland Cement Industry', *Geography*, 53, 1968, p. 84.

Chapter 3

THE INFLUENCE OF POWER AND GEOGRAPHICAL INERTIA: THE TEXTILE INDUSTRY

Technological progress has ensured that considerations such as the cost of labour, transport and materials, or merely presence within a manufacturing region, weigh more heavily in location decisions than does the cost of energy. Developments in the field of energy have all tended to confer mobility on industry. Electric power can be transmitted by wire over long distances, oil as a fluid is eminently transportable, and there have been improvements in the methods of transport. There are some exceptions to these generalisations, for we have already seen how the use of electrolysis makes copper refining sensitive to the cost of electric power, and in Chapter 4 we will see that the same is true of aluminium smelting. But apart from the electro-smelting and electro-chemical industries, there are now no industries which react to the need to minimise the cost of power by constructing plants close to the source of that power. Thus in order to study the influence of power as a restrictive location factor it is necessary to examine the great sources of power of the industrial revolution, water and steam. This can be done by considering the present-day distribution pattern of one of the foremost industries of the 19th century, the manufacture of textiles. The distribution of the industry in the advanced countries has barely changed for more than a century, and in order to explain its modern location it is necessary to look at the influences at work at the time when the industry was youthful and when the sources of power were anything but mobile.

Even in the Middle Ages when methods of transport were rudimentary there was evidence that cloth manufacture could be regarded neither as material- nor market-oriented. The Flemish clothiers used English as well as local wool, they imported much of their dyestuffs and their manufactures were exported throughout Europe and the Mediterranean. This was possible because both materials and products have a high value in relation to their weight. Water-driven fulling mills were in use at this time, but such mills could handle the output of a large number of weavers, and even in Flanders, which is short of swiftly running streams, cloth manufacture was never oriented to sources of power. The existence of specialist production centres was a function of the development of local skills and of considerable entrepreneurial ability involving finance, organisation and knowledge of the market, coupled with a strategic position in respect of trade routes. Mechanisation of the industry led to the more widespread use of water to power the new machinery towards the end of the 18th century. The consequence was the transformation of what was essentially a domestic industry into a factory industry whose plants had no choice as to their location, for they were drawn inexorably to water power sites. The subsequent use of steam power did not have quite the same revolutionary effect upon the distribution of the industry, although there are some important concentrations of the activity on coalfields, especially in Britain. Textiles can therefore only be regarded as power-oriented at the water power stage, but the fact remains that mills built up to the end of the 19th century were either at water power sites or on coalfields, or with good access to them. The electric motor and the easy transmission of electric power by wire have since removed power from the list of vital locational factors, and its place has been taken by labour, the importance of which is illustrated in Table 3.1.

TABLE 3.1

Labour and power costs in the cotton industry, 1951
% value of finished product

	Labour	Power
Spinning mills	63	3
Weaving mills	27	7
Finishing mills	39	9

Source: R. Robson, 'Location and Development of the Cotton Industry', *Journal of Industrial Economics*, 1, 1953, p. 101.

New mills are labour-oriented, and this has resulted in striking growth of the industry in low wage areas, for instance in the U.S. South, Japan, Hong Kong and Portugal, but the large majority of mills in Western Europe have not been recently established, and date from the water and steam power eras of the last century. The traditional areas of textile manufacture are still so engaged, and over the years have developed great geographical inertia. However, some traditional areas have failed to hold the activity with which they were associated—pig iron production in the Black Country is an example—and it is necessary to establish why textiles, almost alone of the important 19th-century industries, have not undergone fundamental changes in their distribution in Western Europe.

THE CAUSES OF INERTIA IN THE TEXTILE INDUSTRY

(i) *The absence of transport-orientation*

Many of the industries of the last century were concerned with the processing of low unit value materials and they used large quantities of coal for fuel and power. These industries, for example, iron and steel production, are still transport-oriented, and have reacted to changes in the origin and nature of their raw materials and energy requirements by shifting their location to keep transport costs as low as possible. Textiles were unusual among 19th-century industries in that they never exhibited this transport-orientation. Thus the average freight rates on raw cotton moving from New Orleans to Liverpool between 1886 and 1905 were only 3·1–5·4% of the landed price.[1] The cost of labour rather than transport is of greater significance to textiles, and since very few major areas of production are growth areas—some are regions of indifferent economic health such as Lancastria, French Nord and the Vosges mountains—it has not been necessary to consider migration to seek areas of low wages. Mills at water power sites in rural areas, for example in the valleys of the Black Forest, the Upper Neckar basin and Hesse in West Germany and the Tweed and Derwent valleys in Britain, have a similar advantage for there is little alternative employment available. The relatively unskilled and light nature of much of the work makes female labour particularly suitable. 60% of British, and 78% of Italian textile labour is accounted for by females who are paid lower wages than men.[2]

(ii) *The size of plant*

In industries such as iron and steel, oil refining and brewing, the unit cost of production falls as the size of plant rises. In textiles an increase in the size of the mill does not result in appreciable economies, and no process need be carried out on a large scale to be profitable. There is therefore no technical reason for the existence of large mills. The demand for different types of cloth ensures that production runs can seldom be very long, particularly in woollens and worsteds, and this is conducive to small mills rather than large, mass-production plants. The Colne valley in Yorkshire has 35 woollen mills, large by the standards of the industry, but their average labour force is only 289.[3] Since 19th-century mills are always impressively massive structures, and since the optimum size of mill is no larger now than it was a hundred years ago, century-old mills are still eminently suitable for current needs. Had they been too small or unserviceable, new building would have to have taken place, possibly outside the traditional areas.

(iii) *The age of the industry*

The mechanisation of the spinning and weaving processes had been achieved and had attained a high level of technical stability well before many present industries had ever been established. It follows that new areas of technical innovation in a mature industry are limited, and while there have been improvements, for example, high-speed looms, the developments that have taken place are not always sufficient to justify the scrapping of old equipment. The result has been the continued use of old machinery in old mills, the cost of which has long been written off, allowing such mills to continue in operation on slender profits. If new machinery was sufficiently advanced to give real advantages to mills using it, mills retaining old equipment would be obliged to close or modernise. As it is, old mills with old machinery are still viable, although this is less true of cottons than of woollens and worsteds. Also to be considered under this heading is the fact that although the textile industry was the leading sector in many countries for much of the 19th century and expansion was therefore the rule, it cannot now be seen as a growth industry. There is no expansion which, if it had occurred, might have caused building outside the traditional areas.

(iv) *External economies*

One of the advantages of the regional specialisation characteristic of the textile industry is the great strength of the external economies available to firms in the cluster. The greater the extent of the regional specialisation, the more valuable will the external economies be, and the greater will become the geographical inertia of the region. We identified five types of linkage between plants in Chapter 1, and three of these are present in textiles: vertical, diagonal and information linkage. (a) Vertical linkage. In cottons, finishing and printing are carried out by specialists. In woollens, dyeing and sometimes finishing are separate activities. In worsteds, combing and very often spinning and weaving are in the hands of different firms. With such disintegration at the level of the firm there are obvious gains to be had from proximity. (b) Diagonal linkage. Most medium-sized firms employ their own mechanics, but adjustments of more than a minor nature need the services of specialists and of spare part suppliers. Few mills can afford to stock all the spares they are likely to need. Such support industries are to be found in the textile areas rather than elsewhere. Table 3.2 shows the strength of the

West Riding in respect of various wool textile support activities. Lancashire is also shown since many firms service both wool and cotton textiles. (c) Information linkage. Plants outside the main manufacturing areas are less likely to be fully conversant with the state of either the market or the going price of materials, which fluctuates daily, and they may be forced to rely on agents for this information. Central information

TABLE 3.2

Firms in Britain supplying the Wool Textile industry, 1969

Service	West Riding	Lancashire	Elsewhere	Total
Textile brushes	13	9	—	22
Wool-combing machinery	11	—	—	11
Carding machinery	11	5	3	19
Feeding machines	11	4	—	15
Skip makers	11	5	1	17
Warping machines	9	5	2	16
Tentering machinery	7	—	1	8

Source: *Skinner's Wool Trade Directory of the World, 1968–9*, Bradford, 1969.

agencies have been set up by the larger cotton firms, rendering distance between the main manufacturing regions irrelevant in this context, but this is unusual in wool textiles. Other external economies helping to prolong the attractiveness of established districts include the availability of skilled labour for certain processes and of mills to rent at low prices. The latter facilitates entry to the industry by small firms such as specialist spinners and commission weavers, and their presence further increases the geographical inertia of an area.

(v) *Electric power*

Textiles are more concerned with the use of energy as power rather than as fuel, with the result that the introduction of the electric motor towards the end of the 19th century was particularly useful to the industry. Mills not on coalfields had higher coal costs than those more fortunately located and by using electricity they were able to reduce their power costs. This assisted the continuation of the textile industry in rural areas, many of which were developed prior to the steam era. Electric power confirmed the existence of mills in the pre-Alpine areas of Europe for they were able to replace their water turbines with electric motors deriving their power from water-driven generators.

Having considered the reasons for the retention of textile production by the traditional areas, we turn to look at the reasons for the selection of these regions in the first place. Comment will be restricted to the cotton and wool textile industries.

WATER POWER AND LOCATION

Fulling was the first textile process to be mechanised, but the medieval fulling mill did not disturb the distribution of the industry which, apart from a few specialist areas such as Flanders, was broadly correlated with the distribution of population. The area of important innovation began in the 18th century, very largely in the county of Lancashire and very largely from within the cotton industry.

(i) Cotton textiles

The first major innovation was the flying shuttle by John Kay in 1733, followed by Hargreaves' spinning jenny in 1765. Although these machines improved productivity, they could be used in a cottage, and it was Arkwright's water frame spinning machine in 1769 that began the transfer of workers from cottages to factories. Initially Arkwright employed six horses to provide the power in his Nottingham mill (he was forced to leave his native Lancashire), but by 1771 he had built the first water-driven cotton mill, at Cromford, Derbyshire. Further stimulus for the use of water wheels was Crompton's spinning mule of 1779. Watt patented his method of rotary action in 1781, making it possible for steam rather than water to be used as power, but the immediate result was not dramatic. The early steam engines were unreliable, they were voracious consumers of coal which was expensive to move in relation to its value, whereas water was free, and there was prejudice against steam engines on the grounds that they did not provide the smooth, regular motion of the water wheel. Arkwright's first water wheel at Cromford produced about 9 kilowatts/12 horsepower, but within 25 years wheels generating 60 kW/80 hp were installed, and by 1820 75 kW/100 hp wheels were being built.[4] Until steam engines capable of producing equal power could be developed, water mills had advantages of size over steam mills. The consequence was that in Britain the use of water power continued to be extended until about 1830, although after 1800 the steam engine gained ground.[5]

The best water power sites were quickly developed and mills penetrated into remote upland areas in their search for power. Minor streams, such as the Spodden in Lancashire, yielding 325 kW/428 hp at 18 sites over a distance of 8 km/5 miles,[6] were utilised in many rural areas, irrespective of the absence of skilled workers, or in some places, of any workers at all. Consequently mill owners had to provide new settlements for their workers, and some of these industrial villages remain, for example, Cromford, Milford and Belper in the Derwent valley in Derbyshire. Cotton mills sprang up in Durham, Cumberland, Westmorland, North Wales, Warwickshire, Staffordshire and in the Clyde valley, in addition to those in Lancashire and Derbyshire, during the water power phase. However, these areas found themselves incapable of meeting the competition provided by Lancashire which, although it was an area of important water power sites, is also a coalfield and came to possess remarkable advantages for cotton textile manufacture.

Perhaps the greatest influence water power has had on the present distribution of the cotton industry is the way in which the possession of water mills gave impetus to the expansion of steam-driven mills in Lancashire. If the county had lacked cotton manufacture prior to the steam era, this would have been a considerable disadvantage to the growth of the industry. Certainly many of the innovations originating in Lancashire, specifically designed to improve productivity in cotton textiles, would have been initiated elsewhere. Outside Lancashire the impact of water power on the current geography of the industry in Britain has been small. Lancashire is examined below under 'Steam Power and Location'.

On the continent of Western Europe the mechanisation of the industry took place more slowly than in Britain. In France, for instance, the replacement of hand spinning by power spindles was not effected until the years between 1815 and 1830, and even as late as 1856 there were still 8657 hand looms out of a total of 26 796 in operation in the leading cotton manufacturing *département*, Haut Rhin.[7] In Germany the first cotton spinning mill using Arkwright's water frame was not established until 1794, appropriately enough at Kromford, near Dusseldorf. Because of the shortage of coal in France and Germany until well after 1850, water remained a vital source of power for much longer than in Britain. Indeed, water power was still dominant in Alsace at mid-century, and this region then possessed no less than one-third of all French cotton spindles.[8] Switzerland lacked coal, but possessed abundant water power supplies, and here too water power was of much greater significance than in Britain. The same was true of Italy, but here the cotton industry did not really establish itself until about 1875. There was much incentive therefore to persevere with the technology of water power, and it was on the continent, particularly in France, that innovation in this field was most advanced. In 1825 the Frenchman J. V. Poncelet designed an undershot wheel with curved vanes which was three times more efficient than ordinary wheels, and two years later Fourneyron produced the first water turbine which improved performance still further. When it

F

eventually became necessary to supplement water power with steam, great strides had already been made in the improvement of the steam engine. Watt's engine used 3·4 kg/7·5 lb of coal per metric horse power hour, but by the 1850s only 1·3–1·8 kg/3–4 lb were required.[9] Woolf compound engines, which consumed half the fuel of a comparable sized Watt engine, were much used on the continent. Hence the introduction of steam power in the last half of the 19th century did not create a powerful pull towards the source of the fuel, as was the case in Britain

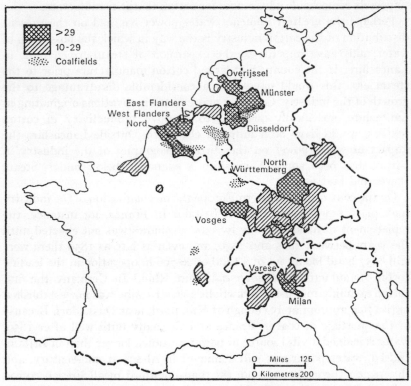

Fig. 49 Distribution of Cotton textile mills by administrative areas in selected West European countries, 1968

where expansion was so much earlier. The electric motor further added to the inertia of the regions rich in water power by completely removing the locational influence of the coalfields.

Of the 28 administrative areas shown in Fig. 49 as possessing more than 9 cotton mills in 1968, 18 are regions of water power, forming an impressive concentration in the pre-Alpine upland areas of France, West Germany, Switzerland and Italy. The French *département* of Rhône might also be included since it has access to both water power and coal.

Only Seine Maritime of the water power areas lies outside the pre-Alpine region. There are, however, areas of abundant water power possessing no cotton mills at all, and it is important to observe that while the availability of water power was a major factor in the location of the textile industry, it was by no means the only consideration. To explain why the manufacture of cotton grew up in one area and not another physically suitable district, it is necessary to consider the special advantages enjoyed by the former. The background to the development of each textile region is unique, but it is useful briefly to examine the factors involved in the growth of one such region. Let us take Alsace and the Vosges mountains as an example.

The Alsatian cotton industry began in mid-18th century as an extension of existing domestic cloth manufacture. The area, which lay along the important routeway of the Rhine leading to and from Switzerland, had a long tradition of commerce and manufacture, giving rise to the accumulation of capital which local entrepreneurs were able to call upon when it became necessary to build water mills in the early 19th century. Swiss capital and technicians were also attracted to the area. With the initiative that many frontier people seem to possess, the engineering industry, based on Mulhouse, diversified into textile machinery, and by the 1840s the town had become a centre of mechanical innovation capable of competing with the Lancastrian textile machinery makers.[10] As in Switzerland and Italy there was specialisation in fine cottons, an area of production that Lancashire, Nord and the Lower Seine districts hardly entered. As in Lancashire, spinning and weaving were carried out in separate mills, leading to improved efficiency. Expansion caused the industry to penetrate the upper valleys of the Vosges in its search for water power sites, and many mills were rebuilt as many as three times between 1815 and 1848 to meet the increased need for power.[11] At this time the industry was growing more rapidly than in the Nord where coal was available, and this must be attributed to the dynamism of the Alsatian businessmen in utilising local advantages to the full. Alsace was lacking the raw materials on which other industrial regions were basing their expansion, and textile production was probably the best outlet for local capital. The same was true of the other pre-Alpine textile regions rich in water power and in many cases with a long history of commerce behind them. The Franco-Prussian war of 1870 caused the Alsatian industry to extend into Lorraine, where it was supported by preferential tariffs introduced by the French government, and a new focus grew up at Epinal. The consequence has been that the *départements* of both Haut Rhin and Vosges are now important producers of cotton textiles. Clearly the presence of water power has not been the only factor at work, but without it there would have been great disincentive for the industry to grow in the manner it did.

(ii) *Wool textiles*

By comparison with cotton textiles, the wool textile industry is much more of a craft activity, requiring a much greater degree of skill. For this reason, and possibly because of a less aggressive approach by entrepreneurs, mechanisation took place more slowly, and mills were smaller than in cottons. In Great Britain power spinning was not adopted by worsted mills until the 1790s, and in woollens the introduction of mule spindles was delayed until the 1820s. Much of the power employed was water, and because of the small size of mill occasioned by the very nature of the industry, water supplies at particular sites were normally quite adequate to meet the power needs of wool textile mills until well into the century. Even in the West Riding with its local supplies of coal there was much incentive to retain water wheels, and as late as 1850 more than one-third of the power available to wool manufacturers in England and Wales was derived from water. Water was very much less important in cottons, as Table 3.3 shows.

TABLE 3.3

Power available in the textile industries in
Britain in 1850 (kW/hp)

	Wool		Cotton	
	kW	hp	kW	hp
Water	4 900	6 600	8 200	11 000
Steam	9 400	12 600	53 000	71 000

Source: D. S. Landes, *The Unbound Prometheus*, Cambridge University Press, 1969, p. 104.

The result was not unlike that experienced by the continental cotton industry, for the later the installation of steam power the less onerous were the costs of fuel. However, it was only by dint of specialisation that the Frome and Tweed valleys, the two most important surviving regions of water power in Britain, were able to compete with the Yorkshire mills. By manufacturing ranges of cloth that Yorkshire spurned, these areas were able to overcome the cost of coal, which was twice as expensive in Gloucestershire as it was in Yorkshire in 1840,[12] and compensate for the lack of the very considerable external economies generated in the West Riding textile district. An examination of the comparative advantages of a region for textiles helps to explain the development of the activity. Thus the Tweed is only one of several valleys possessing adequate supplies of water power in Scotland, but entrepreneurs in other potential woollen regions preferred to invest their capital in cotton, linen or iron and steel production. The Tweed valley, on the other hand, lacked suitable alternatives to woollens which became the activity in

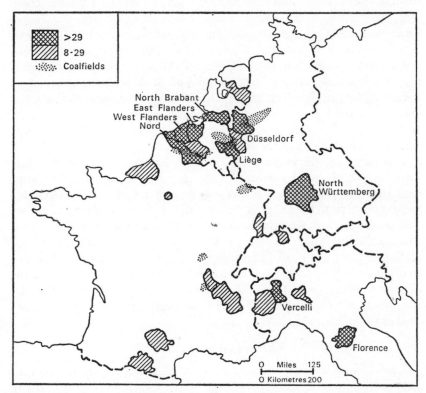

Fig. 50 Distribution of wool textile mills by administrative areas in selected Western European countries, 1968

which it had the least comparative disadvantage. The opportunity costs of woollens in the Tweed valley were low, that is, the income foregone by local capital as a result of remaining in woollens was small, because the area was not particularly suited to other forms of economic activity.

The regional specialisation so marked in Great Britain is weaker in Western Europe. Those administrative areas with more than 7 wool textile mills are mapped in Fig. 50, and comparison with Fig. 51 shows the similarity of distribution with cotton textiles. There are four noticeable discrepancies; the absence of localisation of wool textile mills in southern Germany apart from the North Württemburg *regierungsbezirk*, the presence of isolated wool textile areas of good water supply in France, for example, the *départements* of Tarn and Ariège, the separation of the ancient cloth making district of Florence from the other Italian centres, and the importance of the activity in the Belgian coalfield Provinces of Hainaut and Liège. Some 11 of the 22 administrative areas mapped are areas of water power, and once more it is clear that the inertia of these areas has proved to be greater than in Great Britain where the Tweed valley and West Country mills pale into insignificance beside the strength of those in the West Riding of Yorkshire. As in Britain, wool textiles were slower to mechanise than cotton textiles. In West Germany, for instance, only a few factory centres such as those at Aachen and Augsburg had developed by the 1850s, and it was still possible to use water to power the obsolescent types of machinery employed in many mills until the 1870s.[13] In such cases the steam power stage was quite short for electricity was introduced at the end of the century.

The generally dispersed nature of the domestic activity, the late introduction of power machinery, the retention of water power until well after mid-century and the slow growth of steam mills on coalfields were conducive to the continuation of mills at well-established locations. The consequence is that the present distribution of wool textile mills is fundamentally similar to that of the main concentrations of domestic cloth manufacture in mid-18th century. Growth in some areas and decline in others is largely a function of entrepreneurial behaviour, although the present importance of Tarn and Ariège can in part be accounted for by the formerly large supplies of wool from sheep grazing on the Causses and eastern Pyrenees.

STEAM POWER AND LOCATION

The absence of steam engines and the small power requirements of the first mills may have caused the early textile industry to be oriented to water power, but later technological developments resulted in coalfields and adjacent regions (subsequently referred to as coalfield regions), becoming the most favoured locations for the industry. Nowhere was this more true than in England. Inertia has caused this situation to persist, and Table 3.4 shows that five coalfield counties could claim 80·2% of the workforce of the industry in 1966. On the continent, those areas with large numbers of mills are predominantly coalfield regions. Thus of the 9 administrative districts with more than 29 wool textile mills shown in Fig. 50 (Nord, Vercelli, Noord Brabant, East Flanders, Florence, West Flanders, North Württemburg, Liège and Düsseldorf), only Vercelli, Florence and North Württemburg are not coalfield regions.

The others follow the line of the great north-west European coalfield running between northern France and the Ruhr, by way of Belgium and the Netherlands. It was perhaps a fortunate coincidence that the leading medieval textile region, extending through Flanders to Westphalia, largely lacking in water power, should later be able to make use of local coal for its steam mills and retain its importance in Western Europe.

TABLE 3.4

*Textile Employment in England
and Wales, 1966 (%)*

Lancashire	31·9
West Riding	30·8
Nottinghamshire and Derbyshire	9·8
Leicestershire	7·7
	80·2

There are 10 districts (East Flanders, Milan, West Flanders, Nord, Varese, Düsseldorf, Munster, Vosges, Overijssel and North Württemburg) with more than 29 cotton mills in Fig. 49, and once again the coalfields dominate. Only Milan, Varese, Vosges and North Württemburg lie outside them. In Great Britain the cotton and wool textile districts are firmly rooted respectively on the Lancashire and West Riding coalfields. The use of steam power did not result in the elimination of textile manufacture in regions of water power, although this was very nearly the case in the British cotton industry, but nevertheless coalfield regions held a powerful attraction for steam mills. Four main factors were at work.

(i) *The cost of coal*

In those areas such as Yorkshire and Lancashire that began to use steam-driven machinery before the advent of the railway, the cost of coal was a critical factor. Because the industry was expanding rapidly good water-power sites were rapidly exhausted, presenting entrepreneurs with a choice of setting up at water sites in remote areas or building steam mills in towns. Those who chose secondary water power sites found it necessary to instal steam-driven pumping engines to recycle the meagre summer water flow. Even Arkwright was obliged to do this at Cromford. But coal was so expensive to transport that when the first steam mills were built in Lancashire, a haul of 13 km/8 miles was sufficient to double its price. Coal costs were equal to about one-fifth of labour costs, so that a mill located 8 miles from a supply of coal operated under a penalty equal to a 20% wage increase.[14] Furthermore, we have seen how Watt engines were large consumers of fuel, but many of the pumping engines were built on the Newcomen pattern without a separate condenser and required about 13·50 kg/30 lb of coal per metric horse power hour, that is, four times more than the Watt engines and about eight times more than engines of the 1850s. Under such technological restrictions a location on a coalfield was virtually obligatory for the early steam mills, and certainly desirable for those set up in the first half of the 19th century. In Lancashire, Preston was the only important cotton centre not situated on the coalfield by 1850, and even in this case the town was only 16 km/10 miles from a supply of coal. Settlements of traditional cloth manufacture like Lancaster, Ormskirk and Warrington, away from the coal measures, were unable to retain their textile activities despite the availability of skilled labour.[15] We can extend our earlier comment that textiles may only be regarded as power-oriented during the water power stage to say that this was also true of steam mills erected up to about 1820. The first steam engine to power cotton spindles was built in 1786 at Papplewick near Nottingham, although pumping engines were in use prior to this. As methods of transport and steam engines themselves became more efficient, coal costs declined in importance, so that when steam mills came to be constructed on the continent, it was not essential that they be sited on a coalfield. Indeed, Ruhr coal was shipped up the Rhine and Neckar to feed the engines to be found in the pre-Alpine water power regions.

(ii) *External economies*

Textiles were not the only activity to be attracted to coalfields in order to minimise the cost of coal. Manufacturing processes requiring fuel and power in quantity were drawn to the coal-mining areas which became the great industrial regions of the 19th century. The textile industries were thus able to enjoy the advantages that went with proximity to a wide range of economic activity. The presence of the iron and engineering industries was particularly important, as the Commission set up in 1850 to investigate the causes of distress in the German linen trades discovered. They found that costs were higher in Germany than in England because of the unfavourable cost of iron, coal, steam engines, equipment and of installation. They concluded that 'in England the procurement of all factory equipment is cheaper because of the lower cost of the basic constituent, iron. Also, in England almost every individual piece of equipment is manufactured in large and specialised factories, close to the spinning mills, in a faultless and inexpensive manner.'[16] The English textile machinery industry is essentially a coalfield activity, as we shall see in Chapter 5. An additional advantage was that mills could make use of the existence of the network of canals built to expedite the general movement of materials and manufactured goods. Both the Lancashire and the Yorkshire textile industries benefited in this manner, as did French Nord and East and West Flanders in Belgium. These latter three textile districts are not actually on coalfields, but canals were built to facilitate the export of coal and manufactures through these areas, and mills, especially those making cottons, were able to utilise them for coal supplies.

(iii) *The attitude of entrepreneurs and workers*

Coalfield industrialisation seems to have been imbued with a spirit of confidence and optimism which threw up businessmen of initiative and ability on the one hand and textile craftsmen of real inventiveness on the other. Most of the early innovations in textile machinery originated in Lancashire, the first of the textile coalfield regions. The West Riding workman was more ambitious than his fellows in East Anglia and the West Country, and his was a more fluid economic and social organisation than existed in other British wool textile districts. As Professor Clapham remarks, there was in Yorkshire an 'absence of that corporate conservatism which is often found among the workers in an established *industrie de luxe*'.[17] Coalfields as a source of power had great attraction for textiles, but it was the complete economic environment which set the seal on their desirability.

(iv) *Specialisation within the industry*

The factors considered above interacted to cause the growth of textiles in coalmining regions. In the two principal British manufacturing areas, the sheer size of cloth manufacture emphasised the advantages to be obtained. In both cases there were sufficient mills for very considerable specialisation to take place, further reducing production costs. A mill engaged in a single specialist activity is more likely to be able to execute that activity more efficiently than a mill which spreads its interests over a number of processes. The Lancastrian answer to this proposition was the separation of spinning, weaving and finishing, with like mills clustering together—spinning in the south, weaving in the north and finishing round Manchester—leading to additional external economies. It eventually proved impossible for the integrated firm engaging in both spinning and weaving to exist in competition with the specialist firm.[18] The practice of organising production in specialist mills, a process known as horizontal integration, was also employed in the West Riding worsted industry, but the geographical separation of the stages of production never quite developed as it did in Lancashire. However, the early stage worsted processes were markedly concentrated on Bradford and Shipley. This is still the case, for in 1971 87% of all topmaking, and 73% of all combing firms in Britain were so located.[19] Textile districts must be very large to justify horizontal organisation, and the largest textile districts are for the most part in coalfield regions.

In spite of these powerful influences drawing textiles to coalfields, many of the leading continental manufacturing districts are adjacent to rather than actually on coal measures. They lie in what we have termed the coalfield region rather than on the field itself. The Lille–Roubaix–Tourcoing concentration in French Nord and the Verviers district of Liège in Belgium are both within 30 km/20 miles of a supply of coal, but the Flemish provinces of East and West Flanders and the Dutch provinces of Overijssel and Noord Brabant are up to 80 km/50 miles from the nearest coalfield productive in the 19th century. Why did the introduction of steam mills fail to cause a migration towards the source of fuel as in England? The answer is to be found in the timing of the change to steam power. Just as the tardy use of the steam engine in the water power areas did not cause a shift in location, so for the same reasons when steam power came to be adopted in the districts mentioned, the pull of coal was insufficient to cause a change in the distribution of these well-established areas of domestic production. In the Lille–Roubaix–Tourcoing district the first steam engine was not erected until 1819, and subsequent expansion was slow. As late as 1832 there were only 24 steam engines installed in textile mills in Lille, and by 1856 the mills of the town could muster only a meagre 700 kW/932 hp between them[20]—a power output equal to that of nine large water wheels. Late growth allowed the use of efficient steam engines, coal could be moved by rail as well as waterways, which were particularly well developed in Flanders and the Netherlands, and in no case was coal subjected to really long hauls. The inertia represented by several centuries of cloth manufacture also greatly contributed to immobility. If the switch from domestic to factory production had taken place earlier, migration would doubtless have resulted. As it was, proximity to coalfield-industrial districts was sufficient.

Additional evidence that the continental textile industry did not have to be sited on coal measures is provided by the Ruhr coalfield. Such was the importance of textiles in the area in 1800 that it seemed the industrial future lay in this direction rather than with metallurgy. But gradually textiles migrated from the coalfield and clustered in centres such as Barmen-Elberfeld, Krefeld, München-Gladbach and Munster, peripheral to it. As a corollary of this migration, the metallurgical industry left the textile towns for the coalfield. Opportunity costs of textiles in the coalfield towns were high because greater returns were possible from mining and metallurgy, so textiles moved out.

For what reasons were particular coalfields selected by textiles? Regional specialisation was one of the principal characteristics of British coalfields in the nineteenth century, and the choice of Lancashire for cotton manufacture must be seen in the same light as the choice of the North-East for iron and ships, the Potteries for ceramics and Sheffield for cutlery and quality steels. Simply because industrialisation took place so early and because of the resulting difficulty of transport, communications and the diffusion of ideas, great external economies were obtained by the clustering of plants in the same industry. The railway, motor vehicle and telephone have reduced the friction of distance and made specialist concentrations unnecessary for newer industries, but many of the older activities have remained at historic locations because of inertia. The actual location of the early industries fits 'a logical regional pattern of comparative advantage over the country'.[21] As we have seen in the case of the Ruhr, textiles could not compete with heavy metallurgical industries for local capital and labour, and were therefore excluded from South Wales, the North-East, and after the 1860s from Lanarkshire as well. These industrial districts could have supported a thriving textile industry, for water power, a humid climate and soft water are not exclusive to Lancashire and the West Riding. Opportunity costs for textiles were low in the West Riding and particularly in Lancashire, and in comparison with other British industrial districts they were best suited for textile manufacture. Lancashire, for instance, possessed positive disadvantages for iron and steel production, for not only was the coalfield some distance from a deep sea port, but there was neither local coking coal nor local iron ore.

GEOGRAPHICAL INERTIA AND MIGRATION

However powerful an influence upon the present pattern of location geographical inertia may be, it is not omnipotent and can be overcome. Inertia is at the opposite end of the spectrum from mobility, and Dziewonski suggests that there are four stages in the complete process.[22] Firstly, there is complete stability. Secondly, partial stability develops because of changes in locational advantages between sites. Thirdly, this situation is aggravated and vanishing stability occurs as disruptive location factors come close to overcoming the stabilising factors. Finally stability collapses, inertia is overcome and migration results. It was not uncommon for textiles to migrate in the formative stages of mechanisation. Examples include the collapse of the Lanarkshire cotton and the East Anglian worsted industries, and migration to Lancashire and the

West Riding respectively. Migration in the 20th century is rare, but there are two outstanding instances, both largely caused by wage differentials between established and newer manufacturing districts. One is at the national, and the other at the international level.

(i) Migration of the cotton industry from New England to the U.S. South

New England lacked that most essential ingredient of heavy industry, coal, and cotton textiles were therefore in a strong position to attract local capital. Not only could skilled labour be drawn from the existing woollen mills, and cheap labour from the ranks of immigrants, but also there were great reserves of water power. Additionally the eastern seaboard was the principal market for cloth. It was only in respect of raw cotton supplies that a disadvantage might be thought to exist. Raw cotton was brought in from the South, but this area did not initially participate in manufacturing. Its chief interest lay in agriculture, for Eli Whitney's cotton gin and the growth in demand for cotton made this activity so profitable that it was hardly worth investing in anything else. In other words, opportunity costs in cotton growing were very low indeed. However, from 1870 Southern cotton mills began to expand rapidly and by 1927 their capacity exceeded that of New England. By 1970 the South accounted for 98% of cotton consumed by U.S. mills,[23] representing one of the most drastic industrial migrations ever witnessed. The distribution of mills in 1968 is mapped by states in Fig. 51(a). New England mills tried to adapt to the changing locational advantage by specialising in high-grade cottons and in finishing, but the residual benefits of the region were insufficient to retain these activities and finishing was finally relocated during the 1940s and 1950s. Most of the early Southern mills were built by locals, but later expansion was a result of migration by New England manufacturers, an unusual situation for in previous migrations the industry and not entrepreneurs had moved.

Power costs were hardly a factor in this migration, as Table 3.1 suggests. The benefits of proximity to raw materials were dissipated by the absence of weight-loss in processing and by the need to move the finished goods to the market in the North-East. Transport cost differentials do not therefore provide the reason for the migration. The more enterprising attitude of Southern mill owners was a much more important factor, for their willingness to experiment, for example with the then advanced Northrup loom in 1895, an invention scorned by New England mills at the outset, enabled them to reap the rewards of higher productivity. In 1929, 80% of looms in the South were automatic compared with only 59% in New England.[24] The root cause of the shift, however, was the difference in labour costs between the two areas. Population pressure, poor alternative employment opportunities, the location of plants in rural areas and weak trades unions were all conducive to low wages in the South. Wages paid to textile workers in North and South Carolina in the 1920s were between 20 and 30% lower than those paid in Massachusetts.[25] The differential has since narrowed, but in 1960 it still amounted to 8%. Even if wages in both areas were equal, effective labour

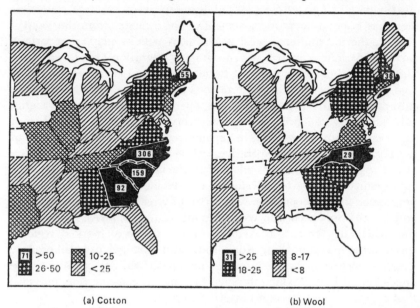

(a) Cotton   (b) Wool

Fig. 51 Distribution of cotton and wool textile mills by States in the U.S.A., 1968

costs would still be lower in the South where labour is much more productive. A mill of 450 looms requires 118 workers in the South, but 158 in New England. Workers in New England enjoy better fringe benefits such as paid holidays, unemployment and insurance legislation than do their counterparts in the South, placing an additional labour cost burden on northern mills. The outstanding advantages for textile production in the South have also caused the wool textile industry to begin to migrate southwards, as illustrated in Fig. 51(b). We may assume that the New England cotton industry is at stage four in Dziewonski's model, but since there has not been quite the same exodus of wool mills, wool textiles are at stages two and three.

(ii) *Migration of the cotton industry from Lancashire to Japan and elsewhere*

Between 1912 and 1967, employment in the Lancashire cotton industry fell from 621 000 to 106 000. At the same time the industry expanded rapidly in countries such as Japan, India and Hong Kong. The international character of this migration allowed those countries trying to encourage a cotton industry to resort to protective tariffs at Lancashire's expense until mills were well established. Since relatively unskilled labour is suitable, cotton manufacture is frequently selected by underdeveloped countries as part of their programme of industrialisation, and since the greater part of Lancashire's output formerly went to these countries, there has been an outward movement of the industry from the county. Thus at the international level government policies play an important part in undermining inertia and encouraging migration. Quite apart from tariffs and other restrictions on trade, however, Lancashire became a high cost producer for the same reasons as New England. Conservative entrepreneurs ran outdated equipment operated by comparatively highly paid labour whose productivity was very much lower than that of Japanese labour. Wages paid to Japanese spinners in 1935 were 20% of those paid to Lancashire operatives, while the figure for weavers was a mere 14%.[26] Lancashire has adapted to the new situation by producing high-quality cottons, by developing the dyeing and printing stages of production using imported grey cloth and by replacing the traditionally horizontally organised firm with fully integrated concerns. At the same time there has been a breakdown of the formerly marked regional specialisation. Japan, Hong Kong, India and Portugal, can still produce cheaper cloth than Lancashire, and migration will not cease until the area's output is approximately equal to domestic consumption, provided that tariffs are high enough to restrict imports.

References

1. F. X. Van Houtte, *L'Evolution de l'Industrie Textile en Belgique et dans le Monde de 1800 à 1939*, Louvain, 1949, p. 76.
2. E. B. Alderfer and H. E. Michl, *Economics of American Industry*, 3rd Ed., McGraw Hill, New York, 1957, p. 343.
3. R. C. Riley, 'Locational and Structural Change in the Huddersfield Wool Textile Industry', *Tijdschrift voor Economische en Sociale Geografie*, 61, 1970, p. 78.
4. R. L. Hills, *Power in the Industrial Revolution*, Manchester University Press, 1970, p. 113.
5. *Ibid.*, p. 93.
6. H. B. Rodgers, 'The Lancashire Cotton Industry in 1840', *Transactions of the Institute of British Geographers*, 28, 1960, p. 138.
7. D. S. Landes, *The Unbound Prometheus*, Cambridge University Press, 1969, p. 160.
8. J. H. Clapham, *The Economic Development of France and Germany 1815–1914*, Cambridge University Press, 4th Ed., 1955, p. 66.

9. D. S. Landes, *op. cit.*, p. 278.

10. *Ibid.*, p. 161.

11. A. L. Dunham, *The Industrial Revolution in France, 1815–1848*, Exposition Press, New York, 1953, p. 110.

12. Jennifer Tann, *Gloucestershire Woollen Mills*, David and Charles, Newton Abbot, 1967, p. 71.

13. D. S. Landes, *op. cit.*, p. 181.

14. H. B. Rodgers, *op. cit.*, p. 140.

15. *Ibid.*, p. 143.

16. H. Kisch, 'Textile Industries in the Rhineland and Silesia, a Comparative Study', *Journal of Economic History*, 19, 1959, pp. 553–4.

17. J. H. Clapham, 'The Transference of the Worsted Industry from Norfolk to the West Riding', *The Economic Journal*, 20, 1910, p. 201.

18. R. Robson, 'Location and Development of the Cotton Industry', *Journal of Industrial Economics*, 1, 1953, p. 107.

19. *Skinner's Wool Trade Directory of the World 1967–8*, Thomas Skinner, Bradford, 1967.

20. J. H. Clapham, *op. cit.*, (1955), p. 66.

21. E. M. Rawstron, 'Some Aspects of the Location of Hosiery and Lace Manufacture in Great Britain', *East Midland Geographer*, No. 9, 1958, p. 27.

22. K. Dziewonski, 'A New Approach to Theory and Empirical Analysis of Location', *Regional Science Association: Papers*, XVI, Cracow Congress, 1965, p. 19.

23. *Statistical Abstract of the United States*, New York, 1971.

24. E. B. Alderfer and H. E. Michl, *op. cit.*, p. 351.

25. J. A. Morris, 'Cotton and Wool Textiles. Case Studies in Industrial Migration', *Journal of Industrial Economics*, 2, 1953, p. 69.

26. E. B. Alderfer and H. E. Michl, *op. cit.*, p. 355.

Chapter 4

MULTI-LOCATIONAL INDUSTRIES

Many transport-oriented industries using large quantities of low unit-value materials, including sources of energy, differ from those industries examined in Chapter 2 in that they do not invariably have plants at the source of their materials. They exhibit a more flexible pattern of distribution, and we find that plants may be located at intermediate break of bulk points, at markets, at historic sites which once supplied materials, at sources of cheap electric power, or at the source of materials, whether they be metallic ores or coal. Because their plants are situated at sites which *can* readily be classified, these industries may be regarded as multilocational.

Three industries are treated in this chapter, iron and steel, aluminium and oil refining. In each transport costs are an important consideration, and this might suggest that it would be preferable to reduce the movement of low-value, weight-losing materials to allow the higher value products to be shipped over long distances. In other words we might expect material-orientation. The Weberian material indices for iron blast furnaces and for alumina production (the first stage in aluminium manufacture) are both greater than 1, yet in both industries there are examples of raw materials and sources of energy moving over greater distances than products. This is not to say that Weber's model has no relevance for the multi-locational industries, but rather that the weight lost by materials is not especially great, allowing a choice as to whether a plant is situated at the source of the raw materials or at some other site. Transport costs even on quite low-value materials may not be especially onerous because of improvements in the methods of transport. Progress in this field may allow a reversal of established patterns so that it becomes preferable to move the raw material rather than the product, as with oil refining. The continuation of plants at raw-material locations long after the local resources that gave rise to them have been exhausted may be justified, not only because it is economically possible to bring materials from elsewhere, but also because of the money that has been invested in the plants themselves. The iron and steel industry provides many examples. The exhaustion of a copper deposit, on the other hand, will automatically result in the closure of the associated copper concentrator. Political interference in the form of protective tariffs may also favour the long-distance movement of materials instead of the import of a semi-finished product in the case of one country, but not in the case of another. Aluminium production is a case in point. It is hardly possible to consider oil refining without reference to politics, while decisions made by individuals in the light of information as they receive it further add to the diversity of the locational pattern exhibited by these industries.

4.1 THE IRON AND STEEL INDUSTRY

Iron and steel production was an essential, and perhaps the most fundamental part of what Wilfred Smith calls the era of steam industrialism of the 18th and 19th centuries. It is not surprising, therefore, that to a greater extent than the other two industries, which are largely products of this century, the iron and steel industry has a complicated pattern of distribution. What in the early 19th century might have been a material-oriented site may now be a market-oriented site following the exhaustion of materials and the development of manufacturing in the vicinity. Because of its antiquity and because of the massive nature of plant and equipment, both expensive and immobile, the industry exhibits great inertia. The life of most pieces of equipment is at least 25 years, and technical modifications constantly lengthen this period. At the same time external economies, such as railway marshalling yards, dockside handling facilities, local skilled labour supply and adjacent research institutes, combine to increase immobility. Consequently the present geographical pattern is a palimpsest created by the superimposition of earlier patterns, themselves a result of changes in technology and resource base.

Existing iron and steel works fall into four categories: charcoal iron sites, coalfield sites, lean iron ore sites and break of bulk sites. It must be remembered that a plant now operating at, say, a charcoal iron site does not necessarily use either charcoal or local iron ore, but that at one time this was the means of production. Each class of site may be seen as a response to technological change. Thus the coalfield works were developed after the introduction of coke as a blast furnace fuel, the lean iron ore plants resulted from the invention of the Thomas process, and the coastal plants were built to use imported raw materials following reductions in the quantity of coke required and the growth in size of bulk carriers. That there are still plants at all four sites is a testimony to the strength of geographical inertia. Table 4.1 illustrates the distribution of British Steel Corporation plants between the four categories of site. It is evident that inertia has not been able to prevent complete migration from the charcoal iron sites, but that iron and steel making is

G

TABLE 4.1

British Steel Corporation plants by site category, 1968

	Charcoal iron		Coalfield		Lean iron ore		Coastal	
	Pig	Steel	Pig	Steel	Pig	Steel	Pig	Steel
Capacity '000 tons	623	441	4340	10871	4457	5827	8917	10320
Number of Plants*	1	2	9	23	5	5	8	9

* Integrated works are counted twice, once as a pig producer, once as a steel maker.

Source: H. G. Cordero (Ed), *Iron and Steel Works of the World*, London, 1969.

still an important activity on British coalfields and lean orefields. However, coalfields seem to have lost their advantage for the production of pig iron to the coastal sites.

PROCESSES

Prior to discussing the different types of site, it is important to consider the processes involved in iron and steel production. There are two main stages, smelting and refining. It is true that some iron ores fed to blast furnaces are concentrated at the mine in order to improve their ability to withstand transport costs, but this is not everywhere the case. Smelting is the first essential process and it is by no means invariably carried out at the source of raw materials. Sometimes the two processes are carried out in the same plant, which is then known as an integrated works. The smelting stage takes place in a blast furnace, into which iron ore, coke, limestone and some scrap iron are charged. The process of combustion is assisted by a hot air blast, although oxygen is coming to replace air. Large quantities of water are required to circulate round the furnace to prevent it from melting, but although 10 tons of water are used for every 2 tons of iron ore charged, the relatively ubiquitous nature of water seldom exerts much influence on location. Pig iron is the principal product of smelting; slag is the other, comprising the impurities. Smelting is a weight-losing process returning a material index of between 3 and 4, depending upon the richness of the ore employed. Iron ore has the greatest locational pull at the present time, and it is for this reason that the last two decades have witnessed the growth of coastal plants using imported ore in Western Europe. The loss in weight of the iron ore during smelting is not sufficiently great, however, for blast furnaces to migrate to the source of the ore. The interplay of the location factors described can be represented by the four-point Weberian figure shown in Fig. 52(a). Scrap supplies largely originate in markets which are normally important manufacturing districts, so the pull exercised by the market and by supplies of scrap coincide. The plant, P, is at a break of bulk point, thus minimising the transport costs on the imported ore.

Pig iron is 95% pure metal, but impurities remain and they must be removed by refining before the metal becomes steel. Three methods are employed. Firstly, by means of a converter through which hot air or oxygen is blown under pressure. Secondly, by the use of an open hearth furnace, normally fired by oil. Thirdly, by means of an electric arc furnace used to produce high-grade alloy steels. Small quantities of iron ore, ferro-alloys and limestone are charged together with much larger quantities of pig iron and scrap. Both the open hearth and the electric arc furnaces can operate largely on scrap, but the converter cannot

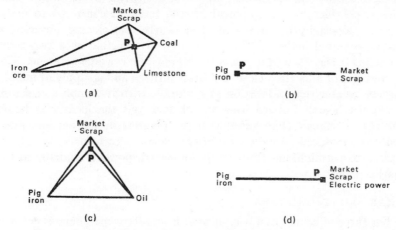

Fig. 52 Locational figures of processes in iron and steel production

accommodate more than one-third scrap in the charge. If the converter is charged with molten pig, no energy is used at all, and the material index is approximately equal to 1. Converters are not as mobile as this index would suggest, for in order to obtain molten pig, the refining process must take place adjacent to a blast furnace, which is far from perfectly mobile. If the converter is at some distance from the supplying blast furnace, it will be necessary to reheat the pig before 'converting' it, in which case the material index will rise to 1·5. The principal justification of the integrated iron and steel works is in fact the avoidance of the loss of heat or, put another way, the reduction of fuel costs. Since the open hearth furnace is fired by oil, its material index of 1·7 is higher than that of the converter, and is higher still if it is not integrated with a blast furnace. Although the electric arc furnace uses large quantities of electric power, the weight-loss involved is negligible, giving this method of refining a material index of a little more than 1, even when the plant is distant from the blast furnace. Not only because refining does not result in appreciable loss of weight, but also because the raw materials and products are relatively high value, the process has a much greater locational flexibility than smelting. In some areas, such as the manufacturing region of northern Italy, steel making is almost completely disassociated from pig iron production, and there are steelworks in relatively small manufacturing towns in the French Alps and in the Massif Central. In the British private sector there are 26 steelworks, not one of which is integrated with blast furnaces.

The importance of scrap in steel making, coupled with the fact that it originates from markets which are often industrial areas, and as such possess considerable geographical inertia, have all conspired to make refining, especially by means of open hearth and electric furnaces, a market-oriented activity. Fig. 52(b) shows converting as a two-point Weberian case when the principal inputs are considered alone. The advantages of a location close to a blast furnace and a supply of molten pig are greater than a location at a market with its supplies of scrap. The open hearth furnace uses oil for fuel and the locational figure becomes a triangle (Fig. 52(c)) with the plant at its market and main source of materials. In the case of the electric arc furnace, the figure shrinks to a straight line (Fig. 52(d)), for electric power is available at the market together with scrap.

Charcoal iron sites

For three millennia iron was smelted from often small deposits of iron ore by means of charcoal. The activity was carried on widely in medieval Europe with concentrations in such areas as the Ardennes, the Eifel mountains, the Sieg, Lahn and Dill valleys in Germany, the Forest of Dean and the Weald of Kent and Sussex in Britain and in Bergslagen in Sweden. Water supply was an important consideration after the introduction of the water wheel to work bellows for the blast and to operate hammers and slitting wheels. This favoured upland areas which could also produce the large quantities of charcoal required; a blast furnace producing 1000 tons of pig per year would use 50 hectares/120 acres of timber in the process. Areas not too distant from markets or with access to consumers by water transport had considerable advantages. Thus pig from the Forest of Dean moved to the Black Country, and Bergslagen pig iron was refined in the Low Countries and England. Hampered by shortages of charcoal and iron ore, by irregular water supply and by a rudimentary transport system, it is not surprising that in the main the medieval iron industry was ephemeral. In very few areas developed at this time has iron making persisted through to the present day, and where this is the case it has largely been a result of the presence of large supplies of high-grade iron ore, and of very considerable modifications to plants to keep abreast of technological change.

The plants at Barrow and Workington in north-west England are British examples of this type of site. They grew up smelting the local, 60–65% rich haematite ore with charcoal. With the introduction of the Bessemer converter, which initially required non-phosphoric ores of the sort found in this district, output soared, and by 1880 the region was the second largest pig iron producing area in Britain. Coking coal was brought in from Durham, although coal from the Cumberland field was later employed. The haematite is now nearing exhaustion and Barrow has lost its blast furnaces; all that remain are two electric arc furnaces. The Workington plant is small but integrated, although the blast furnaces are charged largely with imported ores. One of the three blast furnaces produces specialist manganese pig, but other than this specialisation is not well developed. There is a third plant in the district at Backbarrow making special pig iron in a small charcoal-fired blast furnace, a true relic of the past. Other examples of this category of site are Siegerland in West Germany, the eastern Pennsylvania district of the U.S.A., including the very large plant at Bethlehem, and Swedish Bergslagen. It is in the latter district that plants approach most closely to the medieval situation. The area was the leading world exporter of bar iron in the 17th and 18th centuries, and the relatively rich ores continued to be smelted in charcoal furnaces until this century. This fuel is in fact still used to make steel of the very highest quality. Coking coal must be imported, but the availability of local scrap, iron ore, hydro-electric power for refining and external economies has ensured that when plants are modernised they are rebuilt at new sites in the same locality. Small quantities of pig are made using electric power rather than coke as a blast furnace fuel at plants such as the Uddeholms works at Hagfors, where iron making has been going on since 1668. These charcoal iron sites have been able to remain in production because, for the most part, their output is specialised, particularly in the case of Bergslagen, helping to increase the power of geographical inertia which overcomes the absence of coal, and now, in Siegerland and eastern Pennsylvania, iron ore as well.

Coalfield sites

The major problem confronting 18th-century ironmasters in Europe, although not in North America, was the growing shortage of charcoal. Forests were becoming depleted after centuries of thoughtless cutting, and in some areas such as the Weald, the claims of rival consumers like the shipbuilders prevailed. British forests were not especially extensive, and by 1740 pig imports from Russia and Sweden were twice as large as the domestic product. During the 17th century many attempts had been made to use coal instead of charcoal, but these proved fruitless, and it was not until 1709 that Abraham Darby successfully smelted iron ore by the use of coke at Coalbrookdale, Shropshire. This innovation was the most important development in iron smelting since the invention of the blast furnace in the 15th century, but diffusion was slow to take place and it did not gain general acceptance in Britain until mid-century. Elsewhere the first coke-fired blast furnace did not operate until 1796 in Upper Silesia. The use of coke had four results. Firstly, since supplies of coking coal were plentiful, blast furnaces could be larger than formerly, indeed the use of coke required a large furnace to permit the greater blast needed to produce the necessary higher working temperature. Secondly, it became possible for several furnaces to be established in the same locality since fuel was no longer scarce, and since Newcomen engines (1708) could be employed to pump back water from below the water wheel to the pond above. Thirdly, a combination of the use of coke and the invention of rotative action by Watt in 1781, removing the need for water as a source of power, allowed smelting to develop in districts such as the Black Country, which were rich in coal but lacking in water power. Fourthly, a coking coalfield location became obligatory, for not only were between 8 and 10 tons of coking coal required to produce 1 ton of pig iron, but 18th-century transport was inefficient and the cost of moving coal over more than short distances by land was prohibitive. The industry was now freed from 'the tyranny of wood and water', but the migration of furnaces from hill regions to the coalfields was not effected immediately. In Belgium the first coke-fired blast furnace was blown in at Seraing near Liège in 1822, but twenty years later there were but 45 furnaces using coke out of a total of 120. It was not until 1860 that the last charcoal furnace was extinguished.

Comment has so far been restricted to smelting. For many purposes pig iron could be used in its crude form, but much had to be refined into wrought iron. This was achieved in a finery which was slow, inefficient and employed charcoal. It was left to Henry Cort in 1784 to develop the dry puddling process for the manufacture of wrought iron by means of coal. It was a fuel-intensive process, making a coalfield location desirable. Cort's own experience supports this. He carried out his experiments at a tiny mill at Funtley, Hampshire. He used water for power, but the need to import coal placed him at a disadvantage in respect of the coalfield iron making districts, and his works never attained more than

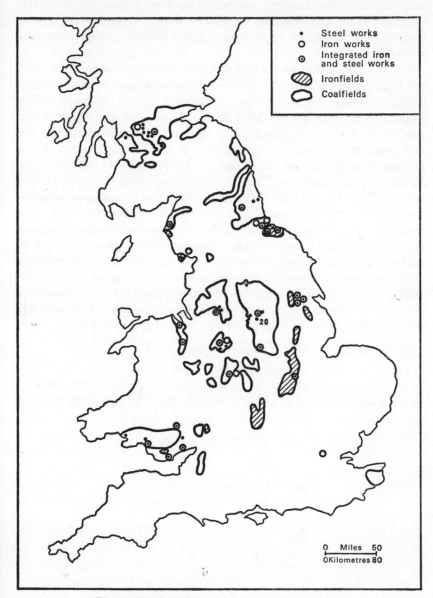

•	Steel works
○	Iron works
⊙	Integrated iron and steel works
▨	Ironfields
⬭	Coalfields

•20

0   Miles   50
0 Kilometres 80

Fig. 53 The British iron and steel industry, 1969

local significance.[1] Ancillary equipment such as bellows for the blast, rollers, cutting and winding machinery were all powered by steam engines which, because of their low boiler efficiency, were voracious consumers of coal.

The size of coalfield works and the possibility of the concentration of production in small areas gave rise to external economies on a scale which had been impossible in the charcoal iron era. Canals, railways, roads, skilled labour, iron ore and coal flows, coke making and maintenance services developed to reduce the cost of manufacture and to increase the attraction of the coalfields. Investment in plant itself was very much greater than previously, encouraging entrepreneurs to be immobile. Further advantages accrued in some areas, for example the Ruhr, Derbyshire and the West Riding of Yorkshire where iron ores, known as blackband and clayband ores, were found interbedded with the coal. The iron industry, with a number of other industries, some of which used iron as their raw material, made an important contribution to the growth of coalfield manufacturing regions which developed during the 19th century.

The attraction exercised by coalfields as a source of coal is now relatively small. It is therefore necessary to explain how this change has been brought about, and to account for the continuation of the industry on coalfields evident in Figs 53, 54 and 55, and in Table 4.1.

(i) *Improvements in blast furnace technology*

We have noted above that early blast furnaces were extravagant users of coal. The weight of coal required to make 1 ton of pig iron was very much greater than the weight of ore consumed. This was conducive to a

TABLE 4.2

Tonnage of coal required to make 1 ton of pig iron, Great Britain

Mid-18th century	8–10
1788	7
1800	5
1840	3·5
1873	2·5
1938	1·7
1970	1·0

coalfield location for in this way movement was minimised. Table 4.2 shows the way in which the coal rate, that is the amount of coal required to produce 1 ton of pig iron, fell quite sharply in Britain down to 1840, thus diminishing the attractiveness of the coalfields. Isard is of the opinion that coalfields had lost their influence on blast furnaces well

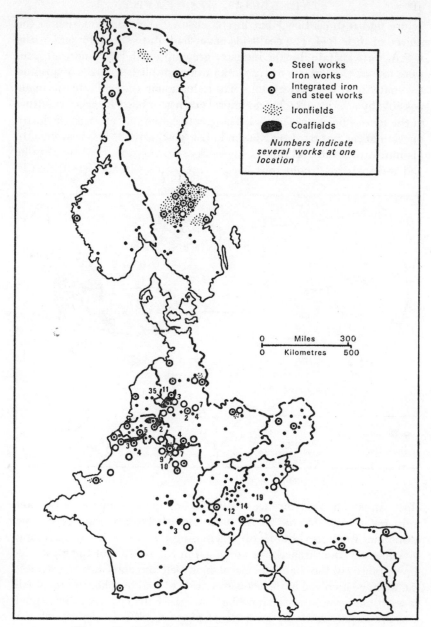

Fig. 54 The West European iron and steel industry, 1969

before mid-19th century,[2] but inertia ensured their continuation at the source of their fuel. The coalfields never had quite the same pull in the U.S.A. as in Britain, for the industry grew up much later and coal rates were low at the outset: many works were established in the 1840s and the coal rate in 1850 was 2·5 tons. The reduction in the coal rate was made possible by a series of technical improvements to blast furnaces resulting in the more efficient use of coal. The greatest step forward was the introduction of the hot blast by Nielson in Glasgow in 1828. The year prior to his innovation the coal rate at his works was 8·05 tons, but by 1833 he had reduced this to 2·9 tons using a preheated blast at 315°C/600°F.

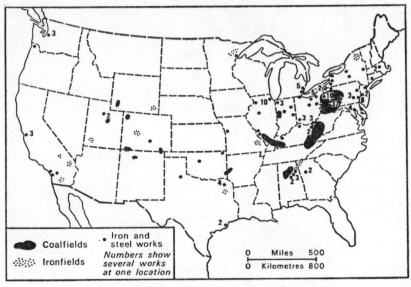

Fig. 55 The iron and steel industry, U.S.A., 1969

Most American blast furnaces used the hot blast from the outset and were not so tied to coal as the early British furnaces had been. Fuel economies were also obtained by increasing the size of the furnaces and by collecting the furnace gases to assist in the heating of the blast. The development of the chamber coke oven in Belgium and Germany reduced the wastage involved in the transformation of coal to coke, and the waste gases could be used in the hot blast stoves. If the coal rate diminished, iron ore requirements for each ton of pig iron fell only slightly when it was possible to obtain richer ores. In Britain, between 2 and 3 tons of iron ore were needed per ton of pig in the 19th century, thus providing ore with at least as great a locational influence as coal over the last half of the period. The response was the growth of plants on lean iron orefields and of plants on the coast using imported ore. In the U.S.A. plants sprang up at break of bulk points on Lake Erie and Lake Michigan using Lake Superior ore. At the same time, once important British smelting areas like Shropshire, Lancashire and the West Riding of Yorkshire lost virtually all their blast furnaces.

(ii) *Technology and refining*

Coal remained an important locational consideration for much longer in the case of refining. In the U.S.A. 3 tons of coal were needed to refine 1 ton of wrought iron in 1850, but in Britain between 5 and 8 tons were consumed, that is, twice as much used to make 1 ton of pig iron. At that time 8 tons of coal were employed to produce 1 ton of steel.[3] Improved refining techniques lagged almost half a century behind those in smelting, and during this time refining was firmly established on coalfields which, as a consequence, came to produce more steel than pig iron. Hence in 1913 the Ruhr made 8·2 million tons of pig iron, but 10·1 million tons of steel. The three principal innovations in refining were the Bessemer converter (1856) which used no coal at all, the Siemens–Martin open hearth furnace (1866) which conserved fuel very much like the blast furnace by the use of exhaust gases to heat the incoming air, and the Héroult electric furnace (1899) which made no direct use of coal. All three could use scrap, which, since it is already refined, reaches its molten state without the expenditure of a large quantity of fuel. These processes caused a rapid reduction in fuel consumption in refining, so that by 1929 only 1·5 tons of coal were needed in Belgium and 2 tons in Great Britain. Since the Second World War open hearth furnaces have been oil-fired with the consequence that coal has no pull whatsoever at the refining stage. Unlike smelting, however, refining has shown little inclination to forsake coalfields in Western Europe.

(iii) *Geographical inertia: blast furnaces and integrated works*

Despite the increasing theoretical flexibility of blast furnaces suggested by Table 4.2, smelting is still carried out on inland coalfields. Indeed, Pittsburgh and the Ruhr are two of the world's greatest iron making districts. In some cases local coking coal has long been exhausted and must be imported. Belgium is such an example. The Charleroi and Liège furnaces were using Ruhr coal before the turn of the century, and no local coking coal has been mined for some time. The cause of this geographical inertia can be seen in the sheer size and physical immobility of the plant and equipment used in the industry. The larger the capital investment, the greater the inertia becomes. Further, new plants suffer from high interest rates on borrowed capital, while old plants are largely written off, allowing them to compete with newer, more efficient works. The cost of purchasing a new site is always considerable, and it is normally between a half and a quarter of the cost to expand *in situ* than to establish comparable capacity at a greenfield site. Thus, although transport costs on the movement of finished steel from plant to market in the U.S.A. account for more than half the total transport costs, emphasising the advantage of a market location, the Pittsburgh district produces far more steel than it can possibly consume.[4] This illustrates the high degree of inertia in the area, which was greatly aided by the Pittsburgh Plus basing-point pricing policy between 1900 and 1924. (See Chapter 1.3.)

In order to overcome their disadvantageous location, inland integrated works adapt to it in various ways. Firstly, they may exhibit a high degree of innovation. Consett, on the South Durham coalfield, was one of the first British plants to investigate oil and natural gas injection in the blast furnace, and also to introduce oxygen converters. Secondly, they may endeavour to reap the economies of large-scale production by means of plants close to the optimum size. In 1968, of the eight largest plants in the European Economic Community, seven were on coalfields, the two largest being Thyssen at Duisburg and Krupp at Rheinhausen with respective capacities of 4·8 and 3·2 million tons. Thirdly, they may merge one with another so that each plant specialises in a particular product, bringing important economies of scale. This strategy has been widely employed in the Ruhr. Thyssen has merged with Phoenix Rheinrohr and with Hüttenwerke Oberhausen, and the Dortmund–Hörder Hüttenunion has joined the Mannesman–Hoesch group and the Dutch Hoogovens plant at Ijmuiden. The latter merger will allow the expansion of pig iron and crude steel capacity at Ijmuiden, where assembly costs are lowest, and finishing at Dortmund near large centres of consumption. Similarly the integrated works at Denain and Valenciennes on the French Nord coalfield form part of the Usinor group which has other plants at Dunkirk and at Longwy and Thionville on the Lorraine ironfield. Fourthly, they may be helped by the form of pricing policy used, as were the Pittsburgh plants at the beginning of the century. At present in West Germany transport costs are calculated from one of two basing points, either Oberhausen or Essen,[5] both of which are in the Ruhr, placing other districts at a disadvantage in respect of transport costs.

(iv) *Geographical inertia: steelworks*

The forces of inertia influencing steel making are not very different from those affecting integrated works, although the scale is somewhat smaller. Capital investment is less, physical immobility is not so great and the area occupied by a steelworks is less than that required for an iron and steel plant. This would suggest, in the absence of any need for coal at all, that steelworks would be able to migrate from the coalfields. What has happened, however, is that coalfields have become industrial areas, generating scrap, and markets at the same time. Oil, oxygen and electric power offer no effective locational pull, and by remaining at historic sites, steelworks can avail themselves of the considerable external economies that have built up over time. Transport costs on pig iron are not especially onerous, and in any case the low cost of scrap gives incentive to reduce the use of pig iron. In 1968 scrap cost £10·50 per ton in Britain, compared with a pig iron cost of £17·50 per ton.[6] An excellent example of a district from which blast furnaces have migrated but which has retained its steelworks is Sheffield. There are 20 steel-making plants in operation, all possessing electric furnaces producing high-grade steels. The St Etienne district with 9 steelworks producing special steels is a further example. Coalfields not well suited to the production of pig iron and standard steels thus adapt to the situation by the manufacture of the highest quality steels, thereby adding to the forces on inertia at these old-established sites.

Clearly geographical inertia is a powerful influence in the coalfield iron and steel districts. In terms of Dziewonski's four-stage model of inertia introduced in Chapter 3, many coalfield blast furnaces are at stage three, for the British Steel Corporation has given notice that the coalfield blast furnaces at Bilston, Brymbo and Rotherham are to be closed. Steelworks on coalfields, on the other hand, are at stage one; between 1943 and 1967, output of alloy steels in Britain expanded 325%,[7] testimony to the strength of the Sheffield steelworks in particular.

(v) *Regional policy*

The final reason for the continuation of iron- and steel-making on coalfields springs from the nature of the coalfields themselves. As a result of their long industrial history, many are now declining areas exhibiting high unemployment which governments are pledged to reduce. Iron and steel plants in such areas thus enjoy the financial benefits of regional planning policy. Social costs are sometimes a factor, and this has particular relevance to the British Steel Corporation as a public corporation. Consett, for example, is the dominant employer in its region, and the effect of closure upon the regional employment situation is partly responsible for the retention of the plant. The establishment of integrated works on coalfields at Ebbw Vale in 1935 and at Ravenscraig in 1962 was a direct result of government concern for local unemployment.

Lean iron ore sites

The third category of site was developed in the last quarter of the 19th century. Three factors were largely responsible for the trend. Firstly, iron ores mined with coal in the Ruhr and Britain were reaching their economic margins, and there was a need to find alternative supplies. Secondly, both the low-cost methods of making steel, the Bessemer converter and the open hearth furnace, were found to be quite unsuited to the refining of pig iron containing more than a trace of phosphorus. Ores free from phosphorus were not abundant, and before the real potential of the two processes could be realised, some means of removing the phosphorus had to be found. This was achieved in 1879 by Thomas and Gilchrist who used a lining of refractory brick made of dolomite that reacted with the phosphorus to produce a good quality steel. Almost overnight the lean phosphoric ores of Lorraine, known as *minette* on account of their former poor iron-making characteristics, and the English Jurassic scarpland ores became desirable raw material. Thirdly, lean ores (Northamptonshire Jurassic is 35% and Lorraine *minette* is 28–32% rich) will not readily stand transport costs, and since by the 1880s the coal rate had been reduced to about 2 tons, there were transport costs savings to be obtained by moving coal to blast furnaces on the ironfields rather than shipping iron ore to the coalfields. If, as in the case of Lorraine, coke rather than coal was dispatched from the coalfields, only about 1·5 tons of fuel were required with 3 tons of ore to make 1 ton of pig iron.

Although the five British lean iron ore plants now produce more pig iron than do the coalfield works, their initial growth was relatively slow, and in spite of the advantages of using the ore close to the mine existing plants on the coalfields brought the ore in for smelting. Some blast furnaces, such as those at Skinningrove (1874) and Redbourne, Lincolnshire (1875), were set up before the invention of the Thomas process, and made pig for foundries and for puddling furnaces. From 1890 they began to smelt iron suitable for the production of steel by the Thomas process. At the same time steel making was introduced as the advantages of integrated works for the avoidance of heat-loss were realised, although Skinningrove did not do so until 1910. Two of the five plants date from this period: Appleby–Frodingham, 1890, and Normanby Park, 1912, both in the Scunthorpe area. Finally the plant at Corby in Northamptonshire was set up in 1936.

It is in Lorraine and Luxembourg that the greatest development of iron and steelworks has taken place. As in Britain, smelting was carried out in advance of the Thomas process, the pig iron being moved to coalfields in Northern France, Belgium and Germany, following the transport cost economies of shipping pig iron rather than *minette*. However, as was the case in Britain, many coalfield works, especially in French Nord and Belgium, considered it worth while to use *minette*, and this is not surprising, for the geographical inertia associated with the coalfields by the last quarter of the 19th century was very considerable, as we have seen. Integrated works were built in due course, first in Lorraine and then after 1900 in Luxembourg. By 1913 the ironfield had a pig output of 10·5 million tons, and as such was a major iron- and steel-producing area, one that had grown with great speed as a result of a single technological innovation. Outside Lorraine and Luxembourg, integrated works have been constructed on lean iron ore sites at Mondeville near Caen in France, at Salzgitter in Lower Saxony and at Amberg in Bavaria, West Germany. The plants at Birmingham, Alabama, are also on lean iron ore, but here they are also in juxtaposition with coking coal, making them difficult to classify.

Ironfield plants possess distinctive characteristics, many of which are locational disadvantages. Firstly, the cost of hauling fuel from coalfields is considerable; much of Lorraine's coke must travel more than 300 km/ 200 miles from the Ruhr and the French Nord-Pas-de-Calais field. Secondly, the cost of local ore is rising much more rapidly than the cost of imported material. Between 1957 and 1965 the price of ores imported into Britain fell 28%, but the price of the domestic product rose 26%, although at Corby the increase was held to 10% by cutting out shaft mining and concentrating on quarrying ores close to the plant. The Appleby–Frodingham plant reduced its consumption of home ore from 100 to 50% in 1966 because of rising local ore costs and because of its proximity to the port of Immingham.[8] In Lorraine, competition from imported ores forced a 20% price reduction of ore at the mine between 1960 and 1968, but this was less than the fall in the price of foreign ore.[9] Thirdly, owing to the large percentage of sterile material in the ore, a proportionately large amount of fuel must be employed in the production of each ton of pig iron. Hence both the coal rate and the cost of fuel are higher than for blast furnaces using rich imported ores. Fourthly, the low iron content in the ore causes a large capital outlay to be made on ore handling equipment, on the blast furnace itself and on slag disposal. It is possible to beneficiate lean ore to improve the percentage of iron in the ore, but this is also true of rich ores. Fifthly, many Lorraine works continue to operate as blast furnace plants only; nine such plants are shown in Fig. 54. They lose the economies enjoyed by the integrated works, and three of them are to be closed. Sixthly, major industrial regions had already been established, for the most part on coalfields, before the growth of plants on lean ironfields. Consequently not only is there a small local market for steel, but also there is a very poor local supply of scrap. This means that the greater part of the steel refined is made from pig iron, often more costly than scrap, and that steelworks not integrated with blast furnaces are the exception. The imbalance between pig iron and steel output noted in Table 4.1 in the case of the coalfield plants is thus much less marked. Inertia is helping to keep the plants at their existing sites, but the problems outlined above are forcing rationalisation to take place. In Lorraine this has taken the form of the closure of small plants, the construction of new oxygen steel-making works, as at Gandrange, and the creation of the huge Wendel–Sidelor firm. The expansion currently taking place at Scunthorpe is both a function of the high site costs of greenfield works and the potential use of ores imported through Immingham.

BREAK OF BULK SITES

We have seen in Chapter 1 Hoover's diagrammatic representation of a manufacturing plant using weight-losing materials located at a break of bulk point between those materials and the market. Since this is an important method of reducing handling costs, and since transport costs account for approximately one-third of the cost of finished steel, we might expect iron and steel plants to occur at points where the flow of materials is broken. Such points arise at the junction of land and water transport, that is, at tidewater ports, lakeside ports or along large rivers. The continued decline in the coal rate, coupled with the absence of a significant improvement in the quantity of iron ore required per ton of pig, have meant that the reduction of transport costs of iron ore rather than of coal are more important. In most cases this has meant that plants have set up where iron ore can be received by water transport and coal by rail. The transport cost of moving the products to markets is such that break of bulk points are chosen either at, or close to, large markets. Break of bulk points have little attraction for steelworks with their overriding need of market locations.

The first plants to be set up according to these principles followed the discovery of ironstone in the Cleveland Hills in Yorkshire in 1851 by John Vaughan. By this time the coal rate had sufficiently reduced to allow blast furnaces to be built other than on coalfields, and rather than establish furnaces on the lean ironstone field, Vaughan chose to locate on Teesside where the iron ore met the flow of coking coal from the South Durham coalfield. Spanish ores were mixed with those from Cleveland, and their transport costs were minimised by a port location. By 1870, Teesside plants were producing 27% of British pig iron. Precisely the same principles governed the development of plants on the shores of

Lakes Erie and Michigan. The iron ores of Lake Superior had been discovered in 1845, and became available in Pittsburgh with the construction of the first 'Soo' canal between Lakes Superior and Huron in 1855. Other ore deposits were discovered and exploited, culminating in 1889 with the opening up of the rich Mesabi deposit. Blast furnaces and steelworks using Bessemer converters and open hearth furnaces, both sparing in their use of fuel compared with the puddling process, were set up at the ore-importing ports of Cleveland, Lorain and Toledo, using Connellsville coal, to meet the growing demand of western markets. In 1880 the first of the many works in the Chicago district was established. They were all on lake-shore sites employing Connellsville, and later West Virginian coal to smelt Superior ores. Chicago is 650 km/400 miles west of Pittsburgh and was thus in a much better position to supply steel to the Mid-West. Pittsburgh suffers from a persistent shortage of scrap, and prices are much higher than in Chicago. The availability of scrap and the demand from automobile plants were two critical factors in the construction of the works at Detroit. A final, remarkable example of the attraction of the lake-shore ports for the iron and steel industry is provided by the migration of the Lackawanna Steel Company from the East Pennsylvanian anthracite field at Scranton to Buffalo in 1901.

Some break of bulk sites are a response both to the growth of markets and to the rising costs of domestic iron ore and fuel, coupled with the decision to base production on imported materials. For the most part plants at coastal locations are a product of this century, and their low production costs have been largely responsible for the decline of coalfield blast furnaces in Britain, and for the adaptation measures that inland plants in Western Europe have been obliged to carry out. In the U.S.A., however, the growth of coastal plants has been restricted to the works at Sparrow's Point, Maryland, which began smelting ore from El Tofo, Chile, in 1912, and the Fairless plant on the Delaware River near Trenton (1952). This situation has arisen because so many of the inland plants are at lake-shore sites, allowing them to take delivery of the recently exploited (1956) Labrador ores by means of the St Lawrence Seaway, completed in 1959. A contributory factor has been the utilisation of the Minnesota taconite deposits, replacing the Mesabi deposits which are becoming increasingly high cost. Coastal plants are peripheral to the main American market, the manufacturing belt; the five States of Ohio, Indiana, Illinois, Michigan and Wisconsin consume 54% of the national output of steel, compared with 21% by the States of New York, New Jersey and Pennsylvania. Further, the strength of the inertia associated with existing inland locations also inhibits much new growth elsewhere.[10] There are at present five coastal integrated works in Britain and ten in Western Europe. Their growth may be considered under four headings.

(i) *The use of imported iron ore*

West European ores are almost entirely lean, and although initially it was possible to use open cast mining methods to ensure low production costs, it is becoming increasingly necessary to resort to the more expensive, labour-intensive shaft mining. On the other hand, as a result of expansion in iron and steel making capacity in the early 1950s, an intensive search for rich, easily worked iron ores was mounted in different parts of the world. By the time the new mines in Brazil, India, Australia, Liberia and Venezuela were in production, demand for steel had fallen away, creating a buyers' market for ore. An example of the way in which prices fell is provided by Brazilian Itabira ores. Their price at the port of Vitoria was £5·50/$14.60 per ton in 1957, but by 1963 the quotation had dropped to £4·24/$11.25 per ton. By agreeing to take delivery of these ores over a long period, a Japanese steel firm was able to negotiate a price as low as £3·20/$8.50 per ton.[11] These trends in the field of production costs have been greatly assisted by even more rapidly falling ocean freight rates. Transport costs account for approximately half the delivered cost of ore, and are at least as important as production costs in respect of delivered costs. Great savings have resulted from the use of larger bulk carriers. For a 8000-km/5000-mile haul in 1962, the freight rate for a 15 000 ton carrier was £1·51 per ton, but when a 65 000 ton vessel was used the cost fell to £0·71 per ton.[12] Other factors are more efficient handling in specially equipped ports, and the long-term chartering of ships at agreed freight rates. As a consequence, iron ore prices at West European ports in 1969 were 40% lower than in 1959, the average landed price having fallen from £6·40/$17 to £3·71/$10 per ton.[13]

Not only is this fall in price most conducive to a coastal location, but plants at such sites are presented with the possibility of a choice of ore in respect of quality and cost. The Ijmuiden plant uses ore from 20 different sources, and Italsider, which controls the Italian plants, does not normally take more than 1 million tons from any one source in the interests of security of supply.[14] Inland plants must face the transfer of ore to barges or to railway wagons, and these small-scale operations largely dissipate the savings achieved on the ocean section of the haul. It has been estimated that plants in the Ruhr pay £0·52/$1.40 per ton more for their imported ore than do coastal plants. By 1970, only 35% of the ore charged into Common Market blast furnaces was domestic in origin.

(ii) *Further reductions in the coal rate*

Improvements in blast furnace technology have further diminished the coal rate, allowing greater locational flexibility in respect of coal supplies. By raising the working pressure within the blast furnace, the speed of the reaction between the gases and iron oxide is increased, with an appropriate saving in fuel. The same effect is achieved by injecting oxygen into the blast furnace. The use of oil, normally obtained from coastal refineries, is a direct substitute for coke, although some coke must still be used. The beneficiation of ore improves its richness and reduces the amount of sterile material that must be smelted. Mesabi taconite, for example, is beneficiated from 25% to approximately 50%. The roasting of fine ores with coke breeze, formerly a waste product of the coke ovens, to form sinter which is then charged into the furnace, also reduces the coal rate. These factors reduce the pull of coalfields, and had it not been for the unwillingness of the Department of Trade and Industry in Britain, and to a less extent the European Coal and Steel Community, to allow the import of cheap American coal, coastal sites would have become even more attractive. In 1967 Durham coking coal was £5·37 per ton compared with a landed price of £4·80 for U.S. coal of higher quality.

(iii) *The influence of the market*

The existence of important markets not served by local integrated works was one of the principal reasons for the establishment of the plants at Sparrow's Point, Fairless Hills, Bremen and Genoa, while the Dunkirk plant is no further from the Paris market than is Lorraine. Markets not only provide scrap for the blast furnace and for steel-making, but the practice of charging *ad valorem* freight rates, making the movement of products more expensive than the shipment of materials, also adds to their attraction. This is particularly true in the U.S.A. Rodgers estimates that transport costs per ton mile for steel in the U.S.A. are three times those for either coal or iron ore.[15] In 1947 Pittsburgh had a freight rate disadvantage of £1·73/$4.60 per ton on shipments of steel to New York, the largest single market for structural steel, compared with the Sparrow's Point plant.[16]

(iv) *Government intervention*

Coastal sites have many advantages for the construction of new plants, and when governments decide to build, or assist in the building of new works, it is not surprising that they should choose such a site. There are two main reasons for government intervention. Firstly, for reasons of national economic security. Thus the Dutch government was eager to reduce the country's dependence on imported steel, and set up the Ijmuiden plant in 1929. Similarly the Swedish plant at Luleå was established in 1940 to produce standard steels which were formerly imported from Germany. Secondly, governments may intervene as part of regional planning policy to aid the growth of areas of low economic activity. Examples are the Italian works at Piombino, Bagnoli near Naples, both dating from the mid-1950s, and Taranto, 1964.

In conclusion it must be observed that not all integrated plants and steelworks fit into the fourfold classification outlined. Those that do not are not numerous, and have grown up in response to local markets, such as the integrated works in the U.S. manufacturing belt at St Louis and Cincinnati. In the Alpine region of Western Europe a number of electric arc steelworks has grown up using hydro-electric power and scrap, but the greatest concentration of such plants is in northern Italy, as can be seen in Fig. 54. Here scrap is in such demand that it must be imported, but this has not caused the steelworks to cluster round the importing port of Genoa. Although they may now be regarded as market-oriented plants, the American plants of Fontana, California, Geneva, Utah, Pueblo, Colorado and Lone Star, Texas were built during the Second World War as part of a government plan for the dispersal of strategic industry. It is unlikely that they would otherwise have been built at that time, and indeed, when the Geneva plant, which cost £76/$202 millions, was sold to the U.S. Steel Corporation in 1946, it fetched only £18/$47 millions.[17]

4.2 THE ALUMINIUM INDUSTRY

In contrast to iron and steel production, the manufacture of aluminium derives from the scientific and technological revolution of the late 19th century, with the consequence that the part played by inertia is proportionately less. Very few plants have been closed down and there are no old-established areas where the industry has been forced to carry out adaptation in order to remain profitable. Aluminium's strength and low density make it particularly useful to the aircraft industry, and its ability to compete with steel for many applications has caused output to rise rapidly and many new plants to be put down. The industry is operated by a small number of large international firms such as the Aluminium Company of America (Alcoa), the Aluminium Company of Canada (Alcan), Kaiser and Reynolds, so that the movement of materials between plants at different stages of the production process is at the international rather than the national level. Despite the recent growth of the industry, plants have, almost without exception, been located at sites which had emerged by the Second World War. Thus plants manufacturing alumina, the product of the first stage of production, are either at the site of bauxite ore, the raw material, or at a break of bulk point near the market where the imported ore is handled. Aluminium plants, which are sometimes known as smelters or reduction plants, are to be found at sites where low-cost electric power is available, whether this be hydro or

TABLE 4.3

U.S. aluminium plants by category of site, 1969

| | Alumina plants | | Smelters | | | |
	Bauxite sites	Break of bulk sites	Hydro	Natural gas	Thermal coal	Lignite
Number of plants	2	6	15	5	3	1
Capacity '000 tons	1130	4420	2292	731	558	275

Source: *Metal Bulletin*, 1969, p. 169, and *Yearbook of the American Bureau of Metal Statistics*,1969 pp. 98–100.

thermal. Alumina plants provide a choice of location, and since they are not invariably close to the bauxite mine, the industry may be regarded as multi-locational. Table 4.3 shows the distribution of the industry in the U.S.A., the leading producer, by category of site. The smelters appear according to the source of the energy from which the electric power is generated, suggesting that smelters also are multi-locational.

PROCESSES

The differing locational characteristics of the two stages of aluminium production are a direct result of the processes involved. Technology is thus an important factor in the location of the industry. The basis of alumina production stems from the fact that aluminium oxide dissolves in heated caustic soda whereas the impurities do not, enabling the alumina content of the bauxite to be separated out. The method was developed by Bayer in 1888. Bauxite is normally employed since it contains between 40 and 60% alumina, although ores such as nepheline, containing only 25% alumina, are used in the U.S.S.R. Bauxite requirements for each unit of output are very much greater than those of the other raw material, caustic soda, or of energy. One ton of alumina requires about 2·5 tons of bauxite, 0·04 ton of caustic soda and 0·225 ton of fuel oil, giving a Weberian material index of 2·76. Great strides have been made over the last two decades in the more efficient use of energy, for example the calorific equivalent of 0·50 ton of fuel oil was needed in the early 1950s, but such is the influential pull of bauxite that this has not significantly reduced the material index. Since the index is greater than 1, and since bauxite is not an especially valuable material (a typical quotation is £2·64/$7 per ton f.o.b., that is, on board ship at the exporting port), we would expect to find alumina plants close to the bauxite mine. This is represented by the locational figure in Fig. 56(a). There are factors which militate against this solution, as we shall see, and alternatively plants may be drawn towards their market, the aluminium smelter, as in Fig. 56(b). Table 4.3 indicates that in the U.S.A. six of the eight alumina plants are sited at break of bulk points to minimise the transport costs on imported ore. In this case the alumina plants are closer to their markets than to the sources of their bauxite.

The reduction of alumina to aluminium is achieved by electrolysis. It was the technical difficulty of carrying out this process at an economic

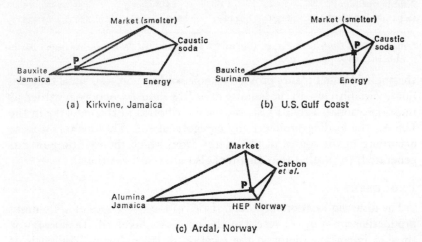

(a) Kirkvine, Jamaica   (b) U.S. Gulf Coast

(c) Ardal, Norway

Fig. 56 Locational figures of processes in aluminium production

cost that delayed the inauguration of the industry until 1886. In this year Hall and Heroult found that by passing an electric current through a mixture of molten alumina and cryolite by means of carbon anodes and cathodes, the oxygen in the alumina would unite with the carbon to form carbon dioxide leaving pure aluminium. The production of 1 ton of aluminium requires 0·03 ton of cryolite, 0·04 ton of aluminium fluoride, 0·6 ton of carbon electrode made from petroleum coke and pitch, and 2 tons of alumina, giving a material index of 2·67, exclusive of electric power. Electric energy cannot be included in the material index since it has no weight, but in fact power is the most important locational consideration, for aluminium electrolysis is particularly energy-intensive. Between 17 000 and 18 000 kilowatt hours are required in the production of a ton of aluminium, or approximately sixty times the amount of energy used in the manufacture of a ton of steel. Electric power accounts for 23% of the value of the product in the U.S.A., and unfortunately off-peak supplies are not attractive because electrolysis is a continuous process.[18] Alumina accounts for 34% of total costs in the U.S.A., but although there is a 50% loss in weight, alumina is a relatively high-value commodity, varying between £20·75/$55 and £27/$72 per ton at the alumina plant, so that it can stand transport costs. The transmission of very large quantities of electric power, on the other hand, is expensive, and these costs can be saved by a location close to the generating station. Because they are more intensive users of electric power than copper refineries, aluminium smelters tend to be less close to their markets, since it is preferable to move finished aluminium from a low cost electric energy site to the market, than to transmit electricity long distances. Fig. 56(c) shows a typical locational figure for countries in North America and Western Europe where hydro-electric power is inexpensive. The significance of cheap hydro-electric power is underlined by the countries like Canada and Norway which possess no bauxite, have poorly developed alumina capacity and yet produce far more aluminium than they consume. In the case of Norway, 80% of the aluminium output is exported.

From what has been said it is clear that the material index has limitations as a means of understanding the location of alumina plants and smelters. There are restrictions on the use of the index when the energy used is electricity, and when the material being transported is of high value, there is little incentive to limit its movement. Both stages of production have indices greater than 1, implying that plants ought to be at a material or energy location, yet it is only in the case of smelting that this applies. We now turn to the examination of the rationale behind the main categories of site taken up by the two sectors of the industry.

ALUMINA PRODUCTION

(i) *Break of bulk sites*

Despite the loss in weight sustained by bauxite in alumina production and the attendant addition to transport costs resulting from the construction of alumina plants away from bauxite deposits, it is only since the 1950s that there has been an expansion of these plants at the source of their ore supplies. Prior to this alumina plants were normally at break of bulk points in the advanced industrial nations. There are four main reasons for this situation. Firstly, during the early years of this century when the industry was in its infancy, the required technology and capital were in the hands of a few firms in the advanced countries, most of which do not possess bauxite. Sometimes these firms were national monopolies like Alcoa, and there was an absence of the need to seek the lowest cost production sites on an international basis. Although alumina manufacture was much less efficient than at present, for example, between 1900 and 1909 6·3 tons of bauxite were required to make 1 ton of alumina,[19] coastal or riverine plants were established at Newport, Mon (1914) and Burntisland (1917) in Great Britain, Bergheim (1915) in West Germany and at Arvida (1928) in Canada. All these countries lacked bauxite. Even in the U.S.A. the East St Louis alumina plant (1902), which was closed in 1957, was located some distance from the Arkansas ore deposits. Only in France at Salindres (1888) was an alumina plant set up at the theoretical location on a bauxite deposit. Secondly, the economic environment of the then 'colonial' bauxite producers such as Surinam and Guyana militated against industrialisation, and firms preferred to expand within the developed countries. Thirdly, the military uses of aluminium not only resulted in governmental support for the industry, especially in Germany, Italy and Japan, but also caused governments to institute preferential tariffs in favour of imported bauxite rather than imported alumina, to encourage alumina production as well as smelting. The three West German alumina plants at Schwandorf (1937), using Hungarian brought up the Danube, Ludwigshafen (1938) on the Rhine and Lunen (1939) on the Lippe Canal, originated in this way. The plants at Porto Marghera (1928 and 1937) in Italy fall into the same category. The U.S. government set the tariff on imported alumina at a very high level. In 1956 the tariff was £1·88/$5 per ton, higher than the combined cost of shipping the alumina from Jamaica and of U.S. port dues (£1·27 + £0·37 = £1·64)/($3.38 + $1.00 = $4.38 per ton).[20] For this and other reasons, imports of alumina were small, and coastal alumina plants such as those at Mobile (1938), Baton Rouge (1943) and La Quinta, Texas (1953) were built. Fourthly, American domestic ore supplies proved to be incapable of meeting demand after 1923, and since then there has been an increasing reliance on imports. In 1969 1·7 million tons of bauxite were mined in the U.S.A., but imports totalled 11·2 million tons, providing further impetus for break of bulk plants. Of the large aluminium producers, only France does not rely on imported bauxite and none of her alumina plants is on the coast.

The four points considered help to explain the existence of alumina plants at break of bulk points, but there is no doubt that in the 1950s, purely on the basis of cost, it would have been preferable for the U.S. aluminium companies to have processed their bauxite in the supplying country. In 1956 there would have been a saving of £2·14/$5.68 per ton of alumina had Jamaican alumina rather than Jamaican bauxite been imported through the Gulf Coast ports.[21] Costs do not seem, therefore, to have been the critical consideration. Reluctance to invest abroad, the absence of external economies in the bauxite supplying countries, the availability of low-cost natural gas in the Gulf Coast area and the possibility of diversifying into the chemical industry to secure supplies of caustic soda, were some of the factors which influenced American firms to locate their alumina plants within the U.S.A. However, the removal

TABLE 4.4

Alumina-bauxite and aluminium-alumina quotients for leading bauxite and aluminium producers, 1970

	Alumina-bauxite Quotient	Aluminium-alumina Quotient
Jamaica	0·35	—
Australia	0·52	0·21
Surinam	0·33	0·13
Guyana	0·16	—
France	0·74	0·84
Jugoslavia	0·14	0·84
Hungary	0·49	0·33
Greece	0·31	0·61
U.S.A.	6·94	1·26
Guinea	0·55	—
India	0·50	1·18
Italy	3·18	1·03
W. Germany	378·00	0·90
Canada	—	1·92
U.K.	—	0·81
Japan	—	1·26

Source: *Yearbook of the American Bureau of Metal Statistics for 1970*, 1971. *Metal Statistics 1960–1970*, 58th edition, Frankfurt am Main, 1971.
Raw data converted to aluminium content before division.

of the $5 (£1·88) tariff on imported alumina in 1957 created a differential of $10.68 (£4·03) per ton, or 24%, and coupled with the considerations examined below, this proved too disadvantageous for the further construction of alumina plants. Two were in fact completed after this date, Point Comfort (1958) and Gramercy (1959), but they had been planned prior to 1957. Figs 57 and 58 show the distribution of alumina plants in Western Europe and the U.S.A.

Alumina plants at break of bulk points are most well developed in those countries relying on imported bauxite. The relationship between domestic bauxite output and alumina capacity can be represented in the form of quotients. Thus if, after divided alumina capacity by domestic bauxite production, the quotient is greater than 1, we may assume that the surplus alumina capacity is fed by foreign ores and is located in coastal or riverine plants. Table 4.4 indicates that predictably the U.S.A. has a high quotient (6·94), as does Italy with 3·18, and that the quite remarkable dependence of West Germany on foreign ores is underlined by its quotient of 378·0. It is thus no surprise to find that the four German plants are oriented to water transport. Important bauxite importers such as Canada and Japan have coastal alumina plants at Arvida, Shimizu, Yokohama and Kikumoto, but cannot be allocated a quotient since they lack bauxite production.

(ii) *Bauxite sites*

Mention has been made of the alumina plant on one of the French bauxite fields at Salindres. It was inevitable that others would be developed on the French deposits and there is now a total of three. In the same way Arkansas came to possess two plants, at Hurricane Creek (1943) and Bauxite (1952). However, the first alumina plant to be built at a foreign source of bauxite supply was Alcan's establishment at Kirkvine, Jamaica, in 1953. This was followed by a further plant belonging to the same firm at Ewarton, also in Jamaica, in 1959, and by plants in Guinea (1960), Surinam, Guyana (1961), Greece (1962) and Kwinana in Western Australia in the mid-1960s. Many others are in the process of construction, and there have been reports that three plants are to be built in Jamaica alone. There are several reasons for these developments.

Firstly, firms in the industry have become increasingly international as they have sought to control overseas sources of bauxite and foreign markets for their aluminium. The early reluctance to become involved abroad has diminished since the mid-1950s. Alcan had less hesitation in investing abroad than American firms for Canada has no bauxite at all, and consumes only one-fifth of her aluminium output, so the firm was traditionally involved in foreign supplies. The decision to build a smelter at Kitimat in British Columbia, distant from the alumina plant at Arvida, was further justification for a Jamaican alumina plant, allowing alumina to reach Kitimat by sea rather than by the more expensive rail haul across Canada. The discovery of very large bauxite deposits in Australia, with its 'safe' investment climate has added to the other incentives to build plants abroad. Secondly, although alumina has a higher value per ton than bauxite, it needs much more careful treatment and is not amenable to bulk handling as is bauxite. As a result the ocean freight rates for the two commodities do not substantially differ, but since the metal content of alumina is at least twice that of bauxite, it is obviously preferable to move alumina rather than bauxite. Thirdly, the difficulty of increasing sales within the U.S.A. and other advanced countries has prompted firms to enter foreign markets by building smelters in countries with promising potential consumption. These smelters are often best served by alumina plants in these countries. The Alcan alumina plant at Muri in India and Alcoa's plant at Kwinana are examples.

The fourth, and particularly important point, is the attitude of the bauxite-producing nations towards the aluminium companies. By requiring firms exploiting bauxite to build alumina plants as part of the contract for the mining concession, bauxite-producing countries are able to share in the profits of alumina manufacture, diversify exports, improve their ability to earn foreign exchange and at the same time provide some local employment. This has happened in Jamaica, Surinam and Australia. Firms setting up in emergent countries have to face high total labour costs because of the need to employ a greater number of workers than would be necessary in advanced countries. Construction costs, maintenance costs and the cost of importing caustic soda are relatively high, tending to offset the transport advantages of a location at the bauxite mine. Such problems weaken the economic case for the establishment of an alumina plant in emergent countries, but the aluminium companies do not have much choice since they depend very largely on these countries for their bauxite. Whether or not a plant is built will depend on the pressure the host country decides to exert. Guyana is taking a very strong line. In early 1971 the government was considering going one stage further than merely requiring bauxite to be produced *in situ*, and was planning the nationalisation of the Alcan alumina plant at Mackenzie. It remains to be seen whether nationally owned aluminium industries in the emergent nations will be able to expand their alumina production as quickly as has proved possible under the present arrangements. Whatever happens in the future, there is already considerable evidence that the Weberian least cost approach is not the only method of understanding the geography of an industry in which so much depends on decisions by firms and by governments.

The extent to which the bauxite mining countries have been able to expand alumina output may be judged from the alumina-bauxite quotients in Table 4.4. Quotients less than 1 indicate an excess of bauxite over alumina production, and it is interesting that in spite of the points made above, many of the principal bauxite-producing countries have very low quotients. Jamaica (0·35), Surinam (0·33), Guyana (0·16) and

Greece (0·31) have had no great success as yet in attracting alumina plants to match their bauxite production. Australia (0·52) has done rather better, undoubtedly because it is a 'western' nation easily capable of attracting investment. Guinea has been most successful in establishing alumina capacity with a quotient of 0·55. Both the French aluminium firms Pechiney and Ugine are part of the consortium that operates the Guinea plant at Fria.

(iii) *Intermediate energy sites*

This is not an important category of site, and at present there is only one alumina plant that may be so classified. This is at Gladstone, Queensland. It is located neither at the source of its ore, which is shipped from Weipa, nor at a break of bulk point in that the alumina is not transported onwards by rail or barge, but continues its journey by sea, often to foreign smelters. It was originally intended that the plant be built at the Weipa bauxite deposit, but the availability of low-cost coal near Gladstone proved more attractive. The justification for creating a category for a single plant is that Gladstone is the world's largest alumina plant.

ALUMINIUM PRODUCTION

It has been noted that aluminium smelters are oriented to low-cost electric energy sites, and that in most cases this energy is developed from water power. However, it does not follow that cheap electric power is restricted to the advanced countries, and it is possible to recognise two types of area within which smelters are located.

(i) *Electric power sites in the advanced countries*

The developed economies present many of the advantages for aluminium as they do for alumina production. The problems of raising capital are not great, the most advanced technologies are available for plant construction and operation and there is no shortage of skilled labour. The countries of North America and Western Europe have a safe investment climate, and the strategic nature of the industry has caused governments to encourage it. As Huggins remarks of Germany, she came to 'attribute a glamorous and important part to the national production of aluminium during a war effort twice in the same generation'.[22] The industrial nations are the main consumers of aluminium and there are foreign exchange savings to be obtained by purchasing alumina rather than the very much more expensive aluminium, which has a market price of about £207/$550 per ton. This was one of the arguments used by the British government in 1967 to justify the construction of smelters at Holyhead, Lynemouth and Invergordon. At that time existing British plants were capable of meeting only 10% of the national consumption. Although aluminium is a valuable commodity, it is desirable to avoid long transport hauls, for shippers have reacted to its high unit value by charging high freight rates. Table 4.5 shows that the difference in the rates charged on alumina and aluminium on ocean hauls is particularly great; it should be borne in mind that freight rates are not always a function of distance. The cost of moving aluminium to the fabricating plants at the market can be minimised by smelting at the market. Petroleum coke for the carbon electrodes is provided by oil refineries which are well developed in industrialised countries. When demand from smelters is sufficient it becomes justifiable to set up a specialist plant converting petroleum coke to carbon, thereby giving the aluminium smelters increased external economies of scale. Such a plant exists at Botlek in the Netherlands.

TABLE 4.5

Freight rates on alumina and aluminium,
mid-1960's ($ per ton)

Transport method	Haul	Cost
	ALUMINA	
Ship	Jamaica–Louisiana	2·25
Rail	Alabama–Oregon	13·51
	ALUMINIUM	
Ship	Quebec–Netherlands	18·50
Rail	Washington–Illinois	23·65
Barge	Louisiana–Ohio	8·00

Source: S. Brubaker, Trends in the World Aluminium Industry, John Hopkins, Baltimore, 1967, p. 159.

Whatever the importance of the factors considered above, it is the availability of low-cost electric power in the advanced countries that has been a critical issue in the development of smelters in these countries. The early centres of this branch of the industry were Niagara Falls, the Swiss, French and Italian Alps, Bavaria and the highlands of Scotland. Subsequently plants have grown up in advanced countries such as Canada, Norway and Austria lacking both bauxite and demand for aluminium. The Pacific North-West of the U.S.A. also falls into this category. Figs 57 and 58 show the distribution of smelters in Western Europe and in the U.S.A. The areas possessing plants are adjacent to markets, but more particularly they enjoy the appropriate physical

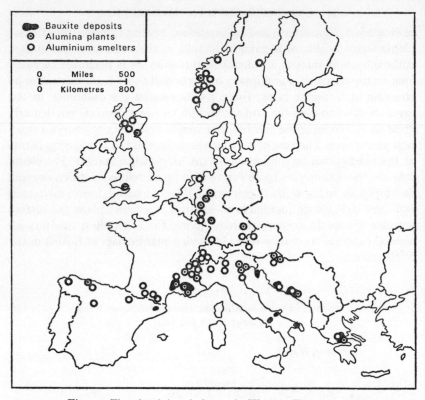

Fig. 57 The aluminium industry in Western Europe, 1969

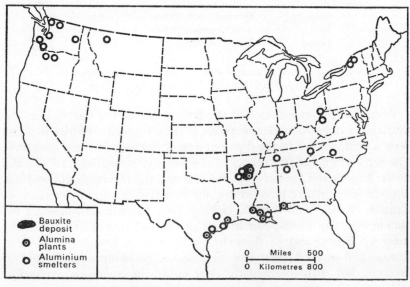

Fig. 58 The aluminium industry, U.S.A., 1969

environment for the production of low-cost hydro-electric power. To realise this water-power potential, aluminium firms are prepared to invest heavily in the construction of new settlements, transport facilities, power stations, dams and sometimes even the reorganisation of drainage systems, as at Kitimat, British Columbia. It is recognised that hydro-electric power could be generated in many tropical, bauxite-mining countries at equal cost, but in the absence of the other advantages of the advanced nations, firms have not been eager to avail themselves of these sources of power.

Table 4.3 indicates that while most smelters in the U.S.A. use electricity generated from water, this is not the only source of energy. This situation holds for many other advanced countries, where thermal electric power is becoming increasingly important. The dwindling number of hydro-electric power sites in the U.S.A. and Western Europe has caused aluminium companies to investigate the use of coal, lignite, natural gas and nuclear fuel for power generation. This trend has been assisted by the fall in the cost of thermal electricity as a result of the rise in the size of generating sets and other factors conducive to improved efficiency. In many cases it is possible to locate the generating station at an energy source which is close to an important market. Examples include the Ruhr coalfield, the Ville field in West Germany and the West Virginian coalfield. In this way the cost of transporting aluminium to the fabricating plants can be drastically reduced. Table 4.5 illustrates the transport cost burden faced by smelters in the Pacific North-West on the shipment of their output to the manufacturing belt. Since, theoretically, there is virtually no restriction on the number of thermal power stations that can be built, there seems to be little incentive for the aluminium firms to search outside the advanced countries for low-cost electricity. Government support for the construction of smelters has worked in the same direction. To encourage Alcan to build a smelter at Lynemouth, Northumberland, an area of declining coal production, the price of coal to be supplied to the firm's power station was set at a low level. This could be justified since not only would jobs be created at the smelter, but also 1000 miners would be ensured employment in the vicinity. Table 4.4 shows that aluminium-alumina quotients greater than 1, that is where there is an excess of aluminium over alumina production, are scored by advanced nations, with one exception. Canada heads the list with a quotient of 1·92, followed by the U.S.A. (1·26), Japan (1·26), and Italy (1·03). India (1·18) is the exception. West Germany (0·90) only just fails to qualify.

The evolution of the distribution of smelters in the U.S.A. provides a striking illustration of how sensitive these plants are to the cost of electric energy, and of the growing importance of thermal electricity. Because power comprises such a large proportion of total costs, a small change in the price of electricity greatly affects production costs. At one time the Niagara Falls and St Lawrence areas had ample supplies of cheap power, but save for the plants at Massena (1903 and 1959), the industry has been forced out by other industrial consumers prepared to pay higher prices for electricity. Smelters migrated beyond the manufacturing belt to the Tennessee valley area during the First and Second World Wars, and established themselves at Alcoa (1914), Badin (1916) and Lister Hill (1940). Expansion of demand during the Second World War, coupled with very low power costs which offset the distance from both alumina plants and markets, caused the colonisation of the Pacific North-West during the 1940s and 1950s. In 1954 power costs in the Tennessee Valley Authority area were £33·28/$88.20 per ton of aluminium, but the price in the Pacific North-West varied between £18·68/$49.50 and £22·07/$58.50 per ton.[23] In the late 1940s the low cost of the natural gas available at the Gulf Coast, coupled with the low initial cost of the gas engines used for generation, caused yet another cluster of smelters to grow up. The cost of power per ton of aluminium in 1954 was $72.00–$78.30, higher than the Pacific North-West prices, but alumina was supplied from local plants and water transport could be employed on the haul to market. There are three plants: Point Comfort (1949), Chalmette (1951) and San Patricio (1952). In 1952 the Rockdale, Texas, plant opened. Local lignite deposits were used to produce power only slightly more expensive than that generated in the Pacific North-West. The fear that the cost of mining lignite would rise steeply prevented other plants from employing this source of energy. The final stage came in the late 1950s with the use of West Virginian coal mined by open cast methods at very low cost, piped in the form of slurry to smelters on the Ohio River. The plants are at Ravenswood (1957), Hannibal (1958) and Evansville (1960).

(ii) *Electric power sites in the underdeveloped countries*

Among the non-Communist countries of the world, there are only 12 aluminium smelters outside North America, Europe, Japan and Australia. In contrast with this meagre development, there are 24 such plants in the U.S.A. alone. The advantage of the advanced nations for the manufacture of aluminium have been noted, and in spite of the potential availability of low-cost hydro-electric power in many emergent territories, where smelters have arisen it has been more a result of politics or governmental regional development policy rather than of economics. The bauxite-producing countries are able to ensure that alumina plants are built by the aluminium companies, and it is a logical step that the construction of smelters be made a condition of mining concessions. However, with some exceptions, for instance Alcoa's smelter at Paranam, Surinam, using water power from the Brokopondo Falls on the Suriname River, this has not yet occurred. More usual is the establishment of a smelter as an integral part of large, often prestigious hydro-electric power projects set in motion to help diversify the economy and to provide local employment and foreign exchange. The smelter at Edéa, Cameroun, was set up by the French government in 1960, before the country became independent, as part of its policy of colonial industrialisation. The plant, based on water power from the Sanaga River, is run by Pechiney and Ugine, although the Cameroun government now has an 8% share of the capital. Initially alumina had to be brought from France, where the finished aluminium was returned, suggesting a high element of transport cost. Alumina now comes from the Fria, Guinea, alumina plant. The absence of both bauxite and alumina capacity from the country gives added point to the fact that the plant was built to utilise available water power. The second African smelter at Akosombo, Ghana, is a further example. The dam on the Volta River was jointly financed by the World Bank, the American, British and Ghanian governments, and the smelter is operated by Kaiser and Reynolds. Although there are local bauxite deposits, these cannot be used *in situ* since as yet there is no alumina plant. An interesting portent for the future is the smelter on Bahrein Island, opened in 1971. It was introduced by the government as a means of utilising the huge reserves of natural gas the country possesses and to widen the range of industrial activity. Alumina is brought from Australia and the finished product is shipped to Europe.

That smelters are poorly developed in the emergent nations is supported by the aluminium-alumina quotients in Table 4.4. Surinam has the very low quotient of 0·13, but Jamaica, Guyana and Guinea have no smelters at all and therefore fail to score. Once againI ndia is an exception, for the government has developed the industry to use indigenous bauxite, water power, coal and lignite resources. The Australian quotient is low (0·21), but this may be expected to rise for the industry is expanding rapidly.

4.3 OIL REFINING

Although the first commercially viable oil well was sunk as early as 1859 in Titusville, Pennsylvania, and an elementry form of refining was carried out to separate the unwanted constituents from the saleable oils, oil refining may properly be regarded as a 20th-century industry. In the inter-war period it grew most rapidly in the most advanced country and leading producer of crude oil, the U.S.A., which by 1938 claimed 61% of world refining capacity. As Western Europe has followed the U.S.A. into what Rostow calls 'the age of high mass consumption' characterised by near universal ownership of a motor car, and by the use of oil rather than coal in most industrial processes, oil refineries have proliferated here too. In 1938 Western Europe possessed a mere 4% of world refining capacity, but by 1970 this had risen to 28%, and the absolute figures had increased from 15·9 to 705·9 million tons. Industrialisation in other parts of the world will similarly lead to further expansion of the industry.

Oil refining is largely in the hands of a small number of firms, mostly American, which are not only international in the scope of their operations, but are also vertically integrated, owning oil concessions, tanker fleets, refineries and retailing facilities such as petrol stations. Because they are international companies of great size, they are able to consider alternative sites for their refineries on an international scale. Should one of the 'majors', as the large firms are known, find that there are savings to be obtained by building refineries in Western Europe rather than in the Middle East, this change in locational advantage can quickly be acted upon. Non-integrated companies and nationally owned organisations do not normally have this flexibility and must work within the confines of one country. As a consequence of the scale of the operations of the majors, the various categories of site taken up by the refineries are at the international, or even subcontinental level. Oil refining is a transport-oriented activity, and whether the plant is located at an oilfield, a market or an intermediate point between the two will largely depend on the comparative transport costs of crude oil and refined products. The least-cost solution has changed from oilfield to market sites over the last two decades, but inertia, coupled with political considerations, ensure that oilfield refineries still exist. The industry is therefore multi-locational in nature.

The threefold classification of refinery locations is sometimes elaborated to distinguish between resource refineries, to be found on oilfields, and seaboard export refineries which are linked with their oilfield by pipeline and which despatch most of their products to distant markets by tanker. Many Middle Eastern plants, such as those at Abadan in Iran, Mena Abdulla, Shuaiba and Mena al Ahmadi in Kuwait are seaboard export refineries, but there are also refineries at inland sites, such as Daura in Iraq, whose function is similar to that of the coastal refineries. Since both types of refinery have the same economic and in many cases political characteristics, it is preferable to regard them as resource refineries. Many market refineries, for example those at Rotterdam-

Europoort, serve local markets in addition to consumers outside the Netherlands, so they are simultaneously market and intermediate refineries. Truly intermediate plants are few in number and are to be found at points such as Augusta in Sicily where the local demand is very small. It is therefore more convenient to consider the market/ intermediate plants as market refineries. It must be pointed out that the three suggested classes of refinery are somewhat arbitrary, for the process of economic development sometimes causes refineries to belong to more than one category. Thus the U.S. Gulf Coast refineries initially

TABLE 4.6

*Production, refining and consumption in the Middle East,
Western Europe and Latin America, 1938–1970 (million tons)*

	1938	1950	1960	1970
	MIDDLE EAST			
Production	16·2	88·4	264·3	712·5
Refinery cap.	14·0	48·7	79·4	129·2
Consumption	na	12·8	35·2	51·0
	WESTERN EUROPE			
Production	0·7	2·0	15·3	20·1
Refinery cap.	15·9	46·2	221·2	705·9
Consumption	na	62·0	196·3	628·0
	LATIN AMERICA			
Production	44·2	102·5	194·5	273·2
Refinery cap.	39·8	73·8	161·4	255·0
Consumption	na	41·6	79·5	135·0

Source: *Institute of Petroleum Review.*

belonged to the seaboard export or resource group, but they now also supply products to an increasingly important local market. The Burmese and Mexican resource refineries now export no oil at all and therefore fall into both the resource and market categories. In the light of the difficulty of allocating the appropriate part of the capacity of a refinery to local needs and to distant market needs, it is not always easy to assign refineries to a particular category. Table 4.6 therefore merely indicates the development of production, refining and consumption in the Middle East, a predominantly resource refinery area, in Western Europe, where refineries are almost wholly in the market class, and in Latin America where production and refining are approximately equal.

THE REFINING PROCESS

In both iron and steel and aluminium production there are two quite distinct processes, each with different locational determinants so that different processes are carried out in plants quite separate from each other. In oil refining there is a single process which transforms crude oil into petroleum products, with the result that refineries are all subject to the same kind of technological and economic considerations. In contrast to both iron and steel and aluminium manufacture, there is now virtually no loss in weight during processing, and this helps to create a wide range of choice of location and to make the decision to build at the resource or the market rather more finely balanced than in the case of the other two industries. A further simplifying factor is that unusually for a 20th-century industry, there is only one raw material, crude oil, and the energy required is often derived from products of the refinery process itself, or in the case of the resource refineries, from natural gas from the local oilfield. As a consequence the Weberian locational figures are simply straight lines. Fig. 59 shows the figures for each of the three groups of site. In the case of the resource and intermediate figures several markets are illustrated since the existence of more than one market is the *raison d'être* for this type of refinery. The figures help to emphasise the importance of the comparative transport costs of moving crude and products, for although loss in weight is not now an important issue, the freight rates on products are normally higher than on crude oil. There is thus incentive for the avoidance of long-distance movement of products. We now turn to consider the three categories of refinery.

RESOURCE REFINERIES

Mention has been made of the declining advantages of resource refineries. Table 4.6 indicates that in 1938 some 90% of Middle Eastern oil was refined *in situ*, suggesting that at that time there were powerful incentives to locate plants at the material source. The same was true in Latin America, for in the same year 95% of indigenous oil was locally refined. Venezuela was the leading producer and the Netherlands Antilles the leading refiner. Although consumption data for 1938 are not available, it is fair to assume that local demand was small and that Middle Eastern and Latin American refined oil was almost entirely exported to distant markets. However, as Middle Eastern crude output has risen, refining capacity has lagged so that in 1970 only 18% of the area's oil was locally refined. Furthermore, nearly half of the products manufactured were consumed in local markets, and it is clear that between 1938 and 1970 there was a complete reversal of the respective advantages of oilfields and markets, Western Europe representing the largest market for Middle Eastern oil. Events in Latin America have progressed differently. In 1970, 93% of the area's crude oil was refined locally, and since only half was consumed in domestic markets, there is a conflict with trends in the Middle East. We must next look at the economic advantages of resource refineries and try to account for the differences in the growth of refining in these two important oil-producing areas.

(i) *The economies of large-scale production*

The cost of producing a unit of refined products falls as the size of the refinery increases, provided that the capacity of the plant is fully utilised. Above a capacity of about 3 million tons per year the economies of scale begin to diminish, but the important point is that they do not disappear altogether. Thus if we assume that the capital cost per ton of output for

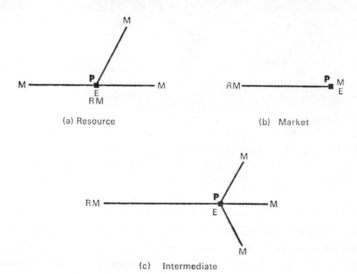

(a) Resource   (b) Market

(c) Intermediate

Fig. 59 Locational figures of the three categories of oil-refinery

a 5 million ton refinery is 100, then the indices for plants of 1 and 3 million tons capacity are 190 and 123 respectively.[24] In order to justify their size, large plants must have access to large markets, and the great advantage of many resource refineries is that they are able to serve several markets by low-cost ocean transport. Middle Eastern and Latin American refineries are able to supply Japan, Western Europe and the U.S.A., as suggested in Fig. 59(a). Indeed the largest refinery ever operated, Abadan, possessed a capacity of 25 million tons prior to its nationalisation in 1951. It now has a capacity of 22 million tons. Other very large resource refineries include Ras Tanura (19·5 million tons) in Saudi Arabia, Aruba (22 million tons) and Curacao (19 million tons),

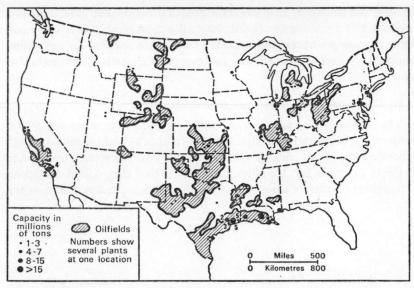

Fig. 60 Oil refining in the U.S.A., 1970. Refineries less than one million tons' capacity not shown

both in the Netherlands, Antilles and Amuay Bay (21·2 million tons) in Venezuela. The six largest refineries in the U.S.A., ranging from 16·0 to 22·4 million tons annual capacity, are all to be found on the Gulf Coast field of Texas and Louisiana (Fig. 60).

(ii) *Demand for different products in each market*

Crude oils have a composition which is related to their origin. Middle Eastern crudes break down into 20–22% petrol, 18–20% middle distillates such as diesel oil, and 43–45% residual fuel oils. This distribution can be changed to some extent by cracking, for example it is possible to obtain 27% petrol from a Middle Eastern crude by this process. Unless demand in a market approximately matches the composition of the crude oil used, a market refinery will be faced with the cost of transporting the surplus products to another market. In the mid-1950s the Norwegian market consumed 70% middle distillates and fuel oils, which would have meant a large surplus of petrol if refining had taken place there.[25] This kind of imbalance in demand for products favours the resource refineries especially when they are well placed to serve several markets in which the demand is for only a few of the main products. Plants in the Middle East can deliver kerosene, used for cooking and lighting, to the underdeveloped nations of India and South East Asia, and despatch fuel oils, which are taking the place of coal, to Western Europe. The importance of refining in Venezuela can partly be explained by the deficit of residual oils on the eastern seaboard of the U.S.A., where refiners have chosen to expand their output of petrol at the expense of heavy oils.[26] Venezuelan crude is much heavier than Middle Eastern crude and is well suited to the production of fuel oils which can easily be shipped in product tankers to eastern U.S.A. The ability of the resource refineries to make use of the varying demand for products in different markets serves to reinforce their size and helps reduce unit production costs.

(iii) *Weight-loss*

Demand for refined products was largely restricted to kerosene in the 19th century, with the consequence that only about 30–40% of each unit of crude oil could be sold. As late as 1899 58% of American demand was for kerosene and only 16% for fuel oils.[27] With a weight-loss of between 60 and 70%, it was effectively obligatory for refineries to be located on or adjacent to oilfields. The growth in demand for petrol, diesel, lubricating and fuel oils during the course of this century has progressively reduced the wastage incurred during processing, and thus weakened the pull of the oilfields on this count.

(iv) *The use of natural gas as a refinery fuel*

The small demand for natural gas, especially in the Middle East and Latin America, causes its price to be very low at the wellhead. In many areas it is simply 'flared off' as a waste product. This low-cost energy is an important advantage, for if natural gas is not available, about 7% of crude oil supplies are used as refinery fuel. Thus many market refiners have to accept this loss in weight, and the appropriate expenditure incurred on transport. Odell is of the opinion that the availability of natural gas at oilfields could well have slowed down the expansion of market refineries had it not been for political and strategic considerations.[28]

(v) *Action taken by the oilfield nations*

Some refineries in the oil-producing countries owe their existence to action taken by these nations to increase their revenue by moving into refining themselves, and by requiring the majors to build refineries as a condition of the grant of oil concessions. Some employment is generated, but an important factor is the prestige attaching to the possession of an oil refinery. The plants at Abadan and Shuaiba are examples of nationally owned refineries, and the Khafji refinery in the Kuwait Neutral Zone, owned by a Japanese company, was built in the mid-1960s as a condition of further oil winning. The Latin American countries seem to have been more successful than those in the Middle East in developing refineries, following the lead of Venezuela which instituted the Hydrocarbons Act in 1943 requiring concessionaires to refine at least 15% of their crude production within the country. With the exception of Venezuela itself, the five other leading oil-producing countries, Mexico, Argentina, Colombia, Brazil and Trinidad, all had refinery capacity approximately equal to their oil output by 1970. In Africa, the remarkably rapid rise of Libya to the status of one of the world's foremost oil producers has not yet resulted in more than nominal refinery capacity.

American experience suggests that there is a strong case for resource refineries. In 1970, the three leading refining states, Texas, California and Louisiana, all important oil producers, possessed 56% of the country's refinery capacity. On the other hand, the economic advantages of refining in the Middle East do not seem to have been great enough to persuade the majors to establish themselves there on a large scale. The location of refineries must take political, strategic as well as economic factors into consideration, and the combination of these has resulted in the expansion of market refineries in Western Europe rather than in the Middle East, the principal source of their oil.

MARKET REFINERIES

Table 4.6 indicates that West European crude-oil production is small in relation to its consumption. The U.S.A. is a larger market for oil than Western Europe, but the U.S.A. can meet nearly 80% of its requirements from domestic sources, compared with a figure of 4% in the case of Western Europe. The subcontinent is therefore strictly a market in that it produces negligible quantities of crude oil, and the very rapid increase in refinery construction in the area emphasises the advantages of market refineries. Between 1938 and 1970, Western Europe's share of world-refining capacity rose from 4 to 28%, and by 1969 the region had a larger refinery capacity than the U.S.A. (660 compared with 608 million tons), although in 1960 the U.S.A. had a capacity more than twice as large. Well-developed refining complexes have arisen close to the major manufacturing regions. The most important cluster is at Rotterdam-Europoort (55 million tons), followed by Thameside (28 million tons) and Lower Seine (28 million tons). Similar expansion had occurred earlier on the north-eastern seaboard of the U.S.A. on the Delaware River in Pennsylvania (31 million tons) and in New Jersey (27 million tons), using Gulf Coast as well as imported crude oils. There are four main reasons for these developments.

(i) The demand for products

In the 1930s the demand for products in a particular market did not match the constituents of crude oil. Petrol was responsible for 50% of the total demand in Britain in 1938, and because of the then great dependence on coal, the demand for heavy oils was very small. Following the inability of coal to remain competitive, it has largely been replaced by fuel oils, and such has been the growth in this sector of the market for oil that petrol's share of the market for all products has dwindled. The demand for products in Western Europe is now very close to the constituents of Middle Eastern crude, so the need to re-export surplus heavy oils, in some cases back along the route of the imported crude, has been removed. Further, the size of demand is such that the threshold necessary to justify the establishment of a refinery has been reached, not merely in each country, but in many regions within West European countries. The diversification of demand has not been restricted to heavy fuel oils, for the growing sophistication of industrial processes, exemplified above all by the petrochemical industry, has created a demand for virtually all the products of refining, with the consequence that there is now effectively no loss in weight at all. Market refineries can now reap the economies of large-scale production that were formerly the province of resource refineries. Examples of large refineries are Gonfreville (14 million tons), Fawley (16 million tons) and the Shell plant at Rotterdam (17 million tons). It is noticeable that these are not as large as the principal resource refineries, for firms prefer to get as close as possible to markets and therefore construct several medium-sized rather than one very large plant. This is not a consideration for resource refineries. Finally, market plants are in an excellent position to relate their output to changes in local demand by switching to a crude from a different source with a different composition. In the same way they can choose between crudes in respect of cost.

(ii) The comparative cost of transporting crude and products

Central to the expansion of market refining is the lower cost of moving crude rather than products. This is true of both tanker and pipeline transport.

(a) *Tanker transport.* Markets for each individual product are quite small and coupled with the inability of many ports to handle large tankers, the optimum size for a product tanker is about 20 000 tons. Since products must be separated, the scale economies of handling crude are denied to products. Crude oil is regarded as 'clean' cargo, but certain types of products are termed 'dirty', and are penalised by the imposition of freight rates 10% above those levied on crude oil. The differential between the freights charged on products and crude oil is steadily widening, for while the size of product tanker is static, crude tankers are increasing in size because in this way crude can be carried more cheaply. Transport costs form an important part of landed prices, and the oil companies have been eager customers of shipbuilding yards capable of constructing supertankers. In 1960 there was only one tanker of more than 101 000 tons, but by 1969 16% of the world tanker fleet comprised vessels of more than 125 000 tons.[29] An example of the economies of scale in tanker transport is provided by the movement of crude from the Persian Gulf to Western Europe in 75 000-ton and 250 000-ton vessels. The larger ship must travel via the Cape of Good Hope, but even so the freight rate per ton for the larger ship is about 25% lower than that of

TABLE 4.7

Freight rates for tankers between the Persian Gulf and Rotterdam, 1968

| Tanker size | Freight rate (cents per barrel) | | |
	Suez both ways	Suez in ballast, Cape loaded	Cape both ways
50 000	51	—	—
70 000	46	—	—
100 000	—	44	—
200 000	—	33	37

Source: P. H. Frankel and W. L. Newton, 'Economics of Petroleum Refining—Present State and Future Prospects', *Journal of the Institute of Petroleum*, 1968, p. 26.

the smaller vessel taking the shorter route via Suez. Suez has been closed since 1967, increasing the differential still further. Table 4.7 gives further evidence of the advantages of large tankers.

The use of very large tankers has had repercussions on the siting and the size of market refineries. Since supertankers move between a small number of berths, it has proved economic to construct special deepwater facilities to handle them, resulting in the clustering of refineries, as at Rotterdam-Europoort. Large vessels are conducive to an increase in the size of refinery; in order to process crude from a 200 000-ton tanker, a refinery must have an annual capacity of 7 million tons, on the assumption that a refinery would not take more than 10 days' supply in one shipment.[30] As we have seen, the unit costs of production vary inversely with the size of refinery.

(b) *Transport by pipe.* The use of tankers for the transport of crude oil results in the great majority of cases in the location of refineries on the coast. Although it is possible to move products and crude by pipe overland, product pipelines are still something of an exception, and once again we find crude being moved, only this time to inland refineries. Pipelines are characterised by high capital and low running costs, for example the total cost of a typical crude pipeline would be apportioned 65% capital and 35% running costs.[31] The upshot is that in the absence of a large and continuous demand, other forms of transport, especially barges, are more economic. It was not until the late 1950s that inland regional demand for products in Western Europe justified the construction of refineries linked to the coast by pipelines. The 'Trapil' products pipe between Le Havre, Rouen and Paris had been opened in 1953, and a number of product lines were constructed in Britain between coastal refineries and points of large demand, for example the aviation spirit line from Fawley to London Airport, but most pipes laid down in the 1960s were crude pipes. The more important of these are shown in Fig. 61.

Since the refineries linked to these pipes are market refineries in the strict sense that they serve the local area and have no intermediate function such as some of the large coastal plants, it is to be expected that they are smaller than the coastal refineries. Their size is determined by the strength of local demand and the number of firms competing in the local market. In West Germany the greatest regional consumption is in the Ruhr, but four German firms, one small international firm (Fina) and three majors share the market. The largest plant is owned by Shell at Godorf with a capacity of 8·3 million tons. The larger demand for products in the U.S.A. has resulted in the bigger inland refineries having a greater capacity than the leading West European inland plants. Whiting, near Chicago, has a capacity of 15·4 million tons, and Wood River, near St Louis, is rated at 12·6 million tons. Inland refineries lack the flexibility of the coastal plants, for if the yield of products does not match local demand, the cost of moving the unwanted products to another regional market may be prohibitive. They are thus prisoners of the local market, and Frankel and Newton apply the term 'cul-de-sac' to these refineries.[32]

There are four reasons for the movement of crude oil rather than of products through pipelines. Firstly, not all products can be economically pumped through a pipe. Heavy fuel oil, the product demand for which has been growing the most rapidly, flows only with difficulty and is not normally moved more than short distances. Mixing occurs when different products are pumped successively. Secondly, where they are used, product pipelines are of smaller diameter than crude pipes because of the limited demand for products, and they suffer from diseconomies of scale. Thirdly, the total cost of moving the products derived from a unit of crude oil is greater than the cost of moving the crude, largely because heavy fuel oil must be moved by rail or barge. Light products can be moved from Texas to Chicago more cheaply than crude oil, but heavy

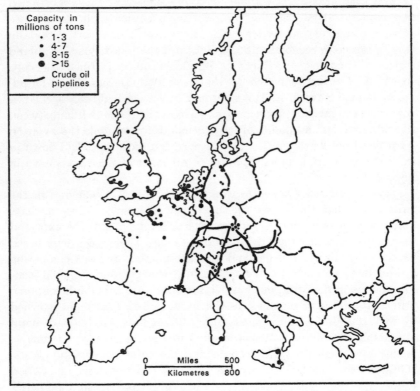

Fig. 61 Oil refining in Western Europe, 1969. Refineries less than one million tons' capacity not shown

oils must be transported by rail and barge, giving a higher total cost for the shipment of products than of crude. Fourthly, incentive for the construction of inland plants can come from a desire on the part of provincial governments to obtain a supply of products at a lower cost in order to encourage industrialisation. The five refineries in the vicinity of Inglostadt, Bavaria, had their origins in this way.[33]

(iii) External economies

The cost of refining oil in areas such as the Middle East is adversely affected by the low level of economic development in the region. Refinery firms must provide all the essential services such as roads, water and electric power supplies, hospitals and houses, the cost of which would be met by other bodies in advanced economies. The cost of capital equipment and of imported supervisory labour is also high. Allied to the external economies available in developed countries is the possibility of entering the petrochemical industry. A number of West European refineries now have their associated petrochemical plants, but the nature of many oilfield regions militates against this trend.

(iv) *Political and strategic considerations*

Despite the economic case made out above for the growth of market refining, 'the influences shifting refineries towards market areas were by no means simply economic, or at any rate had little to do with oil economics proper'.[34] The depression of the inter-war period led some countries to follow a policy of autarchy or self-sufficiency, and in 1928 the first French refinery was completed, although it must have been of doubtful economic viability. This policy caused France to be far and away the most important West European refiner by 1938, with 48% of the capacity of the area. After the Second World War there was an acute shortage of foreign exchange in Western Europe. Governments sought to overcome this by encouraging the construction of refineries and by instituting preferential tariffs in favour of the import of crude rather than products. These incentives towards market refineries were reinforced by the decline of British and French influence and the rise of extreme nationalism in the Middle East, prejudicial to Western business interests. Symptomatic was the nationalisation of the Anglo-Iranian Oil Company in 1951, and the appropriation of the world's largest refinery at Abadan. Firms became most reluctant to risk the loss of expensive capital investment, and governments in the West found further cause to support market refineries since supplies of products from the Middle East could not be relied upon.

Also to be considered under this heading is the construction of small refineries in many of the emergent nations lacking major oilfields. Such countries may therefore be regarded as markets. A refinery is seen by many developing countries as a symbol of progress, and thus the political justifications transcend the dictates of economics. Tariffs of up to 40% have to be employed in Central America to protect the output of inefficient refineries, which are frequently well below the minimum economic size because of the low level of demand. The consumption of products in the five countries is 3 million tons a year, that is, approximately equal to the output of the smallest economic refinery, yet there are six plants in the five states with an average capacity of less than 0·75 million tons and with a total capacity of 4 million tons. The plants are not only small but their capacity is under-used, and for each 1% of unused capacity, unit production costs rise by 1%.[35] An alternative strategy is for a government to bargain with an oil company, offering a guaranteed national market in return for the construction of a refinery. Often these plants are uneconomic,but the oil companies hope that the losses incurred in the short term will be offset by the future profits to be made when demand for products does rise to an economic level. The Italian state company, E.N.I., has been involved in such bargains with Ghana, Morocco and Tunisia.

INTERMEDIATE REFINERIES

The function of this small class of refinery is to serve a number of markets which are individually insufficient in size to justify a plant of their own. There is flexibility as to the source of the crude oil processed, and the demand for a different range of products in each market can be met. Intermediate refineries make use of the economies of moving crude in large tankers over a large part of the haul between oilfield and final consumer, and by locating at a nodal point in respect of the several

TABLE 4.8

Intermediate and market refining capacity in Western Europe 1951–1967 (million tons)

	1951	1960	1967
Intermediate refining	13·9	36·8	47·5
Market refining	55·5	160·0	416·3
Intermediate refining as % market refining	25	23	11

Source: as for Table 4.7.

markets concerned, they can minimise the cost of distributing products. As we have mentioned, the major refineries on the coast of Western Europe may be regarded in part as intermediate plants. The Esso refinery at Fawley, for example, serves a local market in central and southern England by road, rail and coastal tanker, but it also supplies products to distant points such as Aberdeen and Inverness, which are within the local market area of the more northerly refineries. More strictly, intermediate refineries are those at Aden, Tenerife in the Canary Islands, Singapore, Milazzo, Augusta and Gela in Sicily where local demand is very small and the great bulk of products are moved onwards to markets elsewhere. To a great extent they depend for their existence on the imbalance of demand for products in particular markets. Consequently, with the removal of this imbalance, the justification for the intermediate refinery is lessened, for it becomes more economic to locate the plant close to balanced markets in order to diminish the distance over which products must be moved. The development of refineries at inland markets in Western Europe has reduced the intermediate function of plants such as those at Antwerp and Rotterdam, and if the demand for products in the Scandinavian countries becomes more balanced, the large North West European plants will fall even more easily into the market category. Table 4.8 illustrates the trend. That part of each refinery's capacity assigned to the manufacture of products destined for distant markets has been computed by Frankel and Newton, and the data in the table show that intermediate refining is of diminishing importance in Western Europe. If the term 'intermediate refinery' had been restricted to plants consigning most of their output to distant consumers, the intermediate refining capacities would be very much smaller.

References

1. R. C. Riley, 'Henry Cort at Funtley, Hampshire, *Industrial Archaeology*, 1971, pp. 69–76.
2. W. Isard, 'Some Locational Factors in the Iron and Steel Industry since the early Nineteenth Century', *Journal of Political Economy*, 1948, p. 205.
3. *Ibid.*, pp. 207–8.
4. A. Rodgers, 'Industrial Inertia. A Major Factor in the Location of the U.S. Iron and Steel Industry', *Geographical Review*, 1952, p. 60.
5. K. Warren, 'The Changing Steel Industry of the European Common Market', *Economic Geography*, 1969, p. 317.
6. E. P. F. Boughey, 'The Place of Scrap in Steelmaking', *British Steel*, November 1968, p. 26.
7. K. Warren, 'Recent Changes in the Geographical Location of the British Steel Industry', *Geographical Journal*, 1969, p. 345.
8. *Ibid.*, p. 357.
9. J. E. Martin, 'New Trends in the Lorraine Iron Region', *Geography*, 1968, pp. 377–8.
10. G. J. Sharer, 'The Philadelphia Iron and Steel District: its Relation to the Seaways', *Economic Geography*, 1963, p. 363.
11. Anon, 'Structural Changes in World Ore', *Steel Review*, April 1963, p. 10.
12. G. Manners, 'Transport Costs, Freight Rates and the Changing Economic Geography of Iron Ore', *Geography*, 1967, p. 266.
13. *The Economist*, London, 11 January 1969.
14. D. K. Fleming, 'Coastal Steelworks in the Common Market Countries', *Geographical Review*, 1967, p. 58.

15. A. Rodgers, *op. cit.*, p. 58.

16. *The Times Review of Industry*, London, February 1960, p. 9.

17. G. Alexandersson, 'Changes in the Location Pattern of the Anglo-American Steel Industry: 1948–1959', *Economic Geography*, 1961, p. 107.

18. A. S. Carlson (Ed), *Economic Geography of Industrial Materials*, New York, 1956, p. 150.

19. *Bauxite, Alumina and Aluminium*, H.M.S.O., London, 1962, p. 35.

20. H. D. Huggins, *Aluminium in Changing Communities*, Andre Deutsch, London, 1965, pp. 45–6.

21. *Ibid.*, pp. 45–6.

22. *Ibid.*, p. 181.

23. J. V. Krutilla, 'Locational Factors Influencing Recent Aluminium Expansion', *Southern Economic Journal*, 1954/5, p. 275.

24. G. Manners, *The Geography of Energy*, Hutchinson, London, 1964, p. 185.

25. A. Melamid, 'Geographical Distribution of Petroleum Refining Capacities', *Economic Geography*, 1955, p. 170.

26. P. R. Odell, *An Economic Geography of Oil*, Bell, London, 1963, p. 143.

27. J. S. Clark, *The Oil Century*, Norman: University of Oklahoma Press, 1958, p. 127.

28. P. R. Odell, *op. cit.*, p. 139.

29. *B.P. Statistical Review of the World Oil Industry*, 1969, p. 23.

30. P. H. Frankel and W. L. Newton, 'Economics of Petroleum Refining—Present State and Future Prospects', *Journal of the Institute of Petroleum*, 1968, p. 26.

31. G. Manners, *op. cit.*, 1964, p. 57.

32. P. H. Frankel and W. L. Newton, 'The Location of Refineries', *The Institute of Petroleum Review*, July 1961, p. 198.

33. P. P. Waller and H. S. Swain, 'Changing Patterns of Oil Transportation and Refining in West Germany', *Economic Geography*, 1967, p. 149.

34. J. E. Hartshorn, *Oil Companies and Governments*, Faber and Faber, London, 1962, p. 77.

35. P. R. Odell, *Oil and World Power*, Penguin, London, 1970, p. 146.

Chapter 5

MARKET-ORIENTED INDUSTRIES

Market-oriented industries, as the term suggests, exhibit close ties with their markets. A common cause is the high cost of transporting the product because of such exigencies as a gain in weight in processing, when the product has a low unit value. Brewing is a case in point. The high cost of building a distribution network ensures that gasworks are centrally situated in their market areas. Both these industries are clearly transport-oriented; as we have noted in Chapter 2 in the case of other transport-oriented industries, following improvements in transport technology, low-value materials and products can be moved over increasingly long distances, thereby reducing the pull of materials and of markets. Transport costs are not the only reason for a location close to markets, however. The textile machinery industry, for example, not only manufactures machines, but also parts for machines, at the same time repairing and servicing machinery. This industry is said to be 'linked' to its market because of the obvious importance of proximity for reasons other than the reduction of transport costs. A further reason for market orientation is provided by the furniture industry which shows a marked preference for large cities. Although there is an increase in bulk during manufacture, transport costs in relation to the value of the product are not especially onerous. The attraction of cities is provided by several interacting factors such as the strength of specialised demand in cities, especially capital cities, the provision of specialist labour and the evolution of great external economies of scale.

It is clear that while beer, gas and furniture are bought by the consuming public, textile machinery is used by industry. This allows a twofold classification of market-oriented industries to be made: those oriented to final markets, sometimes referred to as residentiary industries because the numbers employed correlate with population, and those oriented to intermediate or industrial markets.* Because of technical and other factors, not all residentiary industries have an identical relationship with the distribution of population; some are very closely related to population, with others the ties are less pronounced. Of the three

---

* A third, rather less important category, exists—those industries oriented to resource markets. An example is tin-can production for use by fruit and vegetable producers.

K

residentiary industries examined in this chapter, gas making exhibits the least distortion in that there are in England and Wales very few counties which specialise in the activity. Distortion occurs in brewing as a result of the presence of highly distinctive water at places such as Burton-on-Trent. In some instances distortion in brewing is more apparent than real because the census returns include cider-making and malting and since both these activities are highly localised, specialisation in brewing appears to take place. Such is the strength of the London region in furniture manufacture that it is debatable whether the industry is strictly residentiary at all. It is certainly at the opposite end of the spectrum from gas.

In order to establish whether an area specialises in a residentiary industry it is insufficient merely to consider the numbers employed in that industry. If this were the case, the largest city would always dominate and specialisation would apparently occur. It is therefore necessary to relate residentiary industry employment to the total working population of an area before specialisation can be established. This can be achieved by the location quotient which relates the concentration of an industry in a particular area to the importance of manufacturing in general in that area. The quotient may be computed by using the formula:

$$\frac{\text{Percentage of U.K. (brewing) operatives in county X}}{\text{Percentage of U.K. labour force in county X}}$$

For example, there are more brewing employees in the county of London than in any other (11·52% of the total in England and Wales), but since the county has only 8·07% of the total employed population in England and Wales, the quotient is 1·42, indicating that specialisation exists. Again, Lancashire has the largest employed population of any county (11·43% of the total), but since only 6·59% of brewing employees work in the county, the quotient is 0·57, indicating that brewing is under-represented in the county. From this example we see that when an area's share of employment in an industry exactly equals its share of total employment, the location quotient is equal to 1. If a residentiary industry were exactly to correlate with population, we would find that all areas would score a quotient of 1. Location quotients less than, and greater than, 1 are evidence of distortion from the theoretical pattern of residentiary industries. Thus the quotients returned by counties in England and Wales for gas manufacture are close to 1, and those for furniture show considerable deviation about this value.

We now turn to look at specific market-oriented industries, all of which are seen as they exist in England and Wales, although the principles developed have a wider application.

5.1 TOWN GAS MANUFACTURE

The term 'town gas manufacture' is used to differentiate between gas made in urban gasworks and that made as a by-product in coking plant and metallurgical coke ovens. This is a necessary distinction since

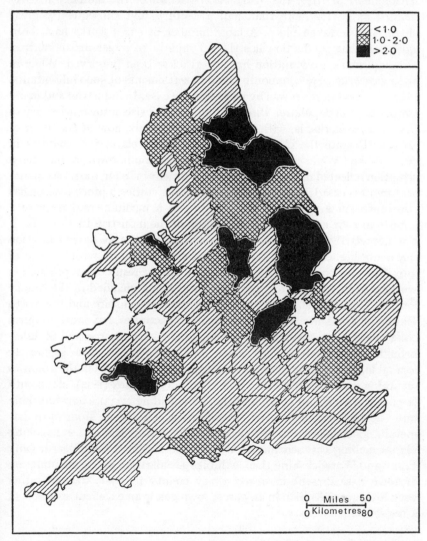

Fig. 62 Location quotient map of the gas industry in England and Wales, 1961

coking plant and metallurgical coke ovens are subject to quite different locational influences which make them other than residentiary industries. The great bulk of town gas is destined for non-industrial markets, hence the significance of the distribution of population to the industry.

Rather more than is the case with other residentiary industries such as baking and brewing, a gasworks by virtue of its size, odour and associated gasholders, leaves its impress on the urban environment. Until it was nationalised in 1949, the distribution pattern of the industry had remained static for more than half a century, but subsequently great changes have taken place. A large number of small works have been closed so that production has shifted rapidly to larger urban centres, although market-orientation has nevertheless been preserved. While in 1949 gasworks were commonly found in settlements of 5000 inhabitants, twenty years later this was by no means the case. In industrial and many rural areas the population threshold, that is, the size of town necessary to justify a gasworks, is, with only a few exceptions, now of the order of 30 000. Despite the changes that have taken place, few counties in England and Wales exhibit marked specialisation in town gas making, a situation reflected in Fig. 62, a location quotient map for 1961. Gas manufacture has ceased in some of the more rural counties, a process which has continued since 1961, but the presence of a medium-sized town in a county in 1961 ensured the continuation of the industry. In 1970, this is not necessarily so. The map shows seven counties as having location quotients higher than 2, the highest being Flintshire with a score of 4·93. The areas of apparent concentration are the result of gas production workers in integrated iron and steelworks being included in the county figures. Thus Flintshire, Northamptonshire, Lincolnshire and the North Riding of Yorkshire, all largely agricultural counties, have metallurgical coke ovens at steelworks at Shotton, Corby, Scunthorpe and Middlesbrough respectively. Were town gas employment data separately available, the quotients would be significantly lower. Of the counties returning quotients between 1 and 2, only four, Essex (1·64), Monmouth (1·96), Warwickshire (1·40) and the West Riding (1·33), show anything but the slightest degree of specialisation. Of these, Monmouth has metallurgical coke ovens at Newport, and the West Riding has 14 coking plants making carbochemicals, run by the National Coal Board. Only Essex and Warwickshire, then, exhibit specialisation in the manufacture of town gas. Present in nearly every county in 1961, demonstrating very little specialisation in any area, town gas is an excellent example of a residentiary industry.

CAUSES OF MARKET ORIENTATION PRIOR TO NATIONALISATION

(i) *Organisation of the industry*

From the first public supply of gas in 1812, production was controlled by a large number of independent companies and local authority undertakings set up to meet local demand. Companies operated in statutory areas at low maximum prices, providing little incentive for amalgamation, while local authorities seem seldom to have been able to sink their differences. In 1945, there were only five Joint Gas Boards involving two or more local authority undertakings, supplying only 1·1% of total gas production.[1] At nationalisation there were nearly 1000 separate gas undertakings.

(ii) *Transmission costs*

19th-century technology carried over into the 20th century, involving low-pressure storage and pumping, and the use of cast iron mains unable to withstand high pressure made gas transmission costs high, severely limiting the distance gas could be sent. On economic grounds alone, it would not have been possible, until the 1930s, to pipe gas from coalfield located gasworks. Studies in the 1930s showed that it had become economically possible to transmit gas over longer distances than was at that time the practice, providing that the quantity of gas was above a certain limit. Shortages of capital, the general economic climate of the period and the fragmented nature of the industry, however, did not favour the development of longer transmission.[2] Thus the basic raw material, gas coal, continued to be delivered to market located gasworks. Not surprisingly, a committee of enquiry reported in 1945 that a national grid, which might have caused the closure of some small high cost works, was not feasible on technical or economic grounds.

(iii) *By-products*

The traditional manufacturing plant produced gas by the carbonization of coal, that is, coal was heated in closed retorts resulting not only in the output of gas, but also of coke, tar and other carbochemicals. For every ton of coal carbonized, 0·5 ton of coke was made, and since the cost of moving coke was close to that of moving coal, it was important that the plant be close to its market for both gas and coke. Transport costs on carbochemicals were less onerous. It was the problems arising from the disposal of coke that kept the optimum size of plant down to levels which, by today's standard, seem very small indeed. In 1945 the optimum size was 0·16 million cubic metres per day (mcmd) 5·5 million cubic feet per day (mcfd); there are now several plants of 3·0 mcmd/100 mcfd in operation.

(iv) *The problems of supplying rural areas*

Since transmission costs were high it was not possible to supply small towns and villages from larger settlements. Small towns thus had the choice of either developing their own plant or doing without a supply of gas. Normally the former solution was adopted, hence the large number of small works in small settlements inherited by the 12 Area Gas Boards at nationalisation. The Southern Gas Board, for example, took over 42 works, out of a total of 67, whose daily capacity was less than 0·01 mcmd/ 0·5 mcfd.

A small exception to the pattern of market location was provided by the use of coke oven gas as a raw material. The principal aim of the coke oven is to provide metallurgical coke for the iron and steel and ironfounding industries, gas being given off in the process as a by-product. This gas can be purified by gasworks in the vicinity of coke ovens, and such works might be held to be material oriented. However, since they supply gas to a local market on the same basis as normal gasworks, they are more properly to be regarded as both material- and market-oriented plants. Examples of such plants occurred on the South Wales, Yorkshire–Derbyshire and Northumberland and Durham coalfields, where colliery and steelworks' coke ovens were able to sell gas in bulk.

The industry was nationalised in 1949 and the substitution of 12 Area Boards for the earlier multiplicity of undertakings removed the

TABLE 5.1

Distribution of gasworks by size of town, Southern and West Midland Gas Boards, 1949 and 1971

		Town Size, population			
	<5000	5000–19 999	20 000–75 000	>75 000	Total
1949	48	38	34	17	139
1971	2	1	2	11	16

Source: Ordnance Survey 10″ Planning Series, *Gas and Coke*, 1949. *Annual Report and Accounts*, West Midland and Southern Gas Boards, 1970–1.

major impediments to progress—the small size of firm and the tiny statutory market areas. It became possible to build plants of optimum size transmitting gas over longer distances and to close many small works. The industry became an excellent example of the effects of govern-

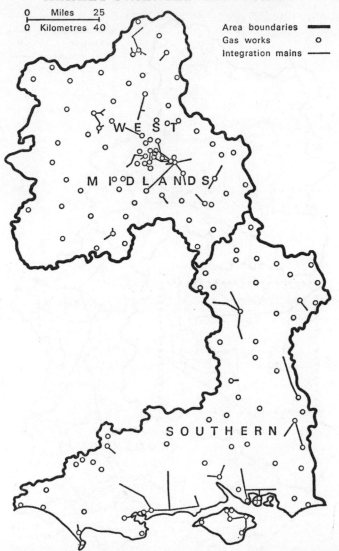

Fig. 63 Gasworks and distribution systems of the Southern and West Midlands Gas Boards, 1949

ment intervention in a mixed economy. Between 1949 and 1971 the number of works fell from 1050 to 118, while the length of mains in use rose from 119 000 km/74 400 miles to 197 152 km/123 220 miles, by far the greater part of the increase being accounted for by integration mains between works rather than town distribution pipes. A comparison of Figs. 63 and 64 gives an indication of the remarkable extension of

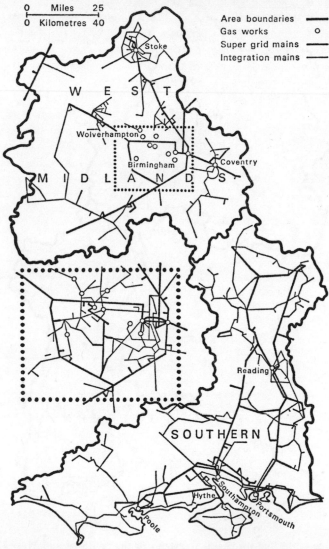

Fig. 64 Gasworks and distribution systems of the Southern and West Midlands Gas Boards, 1969

integration mains in the West Midland and Southern Gas Board areas between 1949 and 1969. As has been mentioned, there was a simultaneous movement to larger towns, a trend clearly evident from the two maps. the precise nature of the trend has been computed for the two Boards, and appears in Table 5.1. Not all Boards have pushed ahead so rapidly.

For example, the Scottish Board is faced with many isolated small markets, and because of the high cost of laying integration mains, there is still justification for these markets to be supplied by small plants. We next consider the technological and economic background to the rapid changes in the distribution of the industry during the last twenty years.

PROCESSES AND THE SIZE OF PLANT

The reduction in the number of manufacturing stations implies that the average size of works must increase, in other words, an inverse relationship exists. The two developments are shown in graph form in Fig. 65. Since it has been noted that the optimum size of plant in 1945 was

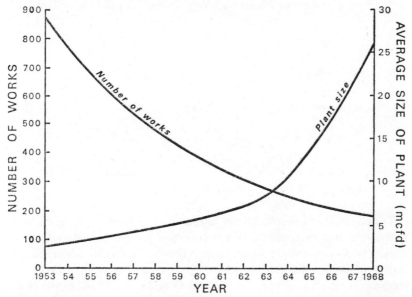

Fig. 65 The relationship between the number of works and the size of plant

0·16 mcmd/5·5 mcfd, and yet the national average was 0·81 mcmd/27·0 mcfd in 1968 (in some Area Boards it was very much higher than this, for example the West Midland Board returned an average size of 2·04 mcmd/68·0 mcfd per plant in 1968), it would seem that gas-making techniques must have undergone radical change. In general, as each new process has been introduced, it has proved possible to increase the size of plant and to cut back the total number of works in operation, although it is important to remember that new transmission techniques have also played a vital part. Large works are desirable since overhead charges in production fall as the size of works rises; labour costs in small works may be 30%, of total production costs, but in new large plants the figure is as low as 7%. In 1958 it was thought that the decreases in overhead costs would fall rapidly up to an output of 0·90 mcmd/30 mcfd after which the rate of decrease would slow down.[3] The West Midland Board estimated that very small works such as those at Church Stretton, Tenbury and Shipston-on-Stour were twice as expensive as those in Birmingham and Coventry.[4] Table 5.2 illustrates the way in which production has been concentrated into larger plants in England, Wales and Scotland between 1953 and 1971.

TABLE 5.2

Gas made by Plants according to size, 1953 and 1971

Size of plant (million therms per annum)	1953		1971	
	n	%	n	%
>10	61	56·3	55	97·3
5–10	57	17·1	9	1·7
1·25–4·9	173	18·7	11	1·0
0·5–1·24	133	4·7	3	—
<0·5	486	3·2	40	—
	910		118	

Source: *Gas Council Annual Reports and Accounts.*

The coal carbonization process had reached its peak of efficiency by the mid-1950s, but even so it was a very expensive method of making gas. Production costs were 5 to 6·25p per therm. Coal costs absorbed 55% of gas revenue, with the consequence that gas prices were tied to gas coal prices which rose 70% between 1951 and 1960. (Power station coal rose only 40% in the same period.) Although it was the traditional process, coal carbonization was not well suited to the daily and seasonal fluctuations in demand which characterise the industry. Further, the demand for gas coke was contracting. New materials and processes were required.

(i) *Coke oven gas*

Although coke oven gas had been bought by the gas industry since 1918, prior to nationalisation its use was limited because of the problems of moving gas more than moderate distances. The coke oven could produce the lowest cost gas—2·7p per therm before purifying—and it was a very attractive source of supply to the gas industry. The development of integration mains and the increased size of market areas encouraged the use of this type of gas, and by 1960 17% of all gas made was derived from coke oven gas. The result was the growth of some large coalfield gasworks based on coke oven gas, especially in the East Midlands and South Yorkshire.

(ii) Oil gasification

During the 1950s experiments were made with processes which used oil as the raw material, although no real progress was made despite the production cost of 3·9p per therm. In 1960 only 2% of gas made derived from oil. New plants using oil in addition to coal (no plant used oil exclusively) were located adjacent to oil refineries or tank farms, as at the Isle of Grain, where the plant is actually on land leased from B.P., and at Partington near Manchester. However, both these examples were also well sited in respect of waterborne coal deliveries. Nevertheless the process exhibited some erosion of market orientation.

(iii) The Lurgi Process

Here coal is completely transformed into gas, without the production of coke as a by-product, thereby removing a powerful market pull. Plants could thus be located on coalfields and the gas transmitted instead of coal, much the cheaper alternative in the 1960s. The process had a very large optimum size, about 3·0 mcmd/100 mcfd, at which size gas could be produced at 3·5p per therm. It looked as though the industry was about to become raw material-oriented. However, the two plants built in the early 1960s at Coleshill, Warwickshire, and Westfield, Fife, were small, with capacities of 0·90 mcmd/30 mcfd and 1·20 mcmd/40 mcfd respectively, and could only produce gas at between 4 and 4·6p per therm. This was less than gas made by the traditional method, but other processes developed simultaneously proved much more efficient.

(iv) The Naphtha Reforming Process

It was the technique of reforming naphtha, a light petroleum distillate supplied by oil refineries, that brought to an end the reign of King Coal. Gas could be made for between 2·5 and 3·3p per therm, half the cost of the coal carbonization method, and significantly below both the oil gasification and Lurgi processes. Capital costs were one third those of a Lurgi plant of comparable size. Plants did not necessarily have to be large to benefit from economies of scale. They were flexible enough to be used for peak loads and base loads, while they occupied only one-eighth of the space of a conventional works of comparable size. Labour costs per unit of output were lower than for the other processes because the process lent itself to automatic operation. A major advantage was the production of gas at high pressure, a factor of vital significance to gas transmission, considered below. Since the supply price of naphtha was linked to oil exploitation costs, which are very much more favourable than coal mining costs, and to ocean freight rates, which constantly improve as the size of tanker increases, the use of the new material was advantageous in yet another respect. Plans to invest in Lurgi plants were scrapped and naphtha reforming plants were hurriedly built to take advantage of this low-cost process. The first plant opened in London in 1964, and by 1969 41% of gas made originated from naphtha and oil compared with 20% from coal which, in 1961, had provided the raw material for 78% of gas made. It is ironic that the invention of the reforming process was accidental as far as the gas industry was concerned. The firm that developed it, I.C.I., was seeking a low-cost source of ammonia for the manufacture of fertilizer, and in the course of experiments discovered that reformed naphtha was an excellent source of lean gas which the gas industry was easily able to enrich.

The sheer size of the naphtha plants very quickly rendered all but the newest and largest coal plants obsolete, and the reduction in the number of works from 272 in 1964 to 118 in 1971 is largely a reflection of the possibility of serving large areas from big naphtha plants. During 1967–8, the South Eastern Gas Board shut works such as Tunbridge Wells 0·15 mcmd/4·9 mcfd, Eastbourne 0·14 mcmd/4·6 mcfd and Bexhill 0·04 mcmd/1·3 mcfd because these areas could better be supplied from naphtha plants such as Croydon 5·55 mcmd/185 mcfd. Even the oil gasification plant at Sydenham 0·03 mcmd/1·0 mcfd, less than 10 years old, was found wanting and closed. Tipton, Staffordshire, is even larger than Croydon with a capacity of 8·46 mcmd/282 mcfd. It is these naphtha plants that have largely been responsible for the movement of gasworks into large towns, and there is not a great deal of evidence to suggest that the source of the naphtha, the oil refineries, have succeeded in exercising an influential pull on gasworks. Naphtha, being a liquid, is much more transportable than coal and can be railed to gasworks in large 100-ton tank wagons, as in the case of Tipton, or piped, as at Southampton and Portsmouth where the source is the Esso refinery at Fawley. Occasionally a new naphtha plant is built at other than an old site, and in these cases the oil refineries succeed in creating material-oriented gasworks. An example is Hythe, adjacent to the Fawley refinery. Hythe has a population of less than 5000, so as we might expect the material-oriented plant represents an exception to the usual gasworks population threshold of about 30 000. Hythe is one of the two plants in operation in 1971 in towns of less than 5000 inhabitants referred to in Table 5.1. The other is Coleshill, Warwickshire.

(v) *Natural Gas*

The use of natural gas in large quantities in this country began in 1964 when the first vessel carrying liquified natural gas arrived at the Canvey Island terminal from Algeria. Natural gas liquifies at a tempera- ture of −161·5°C and its volume is thereby reduced 600 times, making the use of tankers feasible. In spite of the high cost of the two refrigerated vessels and of the Canvey reforming plant, Algerian natural gas costs 2·5p per therm at Canvey, and 3·5p per therm at gasworks after mixing

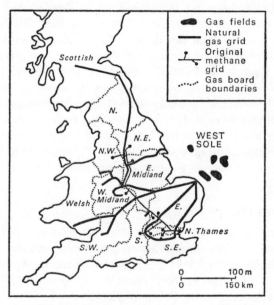

Fig. 66 The United Kingdom natural gas transmission system

with town gas for normal consumption. The two tankers operating a shuttle service between Canvey and Arzew, Algeria, were capable of supplying 10% of Britain's gas consumption in 1964, and for a short while imported natural gas seemed a real solution. Locationally its use disturbed the existing distribution of gasworks in so far as the reforming plant was built at tidewater, and was not therefore market-located. More importantly, however, the 10 gasworks receiving the natural gas by pipe from Canvey (Fig. 66), for the most part located in large towns such as London (2), Slough, Reading, Sheffield, Manchester and

Leeds, have been able to expand at the expense of plants in smaller settlements.

Events moved with quite remarkable speed for the gas industry in the early 1960s, and probably the most far-reaching event occurred in 1965 when an indigenous source of natural gas was discovered in the North Sea by British Petroleum. Gas from this field, West Sole, is landed at Easington, Yorkshire, and gas from the subsequent discoveries further south is brought ashore at Bacton, Norfolk. The negotiated price is 1·19p per therm, although this falls to 0·843p per therm when the offtake by the Gas Council rises above the annual contract quantity. Easington can handle 4·5 mcmd/150 mcfd and Bacton 30·0 mcmd/1000 mcfd, although it is planned to increase this to 120 mcmd/4000 mcfd, equal to the entire British demand in the mid-1970s. Rather than continue to reform natural gas at market-located gasworks, to which it is delivered by pipe, the Gas Council has decided that it is preferable to convert consumers' appliances to burn unreformed natural gas. In the light of the capacity of Bacton, the cost of natural gas and the construction of a national gas grid, this decision is nothing short of revolutionary because it removes the need for gasworks other than at the two purifying plants at Easington and Bacton. If this takes place, the earlier trend of movement of larger settlements will have ceased because the industry will have become material-oriented. It will also represent the extreme case of the rationalisation of an entire industry into what will effectively be one plant.

THE TRANSMISSION OF GAS

The archaic nature of the gas transmission system—cast iron mains with mechanical joints through which gas can be pumped only at very low pressures of up to 2·1 kg per square centimetre (kgscm)/30 lb per square inch—has already been alluded to. In order to concentrate production at a reduced number of works to benefit from the economies of scale, it was vital that transmission costs be reduced if they were not to offset the savings resulting from large works. Welded steel mains working at higher pressures, coupled with the mechanisation of laying, significantly reduced transmission costs. This in turn reduced the cost of making gas since mains linking gasworks allowed a reduction of stand-by plant necessary to cover emergencies, and occasionally helped in the solution of peak demand problems. An example of the latter was the North Wales grid linking the coalfield area in the north-east, with winter peak loads, and the resorts on the north coast, with summer peak loads. Not only pressures were increased, but also the diameter of the pipes and the rates of flow, so that by the mid-1950s it was preferable to transmit gas and the resulting coke to markets more than 80 km/50 miles distant, than to rail coal to a market-located gasworks. Table 5.3 show the variation in transmission costs for particular situations in 1958.

TABLE 5.3

Costs of transmitting gas 80 km (50 miles), 1958

| Size of Pipe | | Pressure | | Flow | | Cost per |
cm	inches	kgscm	lb per square inch	mcmd	mcfd	therm, p.
41	16	3·5	50	3·6	120	0·53
122	48	3·5	50	3·6	120	0·29
61	24	14·0	200	18·0	600	0·25
122	48	3·5	50	7·2	240	0·15
122	48	14·0	200	18·0	600	0·10

Source: J. Burns, *Presidential Address, The Institute of Gas Engineers,* 1958, Appendix. (N.B. kgscm — kg per square cm; mcmd — millions of cubic metres per day; mcfd — millions of cubic feet per day.)

It was the demise of the coal carbonisation process that halted the logical conclusion of the above findings, that gas be made in coalfield works and piped to markets, with the exception of coastal works which should continue to receive coal by coastal colliers. The naphtha-reforming process is a high-pressure system, making gas up to 28 kgscm/400 lb per square inch, and as has been seen, the plants were very large. In order to take advantage of these characteristics, Area Boards constructed supergrid systems (those set up by the Southern and West Midland Boards can be seen in Fig. 64) at about 28 kgscm, although some sections went up to 70 kgscm/1000 lb per square inch, allowing the transmission of gas at low cost. Small outworn gasworks could then be closed, normally becoming points at which the pressure was reduced to allow the gas to enter the older low-pressure distribution mains serving the locality. High-pressure mains assist production and distribution costs in a novel manner. By forcing into the mains more gas than is being withdrawn, the pressure increases and gas is effectively stored in the pipe itself. Gas can then be drawn off at a rate in excess of the inflow during periods of peak demand. This process is known as line-packing. It reduces outlay on storage holders as demand rises, and helps to stabilise production at the works. The best example of line-packing in Britain is the 107 cm/ 42 inch pipe, working up to 50 kgscm/720 lb per square inch, between Portsmouth and Southampton; the principal *raison d'être* of the pipe is storage. The supergrid played just as large a part in the upward movement of the population threshold of gasworks as did the naphtha reforming process itself.

The supergrids of the Area Boards were, for the most part, not connected to each other, as Fig. 64 shows. The import of Algerian natural gas by the Gas Council brought the opportunity of a national gas grid working at 70 kgscm/1000 lb per square inch, allowing gas to be transmitted really long distances, and equally, permitting defreezing to take place at one point. The methane grid, as it is known, is shown in Fig. 60. The advent of natural gas from the North Sea caused the original methane grid to be extended so that all Area Boards can, or will shortly be able to, take delivery of natural gas. An essential factor in the decision to discontinue reforming natural gas at market-located plants, was the possibility of supplying gas to the whole of the country from a limited number of points. Thus improvement in pipeline technology has enabled production to be concentrated in a few large plants; indeed Figs. 63 and 64 indicate that there is a close negative correlation between the length of integration and high pressure mains, and the number of gasworks.

PIPELINES AND MARKET AREAS

Comment on the fragmentation of the industry before 1949, supported by Fig. 63 showing plants and pipelines in 1949, suggest that Losch's idea of plants controlling a market area and competition taking place at the edges of the market area, has some relevance in the gas industry. There are difficulties, however. Because the plants are not evenly distributed, the hexagonal market area shapes would necessarily be distorted, possibly resulting in some areas not being placed within a market area at all. This latter point did obtain in practice, for it was not worth while offering a supply of gas to some rural areas distant from a gasworks. The development of private companies competing for a share of the market in large towns (it is recorded that at one time there were pipes belonging to eight different companies under Whitehall in London)[5] resulted in the institution of a system of areal monopoly rights in 1860. The consequence was that monopolistic competition was impossible since market areas were fixed by law. This being the case, however efficient a shape the hexagon might be, market areas were never hexagonal, rather they assumed, in the main, the shape of local government areas. Fig. 63 illustrates the way in which gasworks were numerous in the Birmingham area in 1949; this is to be expected of a residentiary industry in a densely populated region. The Birmingham area supports Isard's contention that urban market areas are smaller, and plants more numerous, than is the case with rural market areas. Losch argued that the size of market areas would be uniform. Nationalisation merely increased the size of the administrative unit from the local undertaking to the Area Board, there being no competition between Boards. Since Boards possessed many plants, most of which came to be linked as we have seen, the Loschian concept of competitive market areas with plants at their centre was further reduced in significance. With the construction of the supergrid systems, the shape of market areas coincided with the administrative shape of the Boards. Natural gas will cause a further change, for the market area will then become the entire nation. When this occurs, the industry will no longer be oriented to final markets and will have ceased to be residentiary.

5.2 BREWING

In geographical literature it is brewing rather than gas manufacture that is normally quoted as the best example of a residentiary industry. There are many similarities between the two activities, but there are also important differences. In both cases there has been a reduction in the number of plants and a shift to larger towns, but of recent the closure of breweries has been effected more slowly than has been the case with gasworks, and there has not been the rapid migration to higher order settlements, so noticeable in gas making. Raw material orientation has always been more important in brewing than in gas production, helping to distort the pattern of orientation to final markets, while more counties than is the case with gas manufacture exhibit relatively strong specialisation. However, this distortion does not seriously upset the way in which employment in brewing varies proportionately with population, at least at the county level. A correlation of workers in brewing with the employed population by county in England and Wales for 1961 produces a relatively high value of +0·748.

Bearing in mind that a residentiary industry perfectly related to population results in all counties returning location quotients of 1, the extent of the deviation from this pattern in brewing can be seen in Fig. 67. Six counties score quotients greater than 2, indicating considerable specialisation: Suffolk (5·16), Hereford (4·66), Norfolk (3·35), Ely (2·94), Staffordshire (2·50) and Berkshire (2·16). The importance of malting in the two East Anglian counties helps to explain their high quotients. Cider production is a factor in Hereford, and undoubtedly the River Trent and Burton are the main cause of Staffordshire's score. Important specialisation also exists in Lincolnshire (1·94), Nottinghamshire (1·73) and London (1·42). Although it is possible to explain in part some of these high quotients, it is clear that specialisation still exists. Effectively, then, there is concentration on brewing in nine counties

L

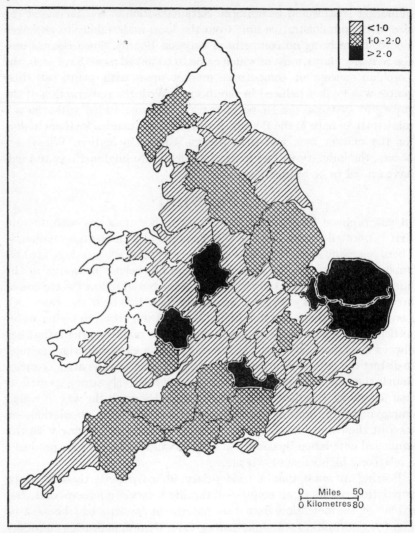

Fig. 67 Location quotient map of the brewing industry in England and Wales, 1961

compared with only two in the case of town gas manufacture. At the
other end of the range, there are only five counties in which brewing is
unimportant, that is, where the location quotient is less than 0·3. This
suggests that brewing is important, without specialisation existing, in
other counties, as is to be expected of a residentiary industry. Brewing
has ceased in some of the more rural counties which lack a town large
enough to justify the continuation of the activity. The location quotient

map does not, however, bring out the changes that have taken place within counties, and it is necessary to relate brewing to the size of settlement in order to trace the migration of breweries to higher order centres.

Table 5.4 traces the changes in the number of breweries in broad classes of settlements in six counties between 1911 and 1967. The counties, Devon, Durham, Hampshire, Staffordshire, Sussex and Yorkshire, include three which are predominantly industrial and three which are largely non-industrial. The total number of breweries has fallen

TABLE 5.4

Breweries by settlement size in six counties,* 1911–1967

	<5000		5000–19 999		20 000–75 000		>75 000	
	n	%	n	%	n	%	n	%
1911	53	16	68	21	70	21	140	42
1967	7	11	10	15	15	23	34	51

* Devon, Durham, Hampshire, Staffordshire, Sussex and Yorkshire
Source: *Brewers' Almanack.*

from 331 to 66 over the period, but the smaller settlements have been less successful in retaining their breweries than the larger settlements. Migration has been much more marked in the non-industrial than in the industrial counties. In 1911 the percentage of breweries in settlements of less than 5000 in Sussex, Hampshire and Devon was 30, 19 and 16 respectively; by 1967 breweries were absent from settlements of this size. That the industrial counties have not entirely followed suit is largely because their population is much more dense, with the consequence that in many cases settlements are only administratively separate, and problems of distance are not so great. Woodsetton, Staffordshire, on the western edge of the Black Country with a population of 3100, is an example of this, as are West Auckland, population 2199, and Castle Eden, population 420, both located on the Durham coalfield amid mining villages.

CAUSES OF MARKET-ORIENTATION

There are four main reasons for orientation to final markets in the brewing industry.

(i) *Water is the basic raw material*

The most important raw material is water, which is ubiquitous, thus allowing other factors to dictate the location of breweries. Although normally water has little locational influence, differences in its chemical composition from place to place sometimes result in the rise of important brewing centres, distorting the theoretical residentiary distribution of the industry. At one time the chemical composition of brewing water was crucial to the character of the beer produced, leading to the significance of towns such as Burton-on-Trent where the water contains calcium sulphate, highly suited to the production of pale ale. Similarly the waters of the Liffey in Ireland gives rise to a dark stout, Guinness, which is now also brewed at Park Royal in London from quite different water. Mains water is now normally employed for brewing and distinctive flavours are obtained by chemical processes. Thus although the nature of the water used is no longer important, water has had a lasting effect on the present distribution of breweries through the medium of inertia. The costs involved in shifting production to another point, coupled with the very success of the firms concerned, result in some breweries continuing their operations at historically significant riverine sites. Examples include Bass at Burton-on-Trent, Watney Combe Reid at Alton on the River Wey and John Smith at Tadcaster on the River Wharfe. Such was the importance of the waters of the Trent at Burton that many large London brewers such as Ind Coope, Truman Hanbury and Buxton, Charringtons and Mann, Crossman and Paulin set up in the town between 1858 and 1875. Burton became the leading centre for brewing research in the 1870s and 1880s, with a highly influential group of scientists, four of whose number became Fellows of the Royal Society.[6] Their research work was in part responsible for the success of their firms, and therefore of Burton itself. In effect they added to the forces of inertia which retained breweries in the town after the significance of the local water had gone.

(ii) *Other raw materials*

These comprise barley, malt, hops and sugar, and they are of minor significance, a significance which is in fact diminishing even further as a result of improvements in processing. About a decade ago, a weight-loss of 10–12% of barley in processing was normal; at present the figure is 5%. Changes in the hopping process involving the use of hop extract have resulted in a 25% reduction in the consumption of hops over the last five years, during which beer output has risen 7%.[7]

(iii) *Weight gain in processing*

Water has a low value per unit of weight, and since it constitutes about 90% of beer, it is important to minimise transport charges on deliveries to consumers following such a great addition to weight and bulk in processing. The Weberian material index lies between 0·2 and 0·1, suggesting marked orientation to markets.

(iv) *Historical nature of brewing*

For centuries brewing was virtually a domestic industry and was restricted very largely to private houses and roadside inns, with the consequence that in the early 19th century there must have been a very high correlation between brewing and population.

THE ECONOMIES OF LARGE-SCALE PRODUCTION

The shift to larger settlements and the concomitant reduction in the number of breweries are primarily the result of economies of scale and improvement in transport technology. It has long been realised that as output rises, the cost of producing a unit of beer falls, but because of the high cost of transporting beer, brewers were obliged to curtail output to prevent transport costs from becoming excessive. This accounted for the large number of small breweries serving local markets in the 19th century. In 1881 there were 16 798 wholesale brewers and 71 876 other brewers. The latter included a large number of licensed premises where home-brewed beer was sold. The problem of supplying anything but small market areas did not prevent aggressive brewers from underpricing, and therefore ensuring the closure of, inns and public houses brewing their own beer in urban areas, where market areas were compact. Thus by 1900 the number of wholesale brewers had fallen to 6447 and other brewers to 12 734. The incentive for small market areas has now been reversed and brewers are seeking to increase output to benefit from the economies of scale as transport technology, and production technology, improve. The result has been the continued reduction in the number of breweries; by 1957 the number of brewers had fallen to 416, a figure which had been further reduced to 211 by 1969. These 211 were grouped in 99 firms, seven of which accounted for 72·7% of national beer output in 1967. These were the firms best able to utilise large breweries, and by implication, to be able to close down their small plants. The details of this concentration of production appear in Table 5.5.

While it must be assumed that at some point diminishing returns will set in, the optimum size of brewery has been steadily moving upwards at such a speed that there are very few breweries fully reaping scale economies. In the mid-1960s an annual capacity of 250 000 bulk barrels was regarded as large. The Whitbread brewery at Luton was planned to produce 750 000 bulk barrels in 1965, but only four years later this had been raised to 1·5 million bulk barrels. It was reported that at this size it would be able to produce beer at half the average cost of the other breweries in the group. Bass plan to build a plant with a capacity of 2·5 million bulk barrels at Runcorn to replace eight or nine plants. Watney Mann anticipate concentrating their production in three main breweries at Mortlake and Isleworth in London and at Manchester, and two smaller breweries at Norwich and Edinburgh. These trends accord with experience in the U.S.A. where the smallest viable plant size is 100 000 bulk barrels, and the lowest average costs are thought to be achieved by plants larger than 1 and smaller than 3 million bulk barrels capacity per annum.[8] It seems that the future distribution pattern will comprise a small number of very large plants.

Since some of the most important methods of increasing production and decreasing costs consist of modifications to processes, a comment on

TABLE 5.5

Principal British Brewery Companies, 1967

	Number of breweries	Production (million bulk barrels*)	% national production
Bass Charrington	20	5·64	18·1
Allied Breweries	12	4·83	15·5
Whitbread	17	3·46	11·1
Watney Mann	9	2·94	9·4
Scottish & Newcastle	4	2·51	8·0
Courage Barclay & Simmonds	5	1·78	5·7
Guinness	1	1·53	4·9
			72·7

* 1 bulk barrel = 164 litres/36 gallons
Source: The Monopolies Commission, *A Report on the Supply of Beer*, H.M.S.O., 1969, p. 5. *The Brewers' Manual.*

these processes will not be out of place. There are three main stages: (a) Mashing. Malt, usually produced from barley by maltsters outside the brewery, is mixed with hot water in a mash tun, a process known as mashing. The resultant extract is called wort. (b) Hopping. Hops are added to the wort which is boiled to extract the oil and resin flavours from the hops. (c) Fermentation. Here yeast is added, so converting the fermentable sugars into alcohol. The fermentation process lasts two to three days. The introduction of continuous mashing and continuous fermentation processes taking the place of the intermittent method has enabled the much more intensive use of existing mash tuns and fermenting vats. A greater output is possible without any extension to the brewery at all, thus reducing the cost of a unit of beer. Similar economies are possible by the use of much larger mash tuns and fermenting vats, especially when the continuous method is employed. In order to find space *in situ* for a new layout or extensions to existing buildings, some breweries have removed their bottling or barrelling lines to nearby premises. Courage have done this in London and Bristol, as have Brickwoods in Portsmouth. The new high-speed bottling and canning lines capable of turning out up to 36 000 bottles an hour must be operated close to their maximum capacity if the advantages of mass production are to be reaped. It is only large plants that can do this. The same principle applies to keg filling and washing plants, some of which can handle 10 000 kegs a day. Advertising by large national brewers has resulted in a larger production of a smaller number of beers, enabling production runs to be lengthened, thus raising the annual capacity of the brewery. A few firms have progressed to the ultimate extreme, they market nationally a beer produced in one plant. Examples are Guinness at Park Royal and the decision by Allied Breweries to produce 'Double Diamond' in one plant.

As the size of plant increases, it becomes increasingly justifiable to introduce costly labour-saving devices. Thus in large plants, labour costs, which account for up to 40% of total costs, are lower than in small plants for each unit of beer produced. Important savings can be made from improved handling of materials. Fluids are much easier to handle and store than solids; thus prior to use sugar is liquified and pumped through the plant. Sugar is now delivered by road tanker and stored in large bins; at one time it was moved in sacks and manhandled about the brewery. The automation of the many valves in a brewery helps to reduce labour costs, as does the non-returnable bottle. Bottles are dispatched in two dozen cases. Unfortunately cases are often returned partly filled, causing time-consuming checks to be made. If the case were the unit rather than the bottle, it would be preferable to return the bottles. However the cost of dealing with partly filled cases is now becoming greater than the cost of replacement bottles, much to the delight of the glass-bottle industry.

Large breweries with low production costs not only have a cost advantage over less efficient plants, but they are able to control larger market areas than their smaller competitors. This is illustrated in Fig. 68. The production costs of the large brewery located at X are lower than those of the small brewery at Y. Production costs are represented by the vertical lines above X and Y. The price of beer is uniform, so the brewer will distribute his product up to the point at which production costs and transport costs, represented by the sloping lines, together equal price. The smaller brewer's market area, M_2M_3, is much more restricted than

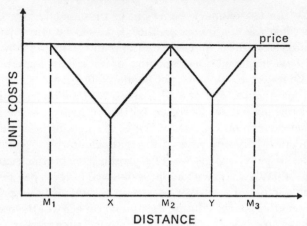

Fig. 68 Production costs and the size of market areas

that of his competitor, M_1M_2. Lacking economies of bulk transport, the smaller brewer's transport cost curves would probably be steeper than those of the other plant, further increasing the differential between the size of the market areas.

TRANSPORT

Storage and distribution costs account for between 4 and 20% of total costs, so that breweries close to the upper limit can fairly be regarded as transport-oriented. It is not surprising, therefore, that when transport was less efficient than it is today, the area over which beer could be delivered was restricted. Without improvements in transport, it would have been impossible to increase the size of breweries because the cost of delivery of the additional beer produced to a larger market area would have been excessive. Transport itself is thus an important contributory factor to the increase in the size of breweries.

Until the 1940s the delivery of beer was frequently effected by horse and dray; indeed Whitbread still employ this method for many central London deliveries. The greater part of beer distribution is now by lorry, which, as it becomes more efficient, allows the market area to be extended and the size of brewery to increase. Beer is normally distributed to public houses or depots in 36 gallon bulk barrels, of which approximately 80 can be loaded on a lorry. A fairly recent innovation is the road tanker, which can carry the equivalent of 120 bulk barrels. The beer is pumped into tanks at either the depot or the public house, thereby reducing the time for unloading at each call, allowing more calls to be made on each trip and a consequent fall in delivery charges. Also, since there are no casks, kegs and crates to be manhandled, tanker crews are smaller than lorry crews, permitting savings in labour costs. The provision of better roads, especially motorways, also improves the productivity of labour. Guinness, whose market area is the largest in the country, makes use of British Rail's Freightliner service.

As market areas increase in size transport costs rise, but such are the advantages of large breweries that the savings more than offset the increase in transport costs. This substitution between production and transport costs has resulted in a 4% reduction in manufacturing costs, set against a mere 1% rise in storage, selling and distribution costs, between 1962 and 1969.[9] A specific example is provided by Whitbread who closed a small brewery with a capacity of 57 000 bulk barrels per annum at Great Yarmouth, thereby saving £100 000 annually in production costs by expanding brewing capacity in London, but incurring an

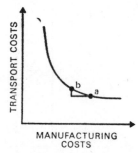

Fig. 69 The substitution curve

additional distribution charge of £50 000. There was thus a net saving of £50 000.

This concept of substitution has been developed by Greenhut. He postulates a substitution curve at all points of which sales are identical. Firms have the choice either of reducing transport costs at the expense of an increase in manufacturing costs, or of reducing manufacturing costs at the expense of increased transport charges. The curve is particularly applicable to brewing since the closure of breweries and the concentration of production at one plant do not necessarily result in greater sales, rather a substitution between inputs as a means of improving profits. The closure of the Great Yarmouth brewery and expansion at London, referred to above, can be represented by a move along the substitution curve from *a* to *b* in Fig. 69.

So far we have assumed the demand for beer to be everywhere equal within the market area. This is very unlikely to be the case owing to differences in population density. The density of population being greatest in urban areas, a brewery located in such an area will be able to supply a large number of public houses at low distribution cost. A rurally located brewery on the other hand must accept higher distribution charges. Aggressive brewers in urban areas have been able to increase their sales by take-overs without being obliged to accept substantially greater distribution costs. This is one of the reasons for the success of breweries located in large towns. Brickwoods in Portsmouth is a case in point. The firm is now the only brewer in the city, having taken over eleven other plants since 1899. The level of population density at points within the market area also has an important effect on the size of the plant as a result of transport costs. We know that as the market area increases in size, transport costs rise, but that these costs are offset by

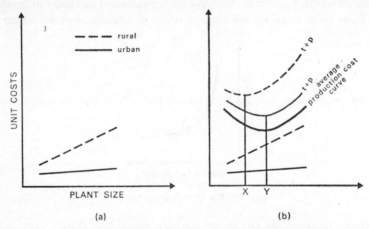

Fig. 70 Transport costs in rural and urban breweries

economies of scale. However, a situation will eventually be reached when transport costs are so large that they are not counterbalanced by economies of large-scale production. When this occurs we can expect the firm to cease further expansion. This point will be reached by breweries in large towns at a very much larger size of plant than will be the case with breweries in small towns. Again we see why breweries shift to higher order settlements and why rural breweries find it difficult to compete with urban establishments.

The way in which transport costs influence the size of brewery is shown in Figs 70(a) and 70(b). A rural brewery has a dispersed market and consequently its transport cost curve rises more steeply than an urban plant; this is shown in Fig. 70(a). Fig. 70(b) incorporates these two transport cost curves with an average production cost curve, which is assumed to be identical for both type of plant. The combination of transport costs and average costs gives two total cost curves, $t + p$, whose shapes differ because of the differences in transport costs between the two plants. The point at which each total cost curve is lowest becomes the optimum size of plant. It can be seen that the most efficient size for the urban brewery Y is larger than in the case of the rural brewery X. It is also evident that the delivered cost of one unit of beer from plant Y is lower than that from plant X, which becomes less profitable to operate.

THE CONTINUATION OF BREWING IN SMALL SETTLEMENTS

From what has been said there would seem to be little cause for the continuation of brewing in small towns, and yet there are many breweries in such locations. Table 5.4 indicates that 26% of breweries in the counties of Devon, Durham, Hampshire, Staffordshire, Sussex and Yorkshire were in settlements of less than 20 000 persons in 1967. In the case of Hampshire and Sussex, there were more breweries in the 5000–19 999 class than in the >75 000 class, although the absolute numbers were small. The detailed breakdown appears in Table 5.6. There are six main influences working against the hypothesis that brewing should take place in large towns and cities.

TABLE 5.6

Breweries by settlement size, selected counties, 1967

	<5000		5000–19 999		20 000–75 000		>75 000	
	n	%	n	%	n	%	n	%
Devon	—	—	1	25	—	—	3	75
Durham	2	40	—	—	—	—	3	60
Hampshire	—	—	4	57	—	—	3	43
Staffs.	1	7	2	12	8	50	5	31
Sussex	—	—	2	40	2	40	1	20
Yorkshire	4	14	3	10	4	14	18	62

Source: *Brewers' Almanack.*

(i) *Brewing is a private sector industry*

The nationalisation of the gas industry allowed great reorganisation to be effected. Small works could be closed as new techniques and the extension of pipelines rendered them obsolete. There was no question of plants lingering on as individual entrepreneurs with large sums of money invested in the company struggled to obtain a profit. Brewing, on the other hand, is part of the private sector, and there has been no national rationalising influence at work. Small marginally profitable plants can continue operations for many years before finally becoming bankrupt.

There are still cases of small breweries in locations that once were highly profitable, but which must now be highly marginal undertakings.

(ii) *Geographical inertia*

It follows from the points made above that there will necessarily be a time lag between the realisation of the diminishing advantages of the site, and migration from that site. The duration of the interim period will depend on the strength of inertia. There are three basic factors at work. (a) The firm will have sunk money into buildings, machinery and perhaps access roads, all of which are immobile, and it is only when replacement is required that these items lose their power to keep the plant at the old site. Replacement may not be necessary for as long as 20 years. (b) There are short-term problems such as labour availability, and, particularly in brewing, the need to reorganise distribution networks at an alternative site. These problems, which can eventually be overcome, are termed frictional. (c) Many entrepreneurs, especially the least dynamic, are satisficers rather than optimisers. They will resist a change of location in the hope that trade will improve.

(iii) *Dynamic management*

The disadvantages of rural breweries can be offset by dynamic management. Breweries in neighbouring larger towns may be taken over and then closed, thus enabling the original brewery to expand, so reducing the unit cost of beer. By being able to supply concentrations of public houses in large towns, some of the friction of distance is removed. Strong's brewery at Romsey, Hampshire, population 6350, is such an example. It was acquired in 1886 by David Faber, a member of the publishing family. Faber possessed not only great personal energy and initiative, but also valuable family connections. Between 1886 and 1965, the firm gained control of, and subsequently closed, 20 other breweries, all but 3 of which were in settlements larger than Romsey. The firm has 65 tied outlets in Southampton, simplifying deliveries to some extent. A second example is John Smith at Tadcaster, Yorkshire, population 4203. Doubtless the firm was assisted by the suitability of the River Wharfe for brewing, but aggressive entrepreneurship has been largely responsible for the development of the firm into Durham, Derbyshire, Lancashire, Lincolnshire and Nottinghamshire. The firm is now the ninth largest in Britain. Behavioural factors are thus of great significance.

(iv) *Nodality*

Neither Romsey nor Tadcaster are distant from major towns. Romsey is 10 km/6 miles from Southampton, population 204 822; Tadcaster is 22 km/14 miles from Leeds, population 510 676. Both possess reasonable nodality in respect of a larger area. Romsey has access to the coastal towns of Poole, Bournemouth and Portsmouth apart from Southampton, while Tadcaster can serve the West Riding conurbation. The development of road transport has assisted this nodality. The same is true of the plants at Knottingley and Wath, Yorkshire, and of the two breweries at Alton, Hampshire, in respect of the towns of the western London region and those of coastal Hampshire. A small town with high nodality may be the lowest transport cost solution, especially when the share of the market in larger towns in the vicinity is restricted. Nodality also helps to explain brewing in some medium-sized towns such as Burton, population 50 751. Because of its location in the Midlands, coupled with its other advantages, once the railway arrived in 1839 the town was able to market its distinctive beer over a large part of Britain.

(v) *Company strategy*

Since 7 firms are responsible for three-quarters of beer output in this country, it is to be expected that these large firms will have plants strategically located in various parts of the country. It is possible that eventually each firm will have one plant, but this is not yet the case. Therefore the existence of a brewery in a small town must be seen against the distribution of other breweries belonging to the firm. A small town may have great nodality in respect of an area the firm wishes to supply, whereas this may not be true of very much larger towns in that area. However, the decision as to where the 'strategic' brewery is to be placed involves the consideration of many factors, some of which relate only to the time in question. These are therefore chance factors. Company strategy helps to explain the continuation of brewing at Tiverton, Devon, population 12 397. Whitbread, wishing to extend its interests into the south-west, took over Starkey, Knight and Ford at Tiverton, and the two Norman and Pring breweries at Exeter, population 80 321, in 1962. Whitbread chose only to use Tiverton. Both Exeter plants were on badly congested sites while Tiverton could be developed, and possessed good nodality in respect of Whitbread's south-western area. A particularly important point, however, is that when Whitbread decided to move into the south-west, these three plants were the only ones available for purchase. Had the Whitbread board resolved to expand at a different time it is possible that a settlement other than Tiverton would have been chosen.

(vi) *Urban land values*

Until recently, breweries have usually been able to expand *in situ* by reorganising their layout, or by moving their bottling lines to nearby premises and using the space made available for brewing. There is incentive to do this owing to the high cost of construction of a new plant at a greenfield site. Further, the cost of the premises of most breweries have long since been written off. There is a limit to piecemeal alterations, however, and it is usually uneconomic to buy up adjacent land on increasingly valuable central area sites. The solution is migration. This is given added force by the very value of the brewery site itself. The Whitbread Chiswell Street brewery, London, E.C.1, on land purchased 230 years ago, has become extremely valuable development property, and the firm is planning a £12 million office block on the site. A new brewery has been built at Luton, a very much smaller town 53 km/33 miles to the north. With a population of 135 000, Luton is by no means a small settlement, but it would seem that as breweries become larger and as urban land values increase, large new breweries, or greatly expanded old ones, will develop in towns peripheral to major cities. The tendency is also an example of substitution between transport charges and economies of scale, and substitution between transport charges and site costs.

MARKET AREAS

A corollary to the increasing size and decreasing number of breweries is the extension of market areas. Greater output must be matched by greater consumption, and since national beer consumption is rising only slightly faster than population growth (beer production rose 8·1% between 1951 and 1961 compared with a population increase of 5·3% in England and Wales), the best way in which firms can expand the market for their beer is to increase the size of their market area. Takeovers are effected not so much to obtain additional production capacity as to obtain control of additional public houses. A purchased brewery is normally closed and its tied outlets, as public houses owned by a brewery are known, are then supplied by the enlarged parent plant, which reaps economies of scale. The process is repeated several times and the market area grows in size. Of great importance to the extension of market areas is the system of tied outlets, which represented 78% of all public houses in 1967. The system essentially developed in the later 19th century as brewers were forced to integrate forwards to preserve and refurbish public houses which, in many cases, had reached such a poor state of maintenance that their licences were in danger of being withdrawn. Had this happened the brewers would have lost their markets. We next relate Losch's ideas on market areas to brewing, and then investigate some empirical evidence on the shapes of markets and on the distribution of beer.

(i) *Hexagonal market areas and brewing*

We know that the model of market areas developed by Losch assumes that, within his hexagonal market area, a brewer has complete monopoly, and that therefore he operates under conditions of monopolistic competition. We saw how in the gas industry there is no element of competition at all. In the brewing industry, while there is competition, it is hardly monopolistic. Monopolistic competition may have obtained in rural areas in the last century, but at present there exists a situation of varying local or regional domination by producers, and a system of overlapping market areas. The penetration of markets by the acquisition of tied houses, reciprocal trading agreements, free houses, clubs, which account for 20% of beer consumed in Britain, and the strength of advertising forcing brewers to sell competitors' beer for fear of driving

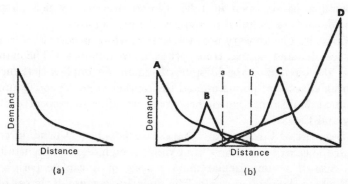

Fig. 71 The demand–distance curve in monopolistic competition

demand elsewhere, have all helped to break down areal monopolies. There are a few areas where the situation approaches monopolistic competition. For example, 90% of the tied houses in Bristol belong to Courage, and in Portsmouth Brickwood have 85% of the tied outlets. In some areas two brewers dominate. In Birmingham Bass have 52% and Allied Breweries have 38% of the tied houses.[10] But even in conditions such as these many other breweries have a share of the market. Portsmouth, for instance, lies within the market area of 10 breweries. It is clear that modifications to the Loschian system are required to take account of overlapping market areas.

Fig. 71(a) illustrates the way in which demand for the product of brewery a declines with distance away from the plant, assuming conditions of monopoly within the market area. This was essentially the basis of Losch's demand cone and hexagonal market areas. A more realistic situation appears in Fig. 71(b) which shows the demand-distance curves of four breweries, A, B, C, and D, all of whose market areas overlap. The area ab is thus within four market areas. It is impossible to define a market area by a line, as Losch argues, because although a degree of domination is possible in the immediate vicinity of the plant, monopoly does not exist even at the plant, as breweries B and C indicate. Domination decays rapidly away from the plant. Demand cones can be developed from Fig. 71(b), but the result is a confused pattern of overlapping market areas lacking a clear shape.

(ii) *Market area shapes in practice*

It is difficult to develop market areas for plants in a competitive situation, but it is possible to construct market area shapes for each plant in isolation. Examples of the principal shapes are given in Fig. 72, in which the skeleton of actual market areas is constructed from depots and bottling plants open in 1968. Closed breweries which have not become depots are included to amplify the market area.

(a) Circular. The brewery is at the centre, which is normally the point of greatest demand, so that transport costs are minimised. The maintenance of the circular shape in spite of expansion implies that mergers have been effected at points around the market area. A good example is Fremlin at Maidstone, which has great nodality in respect of Kent, Surrey and Essex.

(b) Segment of Circle. Many shapes are possible. Depending on the angle at the centre, a brewery can exhibit a high degree of centrality as in the case of a semi-circular market area, or it can be peripherally located where the angle is acute. The underlying cause of shapes of this type is frequently the configuration of the coastline, forcing expansion in particular directions. Transport costs on each unit of beer are greater than in case (a), but in the example shown, Steward and Patteson at Norwich, these costs are offset by the location of the brewery in the largest settlement in the market area.

(c) Discontinuous. Mergers between breweries in towns distant from each other result in a discontinuous market area, the territory between the sectors being served by other firms. Transport costs are offset by increases in the size of brewery, although in the case of the Appleby and Winchester depots of Marston Thompson and Evershed, 250 km/155 miles and 201 km/125 miles respectively from the brewery at Burton, transport costs must be relatively high. Apart from the discontinuous market areas at Appleby and Winchester, this firm exhibits a semi-circular market area, the shape of which is dictated by the direction of mergers rather than by physical factors.

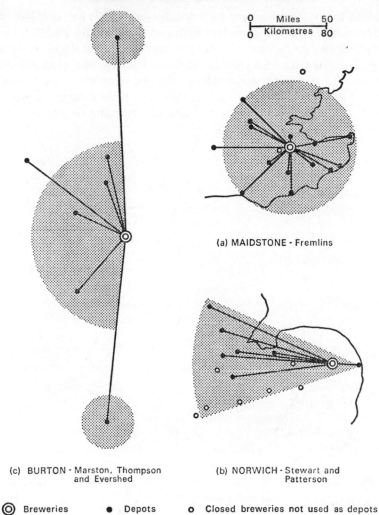

0 — Miles — 50
0 — Kilometres — 80

(a) MAIDSTONE - Fremlins

(c) BURTON - Marston, Thompson and Evershed

(b) NORWICH - Stewart and Patterson

◎ Breweries   ● Depots   ○ Closed breweries not used as depots

Fig. 72 Three cases of market area shapes

(iii) *The distribution of beer within market areas*

With the increase in size of market areas, it has become necessary to set up a number of depots from which public houses can be served in order to minimise transport costs. By this means large market areas can be supplied from one large brewery. Not all firms have adopted the same solution to similar situations, but certain standard solutions can be isolated. In the following four examples, which are illustrated diagrammatically in Fig. 73, delivery is by lorry unless otherwise stated.

M

(a) Delivery from brewery to public house. This is the simplest case and one which was very important in the era of the small firm.

(b) Delivery to outlets from both brewery and from depot(s). In the normal way, depots are former breweries which have been shut following mergers. They are very suitable as depots since they are centrally situated in respect of their former market. This is the most common case, but it is noticeable that firms are increasingly using depots to supply

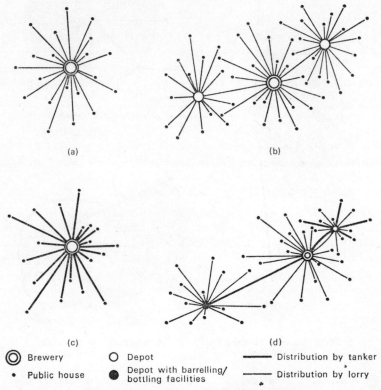

(a)   (b)

(c)   (d)

| ◎ Brewery | ○ Depot | —— Distribution by tanker |
| • Public house | ● Depot with barrelling/ bottling facilities | —— Distribution by lorry |

Fig. 73 Models of beer distribution systems

free houses and irregular demand from hotels, and are tending to supply public houses direct from the brewery. The development of keg beers such as Whitbread 'Tankard' and Watney's 'Red Barrel', which keep longer than normal beer, is assisting the process.

(c) Delivery from brewery to public house by road tanker. The advantages of tankers have been noted above.

(d) Delivery from brewery to depot(s) by tanker. In this case a bottling and barrelling plant is necessary at the depot(s). Some, but not all, beer can be delivered by tanker from the depot to outlets; this is illustrated in the right-hand depot in Fig. 73(d). This is a useful solution, because of the economies of bulk transport, where merger strategy has caused the new segment of the market area to be well beyond, or perhaps discontinuous to, the existing market. It is the solution adopted by Guinness, although the bottling and barrelling are undertaken by other plants, and sometimes rail instead of road tanker is employed.

5.3 FURNITURE MANUFACTURE

We have seen how breweries and gasworks show a tendency to migrate to large towns and cities. Although it is unquestionably a residentiary activity, furniture manufacture does not exhibit this trend because it has with a few exceptions, always been associated with large towns, such as London, Liverpool, Manchester and Leeds. Indeed, where a metropolitan area is the most populous conurbation in a country, it is also the chief area of furniture manufacture. Examples are London, Copenhagen, Lisbon, Paris, Oslo, Stockholm and Vienna.[11] The industry is thus oriented to the largest final market, and it seems to require a much larger population threshold than gas-making. It is impossible to be precise about this since there are examples of furniture plants in settlements very much smaller than the minimum size required to support a gasworks. The advent of the motor vehicle, improved roads, steadily rising rents and other costs in crowded city centres have contributed to a migration from cities to smaller towns within the sphere of influence of the city. This is the reverse of the trend in gas-making, although there are some parallels in brewing where some city centre sites have been vacated.

Both the tendencies referred to above—the concentration of the industry in the largest city, and migration to contiguous areas—can be discerned in Fig. 74, a location quotient map. The counties exhibiting the greatest specialisation comprise a compact, approximately semi-circular shape centred on London. This shape suggests that the River Thames has been a very effective barrier to the diffusion of the industry from its traditional home in the East End of London in a southerly direction. In spite of the unimportance of furniture production in many areas of the city, such is the degree of specialisation in boroughs such as Hackney, Shoreditch, Bethnal Green and Poplar, that London is still able to return the high quotient of 2·20. It is to be anticipated that migration from London would be reflected in relatively high quotients in those counties north of the Thames adjacent to the county of London. This prediction is a reality, for both Middlesex and Essex return a score of 1·82, and indeed the boroughs in which furniture is strong are closest to the East End of London. Thus the Middlesex boroughs of Tottenham and Edmonton lie in the Lea valley, in the east of the county, and Walthamstow, Leyton, and Romford are in western Essex. Hertfordshire, with Welwyn Garden City on the A1 road north of Tottenham

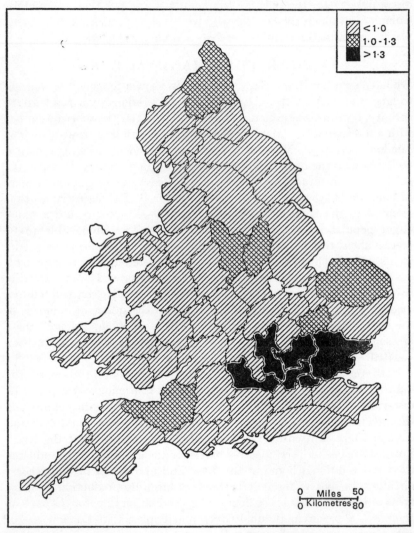

Fig. 74 Location quotient map of the furniture industry in England and Wales, 1961

and Edmonton, represents the most recent stage of the diffusion process, and has a quotient of 1·42. This decline in strength of the location quotients with distance from London, however, is not supported by the two remaining counties in the semi-circle, Buckinghamshire and Berkshire.

Buckinghamshire returns the remarkable quotient of 7·76, a symptom of the outstanding specialisation in furniture-making by the town of High Wycombe. This provides a major exception to the theme of market-orientation in the industry, and since furniture production is a traditional activity of the town, the high quotient is not a result of migration from London. Berkshire may owe its quotient of 1·93 to a process of diffusion from High Wycombe rather than from London. Only six other counties in England and Wales show any degree of specialisation; in the case of Derbyshire (1·04), Northumberland (1·04) and Cambridge (1·07), it is specialisation by the barest of margins. Further evidence of the concentration of the industry into certain areas is provided by the 17 counties with quotients less than 0·3, that is, in which furniture production is unimportant. Brewing and gas-making, both more widespread activities, each claim only 5 counties with a quotient lower than 0·3. Furniture, then, deviates considerably from the theoretical pattern of residentiary industries.

Furniture manufacture exhibits a classical cause of attraction to markets, an increase in bulk during processing of up to five times that of the timber from which the product is made. Virtually no attempt is made to stow one piece of furniture inside another, and single items are packed in wooden crates, foam rubber or corrugated cardboard, thereby adding to the space gained. The very size of furniture vans is symptomatic of the situation. The issue is slightly complicated by a loss of weight in manufacture ranging from 10% to 80%, 40% being the usual figure.[12] There is thus a pull to the source of the timber, that is, primarily West Africa in the case of Britain. However, the advantage of production at the market outweighs those of manufacture at the material source, so that weight-loss plays little part in the location of the industry. If an increase of bulk during manufacture was an important locational influence, as it is in brewing, for instance, we would expect the industry to be much more evenly distributed than is the case. It is therefore necessary to look elsewhere for the underlying reasons for the location of furniture manufacture. This can be done by examining the advantages of London and then investigating the exceptional phenomenon of High Wycombe.

THE ADVANTAGES OF MANUFACTURE AT THE LARGEST MARKET

(i) Ease of access to imported timber

The British furniture industry has never relied on indigenous supplies of timber, and with the exception of such sources as Chiltern beechwood, timber must be imported by sea. Nearness to a port is therefore a significant location factor. Not only is London Britain's first port, but it has traditionally handled a large proportion of the country's timber imports. Thus in 1750, 83% by value of timber imports from British plantations in America, including the West Indies, was brought into the port of London. In 1959 the port handled 65% of British plywood imports, 52% of hardwood imports and 27% of softwood imports. As a consequence, certain docks such as the East India Docks and Surrey Commercial Docks have specialist facilities for the reception and storage of timber. Imported timber is cut into basic shapes at waterside saw mills, and since the furniture industry draws virtually its entire material supply from these mills, there were obvious advantages in a neighbouring location for furniture production in the era when urban transport was effected by horse and cart. The cost of moving timber in London in 1903 reached the fairly high level of one shilling per load per mile.[13] Weight-loss considerations were important at this time, encouraging furniture firms to minimise their material transport costs, especially since material costs account for about half total production costs. Wherever possible water transport was used, adding to the attraction of sites on the river and along the Regent's Canal, completed in 1818. A further advantage of a port location stemmed from the ease with which exports could be effected. In 1888 almost £0·75 million worth of furniture was exported, representing a considerable traffic.

(ii) *The nature of demand in London*

Following its function as capital city, London has always enjoyed a high per capita income compared with the remainder of Britain. During the 18th and 19th centuries, the aristocracy would give individual orders for upholstery and sometimes for complete pieces of furniture; this was known as the bespoke system. The rise in middle-class income in mid-19th century was responsible for the growth of large high-grade retail furniture shops such as Maples, opened in 1841 in Tottenham Court Road. These shops possessed workshops, but much of their work was contracted out, providing much local employment in the furniture trades. By the late 1880s Maples were making purchases from 1000 different furniture workshops, and rich customers were still able to order bespoke goods. High-quality goods allow a greater degree of labour intensiveness than is the case with inferior quality goods. Demand for products of the highest quality was not so marked in other large towns in Britain, with the consequence that there was proportionately less employment in the industry.

(iii) *London and the national transport system*

One of the main factors in the growth of London has been its high level of nodality in the national transport system. Deliveries of furniture to all areas outside the capital could be effected quite easily after the middle of the 19th century by virtue of the main lines built by the principal railway companies between the provinces and London. No other town in Britain had such a transport advantage. This has been perpetuated by the development of a national road, and subsequently motorway, network also focused on London. Road transport has allowed some migration to take place, to be sure, but by reducing transport costs in real terms London has been able to maintain its position of supremacy in the industry. Transport costs for London firms now range from between 2·25% and 4% of wholesale delivered prices anywhere in Britain, assuming the use of motor vehicles. Firms are able to market their goods nationally and yet retain the benefits of a metropolitan location. Firms less nodally sited must either absorb higher transport charges or accept a more circumscribed market area. Because of the low transport costs involved and the benefits of moving furniture in vans following the ease with which it is damaged, market areas tend to be larger than in brewing. The concentration of plants in a few areas ensures that market areas overlap to a greater extent than in the brewing industry.

(iv) *Labour*

The London furniture industry had by 1888 firmly developed in the poorer districts of the East End, such as Bethnal Green, where there was much unemployment partly because of the demise of the silk-weaving industry.[14] To the unorganised and unskilled local workers, willing to work for low wages, were added the Jewish immigrants during the early years of this century. The East End at that time thus had outstanding advantages in terms of low-cost labour, and although not a continuing factor, it at least provided real impetus for half a century.

(v) *External economies*

It has always been difficult to introduce mass production techniques into furniture manufacture because of the very large number of different pieces produced. The demand for variety and new styles inhibits long production runs. Entry into the trade, especially in the 19th century, did not call for large capital requirements, so that the small-sized firm was characteristic. In 1851 more than 90% of the firms, employing 60% of the workers in England and Wales had less than 10 operatives. A century later half the workers were employed in plants with less than 100 operatives. Indeed, such are the problems of integrating production processes under one roof, that the optimum size of firm today lies between 50 and 100 workers.

Parallel with the small size of firm has been a high degree of specialisation between plants. The very large number of plants in London allowed greater specialisation than at other centres, with the consequence that the economies external to the firm were of a high order. Specialisation included turning, fret-cutting, carving, upholstering, french polishing, cabinet making and the assembly of various types of furniture such as chairs, dining tables and even pianos. Such a situation, when each production process is carried out by a separate plant, is termed vertical disintegration. Another well-developed aspect of external economies in London were the dealers who effected sales and placed orders with the furniture makers. Equally important were the diagonal linkages provided by the specialist tool makers, mirror makers, iron and brass founders and haulage contractors. These services were especially well developed by the 1860s in the Curtain Road area of Shoreditch and Bethnal Green. External economies were to be found in furniture production irrespective of location, but since there was more opportunity for their growth in London, similar cost savings could not be matched elsewhere. It is not therefore surprising that the Derby furniture makers complained of the low-cost system adopted in London. As early as 1858 it was reported that the division of labour practised in London allowed the city's furniture makers to underprice competitors in every part of the United Kingdom.[15]

The establishment of such a well-developed system of linkages, comparable with those obtaining in the Birmingham–Black Country metal trades, referred to in Chapter 1, well before the end of the 19th century, endowed the East End of London with a high degree of geographical inertia. The pull of the suppliers and dealers of Curtain Road has declined, motor transport has lessened the need to locate close to the docks, while electric power has assisted the mobility of plants, but the presence in London of skilled labour in an industry which is far from fully mechanised is an important locational consideration. The effect has been to prevent most plants from straying too far from London. Migration induced by rising rents, the physical difficulty of expansion, more stringent fire and ventilation regulations making old buildings uneconomic, and road congestion, has resulted in the colonisation of what was until 1925 cheap land in the Lea valley, only a few miles north of Shoreditch and Bethnal Green. Labour considerations are causing manufacturers to be willing to pay high prices for factory sites near London rather than to seek low cost sites elsewhere. By 1961 approximately one-third of London's operatives were in the Lea valley, which could claim more workers than

High Wycombe itself. The significance of labour as a location factor is emphasised by the practice of plants migrating from London endeavouring to take skilled craftsmen with them. Such an example is that of Conrans, who moved from Camberwell to Thetford in Norfolk in 1963 taking 63 skilled men with them.[16]

The multiplicity of small plants, their great interdependence and inefficient road transport all conspired to cause the agglomeration or swarming of furniture plants in the 19th century. The result was the creation of distinctive manufacturing quarters as that in the East End of London and, later, on a less compact scale, in the Lea valley. Hall has

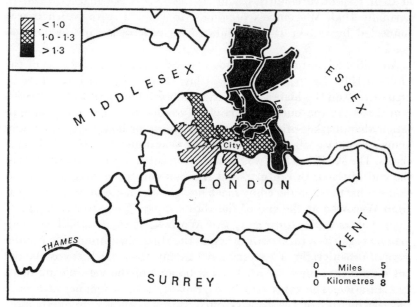

Fig. 75 Location quotient map of furniture production within London, 1951

computed local location quotients for the London boroughs in 1951,[17] and these are mapped in Fig. 75. Bethnal Green and Shoreditch return quotients of 11·2 and 7·2 respectively, indicating the extent to which these areas concentrate on furniture making. Tottenham, Edmonton and Walthamstow in the Lea valley score 7·0, 6·5 and 4·4 respectively. Such distinctive areas can be identified in Boston, Massachusetts, Hartford, Connecticut, Lower Manhattan in New York, Tradd Street in Charleston, South Carolina and in Grand Rapids, Michigan. The industrial quarter is not restricted to furniture, but occurs when old-established industries are characterised by vertical disintegration. Examples include the Sheffield cutlery quarter, the Birmingham gun and jewellery quarter, the clothing quarter of the East End of London and the gold and silver working quarter of Hatton Garden, London.

HIGH WYCOMBE, THE MAJOR EXCEPTION

Although High Wycombe does not accord with the principle that in furniture manufacture the largest towns have the greatest concentration of production, it is by no means unique in an international context. Malines is the principal centre of production in Belgium, Valencia in Spain and Herford in West Germany, but in each case, including that of High Wycombe, these towns are situated in the most populous regions in their respective countries, and to this extent are market-oriented. Certainly High Wycombe's proximity to London, with which it was connected by rail in 1847, facilitated its penetration of the London market.

An initial advantage that London lacked was the beech forest of the Chiltern Hills. In 1949 Buckinghamshire had the largest area of beech high forest and the highest proportion of beech high forest of all British counties.[18] At the outset the High Wycombe industry was material- rather than market-oriented. Rural craftsmen, or bodgers as they were known, would use about 60 beech trees a year from which they fashioned chairs. The Windsor chair was probably invented in the Chiltern Hills at the end of the 17th century, and it is not surprising that when these chairs came to be produced by machines, the first factories were set up at High Wycombe at the end of the 18th century. There were at least 58 chair makers in the town in 1798.[19] Wherever it was established, chair making began as a rural craft, whereas the other furniture-making trades were of urban origin. To a very large extent, then, High Wycombe did not effectively compete with London because of the very nature of its specialisation. The town remained primarily a chair-making area until the last quarter of the 19th century, and has always produced more chairs than London. Other towns in Britain made furniture, but none was such a specialist.

Specialisation would itself not have been sufficient to have carried High Wycombe forward. Innovation by Treacher and Widgington in the form of factory production in the 1790s has been referred to. Other means by which the town's products became exclusive included the use of foreign designers. Dynamism of this sort suggests that an important part of High Wycombe's success can be attributed to behavioural factors. Indeed, the High Wycombe chair makers seem also to have been assiduous salesmen, for in spite of poor road transport, they were marketing their products in London as early as 1728. Oliver comments that 'there is some evidence that the making of Windsor chairs was partly oriented from its early days towards the London market'.[20] Vertical disintegration was no less important a characteristic in chair making than in other branches of furniture production, with the consequence that there was specialisation within chair making, bringing the appropriate external economies. The whole town may be likened to London's furniture quarter. In the 19th century, High Wycombe entrepreneurs were able to pay lower wages than was possible in London because of the absence of unionised labour. It is reasonable to assume equal labour efficiency, so that High Wycombe's production costs were probably the lower of the two centres.

Local materials are now unimportant, bodgers no longer exist, the former almost exclusive specialisation on chairs has gone, and wage rates are negotiated nationally, but such is the extent of geographical inertia built up over three centuries that furniture production continues at this historic location.

5.4 THE TEXTILE MACHINERY INDUSTRY

Not all market-oriented industries are located in respect of final markets; some are oriented to intermediate or industrial markets. Many branches of the engineering industry fall into this category, but unless the distribution pattern of the intermediate market itself is highly localised, it is difficult to discern an orientation to the intermediate market. The textile industry in Britain is highly localised, a few areas such as Lancashire, the West Riding of Yorkshire and the East Midlands specialising in the activity. The textile industry is supplied with equipment by the textile machinery industry which, because it supplies an industrial market with producer goods, is said to be oriented to an intermediate market. The high degree of localisation exhibited by the textile industry allows an analysis of the extent to which the textile machinery industry is located in respect of its industrial market.

Fig. 76 indicates the extent of specialisation in textile production by counties in England and Wales. Only eight counties return location quotients greater than 1. The hosiery district of the East Midlands includes the county with the greatest specialisation, Leicestershire (4·71), in addition to Nottinghamshire (2·76) and Derbyshire (2·61). Woollen and worsted manufacture in the West Riding results in a quotient of 3·40, cotton production in Lancashire brings a score of 2·84, and the same activity in Cheshire causes the county to show a slight specialisation (1·13). Flintshire (1·86), an unusual survival of woollen manufacture, and Worcestershire (1·26), where Kidderminster makes carpets, complete the list. Further evidence of specialisation is provided by the 31 counties which participate in the industry, but in which the activity is unimportant, with the consequence that the location quotient is less than 0·3. Also shown on the map are location quotients for the textile machinery industry. Only four of the eight specialist textile

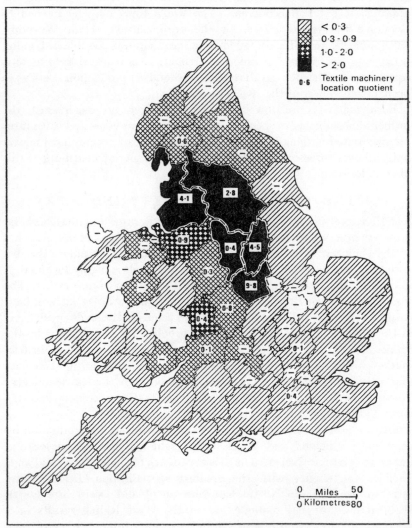

Fig. 76 Location quotient map of the textile and the textile machinery industries in England and Wales, 1961

counties have quotients greater than 1, but it is apparent that, with the exception of Derbyshire, the leading textile counties are also the leading machinery producers. Once again Leicestershire (9·80) exhibits the greatest specialisation, followed by Nottinghamshire (4·50), Lancashire (4·06) and the West Riding (2·81). That there are only four counties specialising in the manufacture of machinery, and that these counties should all have location quotients greater than 2 suggest a very high degree of localisation. Two counties, Cheshire (0·91) and Warwickshire (0·79), have quotients approaching 1. Cheshire is part of the Lancastrian cotton manufacturing region, but Warwickshire, where Coventry claims 84% of the county workforce, illustrates that engineering districts in addition to traditional textile districts exercise some attraction for the industry. Warwickshire is, however, an exception, for elsewhere there is a close correlation between textile machinery manufacture and its market the textile industry.

The orientation of textile machinery to its market is caused by a combination of two principal factors. Firstly, there are obvious advantages in proximity between supplier and consumer, not so much because

TABLE 5.7

Firms making machinery for branches of the textile industry (by county. 1968)

	Cotton	Wool	Hosiery
Lancashire	78	58	6
West Riding	44	57	4
E. Midlands	6	5	49

Source: *Trade Directories.*

of the savings in transport costs, but because of the convenience of being able to install, maintain and repair machinery in nearby premises. Some firms recondition equipment, and in this case the textile industry is both material supplier and market. Textile machinery producers are also more likely to be aware of modifications required by mills if they are close to rather than distant from them. Some machinery is made to specifications provided by customers; here the need for consultation is important. Secondly, the textile machinery industry sprang from the growing sophistication and mechanisation of cloth manufacture in the 18th century. The great innovations of Kay, Hargreaves, Arkwright and Crompton were made from within the textile industry, and it was a logical process that their subsequent large-scale production and further development should be made in the locality. Sometimes other forms of engineering grew out of textile engineering. This certainly has been the case in Lancashire.

When the distribution of the three main branches of the textile machinery industry is considered, the importance of Lancashire causes some distortion of the pattern of orientation to markets. It is to be expected that textile machinery makers for each of the three branches, cotton, wool and hosiery, will be located in Lancashire, the West Riding and the East Midlands respectively. However, Table 5.7 indicates that there are more wool textile machinery firms in Lancashire than in the West Riding, and that not all firms manufacturing cotton textile machinery are to be found in Lancashire. The predicted pattern works very well for the hosiery district, for 83% of the firms making hosiery machinery are found in the East Midland counties. Lancashire and Yorkshire are sufficiently close to be regarded as a single region, and the distortions mentioned do not greatly detract from the choice of the textile machinery industry as an excellent example of orientation to an intermediate market.

References

1. Peter A. Brown, 'Some Geographical Aspects of Gas Production in the East Midlands', *East Midlands Geographer*, No. 5, June 1956, p. 25.
2. G. Manners, 'Recent Changes in the British Gas Industry', *Transactions, Institute of British Geographers*, 1959, p. 153.
3. J. Burns, *Presidential Address, The Institute of Gas Engineers*, 1958, p. 11.
4. G. Manners, *op. cit.*, p. 157.
5. L. T. Minchin, *The Gas Industry*, Harrap, London, 1966, p. 91.
6. E. M. Sigsworth, 'Science and the Brewing Industry 1850–1900', *Economic History Review*, 17, 1965, p. 539.
7. *Financial Times*, London, 2.2.70.
8. Ira Horowitz and Ann R. Horowitz, 'Firms in a Declining Market: the Brewing Case', *Journal of Industrial Economics*, 13, 1965, pp. 145, 149.
9. National Board for Prices and Incomes, *Beer Prices*, Report No. 136, H.M.S.O., 1969, Appendix 1.
10. The Monopolies Commission, *A Report on the Supply of Beer*, H.M.S.O., 1969, p. 52.
11. J. L. Oliver, 'The Location of Furniture Manufacture in England and Elsewhere', *Tijdschrift voor Economische en Sociale Geografie*, February 1964, p. 52.
12. *Ibid.*
13. J. E. Martin, *Greater London, An Industrial Geography*, Bell, London, 1966, p. 10.
14. *Ibid.*, p. 10.
15. *Ibid.*, p. 9.
16. *Ibid.*, p. 185.

17. P. G. Hall, *The Industries of London since 1861*, Hutchinsons, London, 1962, p. 81.
18. J. L. Oliver, *The Development and Structure of the Furniture Industry*, Pergamon, 1966, p. 126.
19. *Ibid.*, p. 29.
20. *Ibid.*, p. 139.

Chapter 6

FOOTLOOSE INDUSTRIES

The increasing technical complexity of manufacturing industry has resulted in a great reduction in the weight of materials required in relation to products. Materials are frequently high-value semi-finished goods in the first place, and as the value added by manufacture has risen, so transport costs have become an increasingly small proportion of total costs. Improvements in the efficiency of transport have also assisted a large part of manufacturing to become insensitive to transport costs. This locational flexibility is emphasised by the absence of the threshold considerations of the market-oriented industries, which require a minimum local or regional volume of sales to justify the establishment of a plant. Markets are both local and non-local, and the latter may be at an international scale. The neotechnic revolution of the present century is causing a very rapid growth of industries which are neither tied to their material sources nor to their markets nor to specific intermediate locations such as break of bulk points. The relative freedom of location enjoyed by these industries allows them to be described as footloose.

Most industries of the phase that Mumford has called the paleotechnic era seldom used more than three materials. Those of the neotechnic era almost invariably employ a much larger number, and the 20th century has witnessed the development of industries producing components, tools and assemblies from a variety of metals, synthetic fibres and plastics, themselves manufactured from other materials. Indeed the greatest market for industry is now industry itself. Because a plant requires a large number of materials, no one supplying plant can exercise a decisive pull on another, but collectively they all influence each other because of the complex linkages between them and the need for contact between producers and consumers. The result is the growth of manufacturing belts within which plants are able to enjoy, and contribute to external economies, such as the availability of skilled labour, efficient transportation facilities and specialist services. Proximity increases the speed of the diffusion of innovations, at the same time stimulating competition and increasing the rate of innovation. The very success of these manufacturing regions breeds further success, and this is seen in the western and southwestern movement of the North American Manufacturing Belt and the northward extension of the English axial belt.

Plants in the footloose industries are not, then, restricted to particular locations, but are free to locate within broad areas. The precise siting of a plant within such an area will depend on behavioural factors. The entrepreneur who built his factory within reach of his favourite golf course was not acting in an irresponsible fashion, providing the golf course was somewhere within the manufacturing belt. Birthplace, for example, is an important consideration. J. A. Piquet found that in a survey of 100 manufacturing plants, in almost all cases the location of the plant was the founder's home town.[1] The automobile industry provides support for this finding, for both Ford and Morris were born in Detroit and Oxford respectively. In many cases firms in the footloose industries show little interest in finding the best location, and spend a relatively small amount of effort in the search, often choosing a site from a few alternatives within what is thought to be the profitable area. The concept of the spatial profitability margin propounded by D. M. Smith has obvious relevance to footloose manufacturing, and the boundary of the manufacturing belt is seen to be the composite margin of profitability of a large number of plants. Having established the area within which it is possible to make a profit, Pred's work on behaviour can then be invoked to explain the site of the plant.

In this chapter three industries are examined. Two of the three, automobile manufacture and shipbuilding, were at one time oriented to materials, but technological progress has allowed these ties to weaken so that many recently developed car plants and shipyards have been sited in respect of factors other than material supply. Some car plants and shipyards have even been set up outside established manufacturing areas. The third example is the railway engineering industry whose distribution has been determined by decisions made by railway companies as to which point was the most suitable on their system as it existed at a particular time.

6.1 THE AUTOMOBILE INDUSTRY

On the world scale the production of automobiles is dominated by a few highly industrialised countries. In 1968 six countries were responsible for 86% of the world output, and one country, the U.S.A., manufactured more than three times the number made by the second largest producer, West Germany. The percentage shares of world output were: U.S.A. 41, West Germany 13, Japan 9, France 8, Great Britain 8 and Italy 7. It is an industry characterised by the most advanced flow-production techniques, high capital investment, a large demand for semi-skilled labour and very large plants which are normally located in the major manufacturing region of the country concerned. This has not always been the case, and in order to show how its present footloose nature has evolved it is useful to examine the industry chronologically. Four distinct eras can be recognised, each with its own pattern of location. Firstly, the experimental period when motor car producers, each making a very limited number of vehicles, sprang up at many dispersed points. From this the second era developed, with the first tentative steps at rationalised manufacture; production was essentially small scale, but definite localisation began to emerge. The third era saw the establishment of large-scale production at a limited number of sites, while the final era witnessed the dispersal of plants away from the concentrations built up in the previous period. After the initial experimental period, we see a concentration upon particular areas, followed by a gradual widening of the area within which the automobile industry could profitably locate as the attractions of the first developed areas have decreased. Orientation to final markets has never been especially important, although there are some advantages in a location central to the national market. The U.S.A. and Great Britain will be used to exemplify the eras mentioned.

THE EXPERIMENTAL PERIOD, 1895–1901

In the initial stages of automobile production, entry into the industry was easy because vehicles were individually made and output small so that the supply of capital was unimportant. Many plants were merely backyard workshops which were sometimes adjuncts of other engineering activities in which techniques were similar. Thus the Humber, Riley, Rover and Singer firms in Britain, and Nash (American Motors) in the U.S.A. grew out of bicycle or motor cycle manufacture. Vauxhall began in electrical engineering and Wolseley in sheep-shearing machinery. Other firms were engaged in carriage and wagon production, as were the Studebaker brothers at South Bend, Indiana, and W. C. Durant, the founder of General Motors, at Flint, Michigan. Access to components was not vital since most firms produced a large proportion of their own parts; the Lanchester company even made their own screws. Skilled labour was an essential pre-requisite, but since output was small this did not preclude firms from setting up in almost any city. The first car made in Britain was a Daimler which ran in 1895, and which was built in Coventry, but by 1901, of the 55 manufacturers who had produced a car, although 18 were in the West Midland engineering and metallurgical district, 14 were in London.[2] Other producing centres included Glasgow, Southport, Cowes, Lowestoft and Bridgwater. A similarly dispersed pattern was to be found in the U.S.A. The Duryea brothers were the first to produce more than one car of the same design, at Springfield Mass, in 1895. In that year there were 40 plants in operation building more than two cars a year. New York City led with 7, but Detroit had no plant at all. By 1900 there were 327 plants making more than two cars a year, with major concentrations in southern New England and on the mid-Atlantic seaboard between New York and Philadelphia. Detroit possessed the single plant beconging to Henry Ford, but production was developing in other mid-western cities, for example Chicago and Cleveland with 26 and 21 plants respectively.

SMALL-SCALE PRODUCTION, 1902–1913

During this period output per plant increased, there was an increased reliance on bought-in parts, and skilled labour requirements were no less important than in the initial period. However, large numbers of skilled operatives were required, and in Great Britain this conferred a considerable advantage on plants in the West Midlands. Not only did the area possess a suitable labour force, a wide range of engineering firms able to supply components, and experience of bicycle production, but also a very high level of innovation. Of the 11 firms producing more than 1000 cars in 1913, 8 were located in Birmingham, Coventry and Wolverhampton.[3] In this year 53% of British car output originated from the region, compared with 4% from London. Fig. 77 illustrates the way in which by 1913 a few plants were responsible for a large proportion of total production. From a total of 149 firms, 11 manufactured 76% of all cars. Of these, two firms, Ford (22%) and Wolseley (10%), made almost one-third of the total. By the end of the period concentration of production, if not of plants, was apparent along an axis between Manchester and London, with the northern segment between the former town and Birmingham being the more important. Despite the advantages of the West Midlands, this situation indicates that manufacturers were able to succeed elsewhere, and nowhere more than in Manchester, where 28% of British cars were made in 1913. The decision by Ford to establish a plant at Trafford Park, Manchester in 1911, largely supplied with components shipped from the U.S.A., suggests that even at this early date proximity to material supply was not absolutely vital.

The geography of the American automobile industry differed from its British counterpart in several aspects. Firstly, it continued to develop at a faster rate, so that by 1914 a total of 469 plants turning out more than two cars annually were in operation. Secondly, the scale of production was larger than in Britain, and symptomatic of this was the introduction by Ford in 1908 of flow production techniques for the assembly of the flywheel magneto for the legendary Model T. Thirdly, there was a perceptible shift in concentration away from the area of initial importance, the eastern seaboard, to the Mid-West in general and Detroit in particular. The latter city possessed 50 plants constructing more than two cars annually in 1914, more than any other city. The use of mass-production techniques reduces the need for skilled labour (at present 65% of the labour force in American automobile plants is unskilled), and this assisted Ford and others to establish themselves outside the older engineering districts. In America, therefore, the end of this period belongs to the era of large-scale production, culminating in the perfection of the moving assembly line at Ford's Highland Park works in 1914.

The westward movement of the industry in the U.S.A. was also a result of wrong decisions on the part of eastern manufacturers to concentrate on the development of steam and electric traction, while makers in the Mid-West chose to develop the internal combustion engine. By the time it was finally accepted that the petrol engine was the most efficient, mid-western producers had built up a long lead. Permeating the whole economic environment of the Mid-West was an intense spirit of resource and enterprise, characteristic of the pioneers, and contrasting with the more conservative approach of the East. Mid-western bankers were imbued with this spirit and capital was not difficult to find. The Hudson company was established in 1909 with capital advanced by a Detroit department store magnate. Access to steel supplies was better in the Mid-West than in the East, not only because of the strength of Pittsburgh, Cleveland and Chicago in this respect, but also because of the Pittsburgh Plus basing-point system which operated until 1924. Additionally the Mid-West possessed much greater nodality than did the east coast for the supply of automobiles to the national market.

While it was predictable that plants in the East would decline, it was by no means inevitable that Detroit should become the major seat of the industry. There is little doubt that Cleveland, Toledo or Chicago, or most other cities in the Mid-West, would have been equally satisfactory. The concentration on Detroit and Lower Michigan was largely the result of behavioural factors, the most important of which was the extraordinarily high level of entrepreneurial and technical expertise to be found in the locality. Other than Henry Ford, who was greatly assisted by some very talented engineers like Charles B. King, there were such as Ransom E. Olds (Oldsmobile) at Lansing, Michigan, the Dodge brothers at Detroit, W. C. Durant (Buick) at Flint, Michigan, Henry M. Leland (Cadillac) at Detroit and Howard E. Coffin (Hudson) at Detroit. Had these men lived elsewhere in the broad area of the Mid-West, Lower Michigan would not have developed as it did. The very success of the area increased the external economies available to plants within it, encouraging the birth of new plants and the migration of others. Thus the Packard company, set up at Warren, Ohio, in 1899, moved to Detroit in 1903. However, the single most important behavioural consideration was Ford's decision to produce a cheap car. Rae comments that 'it was Tin Lizzie who put Detroit finally and unchallengeably ahead of any possible competitor'.[4]

LARGE-SCALE PRODUCTION, 1914–1938

The era of large-scale production was ushered in by Ford in 1914. The techniques used in the assembly of the magneto were applied to many other components, and eventually to the entire car itself. The chassis assembly was pulled along a 75-metre/250-foot route past stockpiles of parts, resulting in the reduction of assembly time from 14 to 6 hours. Conveyor belts were then introduced, and finally parts were supplied to the assembly lines by overhead conveyors. As the term implies, flow production involves the continuous delivery of components to the assembly lines. It also involves a smooth flow of components from the outside suppliers, and in the early stages this could most easily be achieved by reducing the distance between the plant and these suppliers. Large-scale production methods were not introduced into Western Europe until the 1920s. Their introduction had five principal effects on the industry.

(i) *Increase in the size of plant*

Both in terms of the numbers employed, the output of cars and the area of land occupied, plants using flow production methods were large. In 1913 the Ford plant at Manchester produced 6000 cars, but by 1938 the same firm, being the largest producer using a single plant, made 90 000. The trend continues and the present Ford plant at Dagenham has 39 000 workers, makes half a million cars a year and occupies 210 hectares/500 acres. In 1938 the Jaguar company, with 1·1% of British output, was making more cars in its Coventry plant than the second largest producer, Wolseley, in 1913.

(ii) *Reduction in the number of plants*

The cost savings resulting from the installation of flow production lines were enormous; the price of the Model T Ford fell from £358/$950 in 1909 to £110/$292 in 1922, while over the short period 1924–9, the average price of British cars fell 25%.[5] Small-scale producers were quite incapable of matching the prices achieved by large-scale methods, and to remain competitive it became necessary to raise sufficient funds to install assembly lines in retaliation. This many firms were unable to do. The onerous capital requirements also prevented new entrants to the industry from being numerous. By 1934 there were only 53 plants producing more than 12 cars a year in operation in the U.S.A. In Great Britain in 1938 the total had fallen to 42, but as can be seen in Fig. 77, 26 of these could each lay claim only to less than 1% of national output,

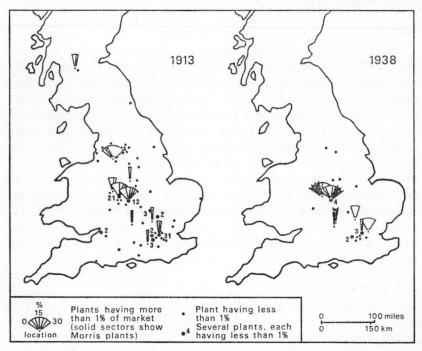

Fig. 77 Automobile plants in Great Britain, 1913 and 1938

and in total they shared only 3% of production. The other 16 plants accounted for the remaining 97% of output. Three plants, at Dagenham (Ford), Birmingham (Austin) and Luton (Vauxhall), manufactured 45% of British cars in 1938.

(iii) *Reduction in the number of firms*

Major producers would frequently absorb their ailing competitors who were unable to find the cash needed to develop mass production, with the consequence that many plants came under the control of one firm. As early as 1927 General Motors, Ford and Chrysler were producing 75% of American automobiles, a figure which had risen to 90% by 1939. In Britain 6 firms, Morris, Ford, Austin, Vauxhall, Rootes and Standard, operating 13 plants, accounted for 90% of output in 1938. The first three of these firms were responsible for 61% of total production.

(iv) *Declining importance of component supplies*

It has been noted how mass production brings in its train complicated flows of components from suppliers to automobile plants. These flows lead to the agglomeration of plants in important areas of component supply, that is Lower Michigan in the U.S.A., and the West Midlands in Britain. A location in these areas assisted the continuation of smaller firms who were often forced to close down elsewhere because of the difficulty in procuring components. For this reason the Jaguar company left Blackpool, where it had been making motor cycle side-cars, in 1928 for Coventry. The largest British firm, Morris, found it expedient to hold three weeks' stock of components rather than the normal week's supply. By 1923 Ford, which had initially used American components, had switched to British components for 83% of its needs. However, as the output of cars rose, the necessary thresholds were reached for mass production of gears, radiators and transmissions by the automobile firms themselves, and the need for proximity to component suppliers became less important. Morris set up body, engine, transmission and later (1946) carburettor plants in Birmingham and Coventry and a radiator plant in Oxford. Ford at Dagenham and Vauxhall at Luton also began to turn out components in their own works. Ford went so far as to install their own blast furnace and produce their own castings as part of a move towards greater independence.

(v) *Declining importance of skilled labour*

Operations such as stamping and pressing were traditional West Midlands skills, but the new large presses, imported from the U.S.A., did not require skilled labour and could be efficiently worked at Luton, Oxford, where Pressed Steel began in the late 1920s, or Dagenham. Other component manufacture involving, for example, very high speed machinery, was new to Birmingham, and was not attracted there. Indeed the rapidly changing technological background to the industry, requiring high productivity rather than quality, made raw, unorganised labour a positive locational advantage. In contrast, the Wolverhampton automobile industry was virtually wiped out by the 1930s largely because of a preference for the use of local skills and batch production rather than mass production.[6] The availability of a large pool of unskilled labour, which could easily be trained, in east London, was a major factor in Ford's decision to move in 1931 to Dagenham rather than some other location when it became obvious that Trafford Park, Manchester, was unsuitable for future expansion.

The period in both the U.S.A. and Britain was one of increased concentration of automobile manufacture into Lower Michigan and the West

Midlands respectively. In 1934, 16 of the 53 American plants producing more than 12 cars annually were in Michigan, while in 1938 the West Midlands were responsible for 60% of British output. However, as mass production developed, the pull of the West Midlands diminished, and part of its growth was due to geographical inertia. Indicative of the growing footloose character of the industry, production in areas strong in engineering tradition, such as Glasgow and Manchester, a very important centre in 1913, had completely ceased by 1938. In their place centres with little engineering background grew up, and by 1938 London (21%), Luton (10%) and Oxford (8%) accounted for 39% of British automobile production. During this era there was indeed a consolidation of the position of the West Midlands, but there were already powerful footloose influences at work.

LARGE-SCALE PRODUCTION SINCE 1939

Most of the trends noted above continued in this period. Most evidently, the number of firms decreased as the optimum size of firm rose. In the U.S.A. General Motors, Ford and Chrysler now have 95% of total output, and there is only one other firm, American Motors, based at Kenosha, Wisconsin, of any consequence. In Britain, four firms, British Leyland, Ford, General Motors (Vauxhall) and Chrysler (Rootes), control 98% of production. This latter figure was shared between 10 firms in 1938, Morris, Ford, Austin, Vauxhall, Rootes, Standard, Rover, Singer, Daimler-Lanchester and Jaguar. Morris and Austin formed the British Motor Corporation in 1952, and acquired Jaguar, which controlled Daimler, in 1966. Leyland, the major British truck firm, took over Standard in 1960, and Rover in 1967, finally merging with B.M.C. to form British Leyland in 1968. Singer was acquired by Rootes, now owned by Chrysler. In contrast the number of plants has increased, as there are now 48 employing more than 1000 operatives owned by the four main groups. These plants are shown in Fig. 78. Some of the other plants appearing in Fig. 78 are also large, for example the Rolls Royce plant at Crewe employs 4500. The pulls provided by component supply and skilled labour continue to diminish in importance.

Locationally, the era since 1939 has been one of dispersal, although there are great incentives to expand production *in situ*. We first examine these incentives before looking at the process of dispersal. The centres of production established by 1938 developed important external economies making them very attractive to continued expansion. By extending existing plants or by building new ones in the vicinity, control of production and flows of information are simplified. Very large plants enable economies of scale to be reaped. However, perhaps the most important

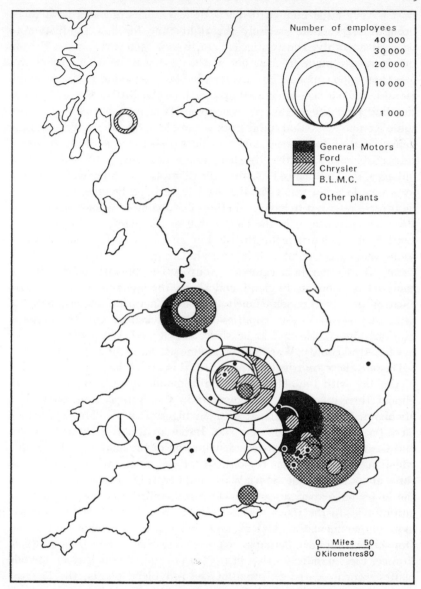

Fig. 78 Automobile plants in Great Britain 1970

reason for expansion *in situ* is the sheer complexity of the flow of components, parts and accessories to the plant. Ford at Dagenham now purchase 65% of the cost of each car from outside suppliers, and while in Europe and the U.S.A. the figure is as low as 25%, the fact remains that a very large number of parts or assemblies of parts have to be brought together at precisely the right time for flow production to proceed smoothly. The average car consists of 2500 parts, and in Britain purchases are made from 24 out of the 38 official industry groups. No less than 1500 suppliers are involved in the production of the Triumph Herald, while a well-integrated firm such as the British Motor Corporation had 4000 different suppliers in 1964.[7] It is not the transport cost of these components that represents a problem, for they are normally delivered at uniform prices, and transport costs are a small proportion of total costs, rather it is that the shorter and the more established are these linkages, the less chance is there of the disruption of supplies. Expansion at a new location results in the need to reshape linkages, and manufacturers prefer not to have to do this. These considerations suggest that there are advantages in the localisation of car plants in specific areas. Lord Stokes, chairman of British Leyland, has said, 'I feel daunted sometimes by the number of factories in this group. I would like to have them all together in a compact group.'[8] The present distribution of component firms in England underlines the attraction of a central location in the London–Manchester manufacturing region; 84% of firms are found in the counties of Warwickshire, Greater London, Staffordshire, Yorkshire, Lancashire, Essex and Worcestershire. The most central county, Warwickshire, alone accounts for 24% of the total.

Despite these centripetal tendencies, this period has seen a loosening of the ties with the older areas of automobile manufacture. Although almost three-quarters of employment in the American industry is in Michigan, Ohio and Indiana, with Michigan alone having 50%, there have been important gains in Ohio, Indiana, Illinois, California, Texas and Georgia. Fig. 79 shows the distribution of the final assembly plants which have largely been responsible for the recent trends. In Britain three areas, Merseyside, South Wales and Central Scotland, of which only the latter has experience of vehicle manufacture, have begun to make automobiles in the 1960s. As can be seen from Fig. 78, Merseyside has more employment than Oxford, and very nearly as much as Luton and Dunstable combined. Perhaps even more remarkable have been events in France. Fig. 80 indicates that in 1955, 13 of the 18 principal automobile plants were in Paris; only one of the provincial plants, the Peugeot works at Sochaux, had more than 3000 employees. A decade and a half later, 5 provincial plants have increased to 48, of which 12 have more than 4000 employees. Only the southern areas of France now lack automobile manufacture. There are two main reasons for these centrifugal movements.

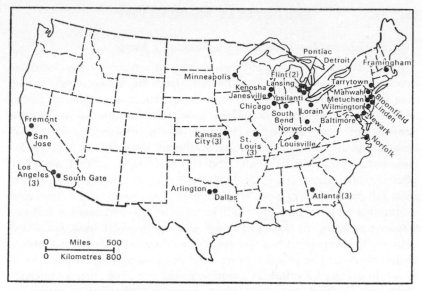

Fig. 79 Final assembly plants in the U.S.A., 1966

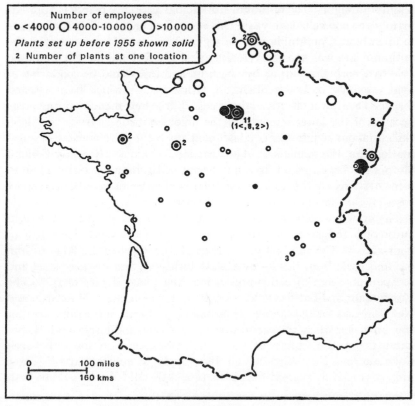

Fig. 80 Automobile plants in France, 1969

(i) *The construction of separate final assembly plants*

As yet this is an American phenomenon as a result of the distances involved in the delivery of automobiles from the Lower Great Lakes area to many parts of the country, and the high level of demand in the nation as a whole. The Lower Great Lakes district now assembles only one-third of American cars as the result of the construction of 30 final assembly plants elsewhere. Especially affluent areas distant from Michigan, such as California, Texas and the east coast, attract assembly plants, while Kansas City, St Louis and Atlanta are useful nodes for regional markets. Engines, transmissions, gearboxes and other sub-assemblies are made in the traditional locations, but since a railway wagon can carry 12 'knocked-down' cars as opposed to 4 assembled vehicles, there are great transport cost economies to be had by assembling at the market. The practice of quoting prices including an element to cover an assumed haul of an assembled vehicle rather than a knocked-down vehicle from the engine plant, provides additional incentive for market assembly plants. These assumed transport costs are termed phantom freights. The optimum size of final assembly plants is approximately 100 000 vehicles a year. This is small enough to allow such plants to operate at a profitable scale in regional markets. If, for example, the optimum size was 500 000 vehicles, no single regional market would be able to absorb this output by one firm, and this would be conducive to final assembly in Lower Michigan. Other factors which have assisted dispersal are lower effective labour costs in the new manufacturing areas because of the lower strength of the unions outside Detroit, very low-skilled labour requirements consequent upon the development of automation, and the refinement of advertising techniques. Recently General Motors has begun to set up a number of body-stamping plants close to some of its regional final assembly plants in order to save the transport costs on the movement of bulky body parts from Michigan.[9]

The growth of separate final assembly plants has given the American automobile industry a location pattern which Hurley has likened to an hour-glass.[10] The top half of the hour-glass comprises the flows of iron ore and coal (Ford has its own blast furnaces), and of sheet steel and components from 25 000 suppliers into the Lower Lakes district. The Buick plant at Flint has linkages with 35 towns between Wisconsin and New England for the supply of machinery, 34 towns in the same area for the provision of metal parts, 9 towns between California and Massachusetts for the supply of tubes and tyres, and 26 towns between Colorado and New England for the supply of rubber parts.[11] These linkages certainly suggest that a location in the Mid-West would be best, although it is equally obvious that Flint need not be that location. The stem of the hour-glass is represented by the plants of Lower Michigan and associated areas. The bottom of the hour-glass is made up of the final assembly plants and the 45 000 dealers who are all part of the marketing machinery, although they belong to the tertiary or service sector of economic activity rather than the manufacturing sector. The continual growth of population outside the manufacturing region of the U.S.A. will lead to an increasing number of plants in the lower part of the hour-glass, further emphasising the footloose character of the industry.

Before leaving final assembly plants, mention must be made of their establishment in countries outside those in which the main plant is located. Apart from the transport cost saving of shipping knocked-down vehicles, firms can take advantage of the lower import tariffs levied on sub-assemblies rather than on completed automobiles. Governments of importing countries make this differentiation to persuade producers to assemble at the market and absorb local labour in the process, thereby assisting the regional and national income. General Motors maintains final assembly plants in Canada, Mexico, Venezuela, Brazil, Argentine, Peru and Belgium, for instance. Ford has such plants in Belgium and the Netherlands, and Chrysler has a plant in Belgium. British Leyland has final assembly plants in Australia, New Zealand and South Africa. In 1968 Belgium (605 600 cars) was the principal site of final assembly operations, followed by South Africa (141 400), Mexico (102 700) and Ireland (50 000).

(ii) *Governmental regional policy*

In the U.S.A. the National Industrial Dispersal Program of 1951 aimed at reducing the number of new plants in established industrial districts, has contributed to some centrifugal movement, but it has been in Western Europe that the automobile industry has been employed as a major instrument of governmental regional planning policy. In Britain, an Industrial Development Certificate (IDC) is required from the Board of Trade before a plant of more than 270 square metres/3000 square feet, in the regions outside the designated Development Districts, may be built. Virtually all car plants in 1945 lay outside Development Districts, and as we have seen there is powerful incentive to expand *in situ*. However, by means of the IDC legislation, during the 1960s the government was able to direct new plants to areas of higher than average unemployment. These plants received building grants and, later, an allocation for each operative employed (the Regional Employment Premium). The vehicle industry was expanding rapidly, its skilled labour requirements are small, and within broad areas it is footloose, so it was very suitable as a 'location leader'. As such it could generate employment not only in its own plants, but also in the supporting industries such as components and the servicing industries such as building maintenance and vehicle distribution. The biggest impact of these policies has been on Merseyside. Ford has its second largest British plant at Halewood, as does General Motors at Ellesmere Port. British Leyland has a small works at Speke. A second concentration has been developed in Central Scotland in the shape of the British Leyland (formerly Pressed Steel) body plant at Paisley, and the Chrysler (formerly Hillman) plant at Linwood. Government policy has succeeded in making the 1970 map of the largest plants very similar to that of 1913. Only the development at Llanelli and Cardiff does not fit this pattern. Areas developed by the government now account for 13% of the industry's labour force, although only 2%, that is the Scottish plants, is more than 190 km/120 miles from the West Midlands.

For the same reasons as in Britain, the French government has used the automobile industry to redistribute prosperity. One of the four major firms, Renault, has been nationalised since 1944, but this has not influenced its behaviour, and it has been no more willing than any other firm to expand outside Paris. Although the policy of persuasion adopted by the government after the war did result in the establishment of a Citroen plant at Rennes in 1951 and the construction of a Renault plant at Flins, 40 km/25 miles from Paris in 1952, in 1954 it was considered necessary to provide firms with financial incentive to set up in the provinces. However, it was the Paris zoning laws of 1959, forbidding the building in the Paris region of new plant with floorspace of more than 500 square metres/5350 square feet, or the extension of existing plant by more than 10%, that precipitated major locational change. The results have been much more marked than in Britain, for not only have 43 new plants been constructed since 1955, but also the majority have been located at points more than 160 km/100 miles from Paris, as Fig. 80 shows. Most have been set up in towns, in some cases very small towns, with little manufacturing tradition, in an effort to stop the drift of population to Paris. The French case would suggest that the area within which location is relatively unimportant is, in Western Europe, beginning to approach the dimensions of the American automotive triangle, whose apices comprise Milwaukee, Cincinnati and Buffalo, and whose sides are between 600 and 800 km/400 and 500 miles in length.

LINKAGES BETWEEN PLANTS

The principal result of the extension of the industry's spatial profitability margins is that linkages, both of materials and information, between plants have become increasingly important. There have always been complex linkages between component firms and car plants, but as the size of firm has grown, linkages between plants of the same firm have developed. An early example in Britain was the linkages between the 7 Morris Motors plants, shown in Fig. 77. Mergers normally result in rationalisation of production with particular plants specialising in certain stages of production to achieve economies of scale. When mergers are effected between multi-plant firms, for example Austin and Morris in 1952 to form the British Motor Corporation, the opportunity for plant specialisation is considerable. In this case the result was the flow of engines and bodies from Coventry to Oxford, transmissions from Birmingham to Oxford, components from Birmingham to Longbridge, and radiators from Llanelli to Oxford and Longbridge. There was an exchange of engines between Longbridge and Oxford, although this might not be expected to happen.

Government restrictions on the extension of plants have served to accelerate the growth of inter-plant linkages. New plants are seldom fully integrated, receiving and dispatching sub-assemblies to other plants in the firm. Consequently as each new plant is built, linkages are generated. New methods of transport have been introduced to assist these flows, and the reduction in freight rates have encouraged other flows. Thus engines and transmissions from Dagenham are sent daily by train on charter to Ford's to Halewood. Specially designed terminal facilities have been constructed to improve the speed of the turn-round. Chrysler uses British Rail freightliners to move sub-assemblies, panels and gearboxes from Linwood to Ryton, near Coventry, returning with transmissions.

By American standards, West European countries are not large, and since all the three major American firms operate in Western Europe, it is not surprising that a series of international linkages, over and above the establishment of final assembly plants, should develop. Thus Ford no longer operates as a number of self-sufficient national firms, but is controlled by Ford Europe. The consequence is international plant specialisation. Containers are sent from Halewood to Genk, Belgium, Cologne and Saarlouis in West Germany, as result of the decision to regard the Escort and the Capri as European models, using the British plants to make certain sub-assemblies, such as engines. The Ford plant at Genk even sends sump tanks for the Maverick to Detroit and engines for the Pinto are made at Dagenham and dispatched to the same destination. The internationalisation of the West European industry has received further impetus from a series of strikes at the works of component suppliers who were formerly virtually monopoly suppliers. Until recently all British Leyland glass was supplied by Pilkington at St Helens,

Lancashire. During a strike at the plant, alternative supplies were obtained from Belgium, and these have been continued in order to secure future supplies. There are many other examples of these international linkages, all of which support the contention that automobile manufacture is a footloose activity.

6.2 THE COMMERCIAL SHIPBUILDING INDUSTRY

The construction of merchant ships is very largely the exclusive province of two areas, Japan and Western Europe. In 1968 Japan launched 51% of world gross registered tonnage, and collectively West Germany, Sweden, Great Britain, Spain, Italy, Norway, France, Denmark and the Netherlands were responsible for a further 37%. Since 1950 several trends have been discernible. The truly remarkable growth of the Japanese industry overshadows all else, for postwar production did not begin until 1950 and yet six years later the country was the leading producer. Japan now builds more tonnage than the rest of the world combined, and her success has contributed to two other trends. Firstly, the decline of the British yards, which were the largest in the world for over a century, and secondly, the recent growth of production in low labour cost countries such as Spain and Italy, better able to compete with Japan.

More than most other industries, shipbuilding has especially critical site considerations because of the need for deep water for launching. The larger the vessel the more influential do these considerations become. However, this does not conflict with the classification of the industry as footloose, for however critical the site considerations may be, this does not necessarily tie the industry to the sources of materials and energy, or to markets. Indeed there is much evidence to suggest that the industry can now be established at any point with suitable deep water either in or proximate to a manufacturing region. The entrepreneur does not have the wide choice available to those setting up plants whose site is much less critical, but the shipyard has increasing mobility in respect of other location factors. To be sure, the industry is not as footloose as, say, the electronic products industry whose materials have a very high unit value, but while there are old yards that appear to be firmly material-oriented, this is usually the legacy of history, for there are many newer yards peripheral to industrial regions and therefore distant from sources of materials. In an industry in which most firms expect to sell a large proportion of their output in foreign markets, there can be no question of market orientation. We first comment on the one time importance of proximity to materials.

INITIAL ORIENTATION TO MATERIALS

In the era of the wooden ship the cost of moving bulky low-value timber was conducive to the establishment of shipyards in estuaries whose rivers flowed through oak forests. Until the Civil War (1861–5) the U.S.A. was the foremost shipbuilder and her principal yards were in New England. In Britain the Thames estuary was especially suitable since wood could be moved down tributaries flowing through the forests of the Weald. Rope and sail making and such ironfounding as was required were associated with shipbuilding. By the late 1850s the iron-hulled, steam-powered ship was seen to be a more viable proposition than the wooden vessel. It was more durable, it was faster, and above all it cost between 10 and 15% less than the earlier type. The later use of steel enhanced these advantages, not least because higher boiler pressures could be maintained, improving speed and fuel consumption. British technology in both iron and steel and steam engine production was superior to that in America, and the country possessed two coastal coalfields where iron and steel manufacture and heavy engineering were well developed. These two areas, Clydeside and the composite district of Tyneside, Wearside and Teesside, differed from the South Wales coalfield, close to which shipbuilding might have developed, in that the latter was not strictly a coastal field, engineering did not establish itself to the same extent, and deep-water facilities were not so suitable. The low degree of locational flexibility obtaining in the 19th century caused the almost complete decline of the Thameside yards following the unsuitability of the area for the supply of materials for iron ships. Although all the larger yards carried out a wide range of ironfounding and metalworking as well as engine building, they relied on local suppliers for their materials. To its great disadvantage, Thameside lacked iron and steel capacity, with the consequence that the basic material would have to have been imported from elsewhere. By 1914 the two main districts were responsible for 89% of British output. Such were the advantages of these two areas that during the 1890s they were able to launch three-quarters of the world tonnage. There were also important yards at Belfast, Barrow and Birkenhead, of which only Barrow is located on a coalfield. Thus even in the last century it was possible to prosper without proximity to coal, iron and steel and heavy engineering.

THE DECLINING LOCATIONAL SIGNIFICANCE OF MATERIALS

In shipbuilding, no less than in engineering in general, the 20th century has seen the loosening of the ties that once bound the industry to coalfields. Steam power has been replaced by electric power as a means of working machinery and dockside cranes. More efficient methods

o

of transport have reduced the formerly high cost of moving bulky
materials. Manufacturing has developed in regions remote from coalfields causing shipbuilding to grow up at new locations. Improved communications have eased the problems of purchasing supplies and dispos-
ing of output. That there are still a few areas fulfilling 19th-century

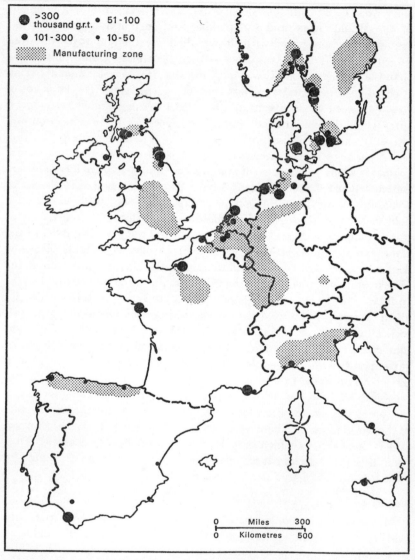

Fig. 81 Principal shipbuilding ports in Western Europe, 1970

location criteria is a function of the geographical inertia that has built up in the traditional centres of production.

Most of the general points made above are conducive to the growth of many manufacturing industries away from coalfields. To account for the growth of large shipbuilding yards at such places as Palermo, Cadiz, Seville, Muroran, Hakodate and other locations some distance from manufacturing regions (see Figs 81 and 82), it is necessary to consider the factors that apply specifically to shipbuilding.

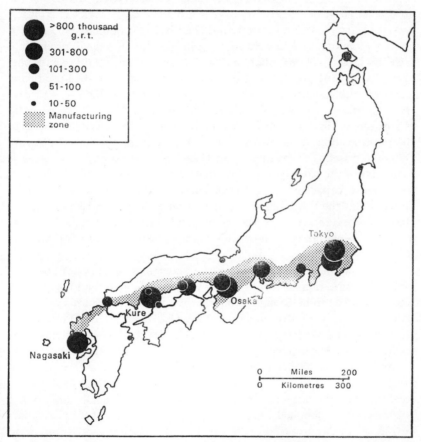

Fig. 82 Principal shipbuilding ports in Japan, 1970

(i) *The supply of steel*

The share of total cost accounted for by steel rises with the increasing size of ship. The steel used in a 20 000 ton dry cargo vessel represents 20% of the total cost. The figure for a 100 000 ton tanker is 26%.[12] Most of the steel is heavy plate and heavy sections for the hull, and ship-building is an important market for the iron and steel industry. In Great Britain shipyards consumed 17% of the national output of heavy plate and 5% of sections in 1964. It is hardly surprising that proximity to iron, and later steel mills was an important consideration for the 19th-century builders, conferring great advantages on coastal iron- and steel-making districts. There is no doubt that the juxtaposition of steelworks and shipyards does help to reduce the delivered price of steel, and that steel supplies are still an important locational consideration. Yards on the north-east coast of England take steel from the large works at Middles-brough, Hartlepool and Consett, and the Clydeside builders are supplied by the plants on the Lanarkshire coalfield. The two great production areas in Japan, Tokyo-Yokohama, with 7 large yards, and Osaka-Kobe, also with 7 yards, are in addition the most important steel-producing districts in the country, with an output of 12 and 9 million tons respec-tively in 1965. The largest single yard, that at Nagasaki, owned by Mitsubishi, is also adjacent to an iron and steel plant. Other examples of the juxtaposition of the two activities are Bremen, Dunkirk, El Ferrol, Bilbao and Genoa. The capacity of these yards in a national context is indicative of the value of adjacent steel making. Bremen and Genoa have the largest capacity West German and Italian yards respectively, Dunkirk has the third largest capacity French yards, and El Ferrol and Bilbao possess respectively the second and third largest capacity yards in Spain. Shipbuilding at these sites clearly has an element of orientation to materials.

Not all shipbuilding is carried on adjacent to steel supplies however. Unlike the situation a century ago, it is now feasible to build ships from steel which has to be brought from distant plants. There are many con-tributory factors. Firstly, since 1945 there has been a marked increase in the number of coastal steelworks, allowing steel products to be moved by means of water transport to shipyards. This is particularly important in Japan, where all the steelworks are coastal, enabling such yards as those at Hakodate and Shimizu, not close to steel plants, to assemble their steel supplies at relatively low cost. The Norwegian, Danish and Swedish yards cannot be supplied from national sources because of the inadequate output of the appropriate type of steel, and therefore rely on Great Britain, West Germany and Belgium for their plates and sections. The recent entry of Spain into large tanker production has created too great a demand for plates for the national steel industry to meet, resulting in the import of 195 000 tons of this type of steel in 1969. Secondly, the estab-lishment of uniform delivered prices for steel has helped to decrease the significance of distance from steelworks; the Aberdeen, Dundee and

Leith yards in Scotland have certainly benefited in this manner. Thirdly, in an attempt to secure outlets for their products, some steel firms have taken over shipyards. Examples such as the purchase of the Barrow Shipbuilding Company by the Sheffield steel-making firm of Vickers, and the control of the Clyde yard of James and George Thomson by the Sheffield firm of John Brown, illustrate the way in which some yards adjacent to iron and steel plants do not always obtain their steel from such sources. The inland Sheffield–Rotherham metallurgical district is in fact an important supplier of steel to shipyards. Out of a total of 39 plants listed in the *International Shipping and Shipbuilding Directory* for 1970, as iron and steel suppliers to the industry, 17 are located in this area. A further 6 are in the West Midlands.

During the 1960s perhaps the most notable feature of the world shipbuilding industry has been the demand for very large tankers and, to a lesser extent, bulk carriers. Many yards have renounced this end of the trade, but those that have continued to build these increasingly large vessels which, as we have seen, require proportionately large tonnages of steel, are by no means all located close to steel plants. Cadiz, Le Trait near Rouen, Emden, Hamburg, Odense, Gothenburg and Malmö are all shipbuilding districts with a capacity of more than 300 000 tons annually, yet they have a common lack of local iron and steel plants. Steel may account for between a fifth and a quarter of the value of a ship, but it is generally losing its importance as a locational factor.

(ii) *The increasing complexity of ships*

For all their size, 19th-century vessels were relatively simple constructions. This century has seen the incorporation in ships of highly complex radio and electronic systems, advanced control gear, air-conditioning plant and sophisticated steering and cargo-handling equipment. Sub-assemblies of this kind are manufactured by specialist firms for whom the shipbuilders may represent only one of many markets. Such firms are distributed throughout manufacturing regions and certainly exhibit no correlation with shipbuilding yards. Bought-in components now account for approximately one-third of the total cost of a ship, and a single yard may place orders with several hundred suppliers and contractors. Fig. 83 shows the distribution of the principal subcontractors involved in the supply of components for a 100 000-ton tanker launched at Barrow in 1966. The location of these suppliers coincides broadly with the manufacturing areas of Great Britain. Clearly the larger the number of suppliers, the more footloose the industry becomes, and proximity to any one supplier diminishes in importance. During the Second World War in the U.S.A. more than 500 plants, located in 32 different states, manufactured components used in the construction of Liberty ships. Over 20 different firms made the engines installed in these vessels.[13] The flow of components to yards also has an international dimension. For example, in 1960 30% of the components used in Swedish yards were supplied by Great Britain. This figure is now nearer 20%, but the flow of German parts to Sweden has proportionately increased. Some

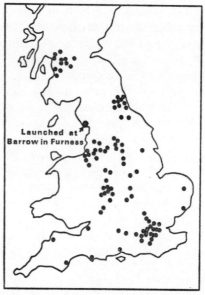

Fig. 83. Principal subcontractors for the *British Admiral*, launched at Barrow, 1966

Japanese yards used British steering gear, pumps and compressors, and it was reported in 1970 that the British Marine Equipment Council had secured £18 million worth of business for most of the equipment for 24 cargo liners and 11 smaller vessels under construction in Brazil. In some cases yards more diversified than normal export specialist equipment to other shipbuilders. Thus the Swedish Kockums yard at Gothenburg has a world market for its echo-sounding equipment.

(iii) *The supply of engines*

The main engine accounts for between 10% and 15% of the total cost of a vessel, and if ancillary engine room equipment is added, the figure may be as much as 20%. In Britain main engines have always been built by the yards themselves, and this remains true of the larger firms. A few engines are built by AEI-EE at their Manchester and Preston plants, but essentially engine building is carried out at the established shipbuilding centres. The situation elsewhere is different since engine manufacture has always been in the hands of specialists. In the U.S.A., Westinghouse Electric and General Electric supply steam turbines and diesels from their inland plants. The largest West European engine builder is Burmeister and Wain at Copenhagen, where the first ocean-going motor ship was launched in 1912, followed by Götaverken at Gothenburg and Sulzer at Winterthur in Switzerland. Certainly those yards using engines made in Switzerland are not located in respect of their suppliers. MAN at Augsburg is another inland marine engine builder. Although the cost of transporting an engine is small in relation to its value, of recent it has become the practice to build engines under licence because of their great size. MAN diesels are built at Barrow by Vickers, Harland and Wolff build Burmeister and Wain engines at Belfast, and Kvaerner make General Electric (America) turbines at Oslo. Many of the engines built under licence are installed in vessels constructed elsewhere. Consequently shipyards, especially those outside Britain, are not especially oriented towards their engine suppliers.

(iv) *Shipbuilding and ports*

By the 1920s shipbuilding was no longer tied to heavy manufacturing districts, and it is hardly surprising that the activity has grown up at commercial ports. Most of these have suitable sites for launching vessels, most carry out ship repair, and whether or not shipbuilding develops is very often a function of behavioural factors, that is, whether or not local shipping or ship repairing interests decide to enter shipbuilding. In this way we can explain the importance of St Nazaire, for long the leading French shipbuilding port, in spite of its being distant from the Nord industrial district. Had close access to manufacturing regions been of paramount significance, then it would have been logical for Dunkirk to have become the leading yard. Dunkirk, however, was never an important port. The commercial ports of Rouen, Antwerp, Rotterdam, Amsterdam, Hamburg and Genoa all have important yards. London, Bristol and Hull, three of Britain's largest commercial ports, have failed to develop shipbuilding this century, largely because of the sheer strength of the existing centres elsewhere in the country.

(v) *Skilled labour*

During the 19th century the presence of a highly skilled labour force conferred a major advantage on the British shipbuilding industry. This labour was highly localised, and was a factor contributing to the geographical inertia of the industry. However, as in automobile production, more sophisticated methods of assembly, in particular the system of constructing vessels in large sub-sections or blocks, causing more work to be given to specialists outside the yard, have resulted in the reduction of skilled labour requirements. Together with the factors considered above, this has allowed firms to be much more flexible in their choice of new yards. Wage rates in many countries are increasing more rapidly than other costs. Between October 1968 and October 1971 alone, wages in the British industry rose 32%, and Japanese yards are experiencing the same conditions. In an effort to find cheap labour, some Japanese firms are constructing new yards in less industrialised parts of the country. Kawasaki is building a yard on the island of Shikoku, Mitsubishi is developing a site south of Nagasaki, and Ishikawajima-Harima is opening a yard near Kure. Countries with low wage rates and poorly developed manufacturing sectors are now being used by shipbuilders in high wage economies. The Wearside firm of Austin and Pickersgill are building (1971) 27 ships in Greece, and negotiations are in progress for the construction of ships in Brazil. Japanese yards have already arranged links with yards in Taiwan and Singapore. These trends indicate the extent to which the industry has become footloose and the degree to which it is possible to expand the spatial margins of profitability.

FACTORS INFLUENCING THE SIZE OF NATIONAL OUTPUT

So far in this chapter we have examined the extent to which selected industries have become increasingly footloose. However, this approach does not explain the level of production in particular countries. Since shipbuilding, unlike automobile manufacture, is not most well developed in the most advanced industrial nation, the U.S.A., but in Japan, a

TABLE 6.1

Tonnage of merchant vessels launched ('ooo gross registered tons)

	1953	1960	1970
Japan	557	1732	10 475
Sweden	485	711	1711
West Germany	818	1092	1687
Great Britain	1317	1331	1237
France	235	594	960
Spain	46	161	926
Norway	118	198	639
Italy	263	434	598
Denmark	142	219	514
U.S.A.	528	485	338
World	5095	8356	21 689

country that has industrialised relatively recently, and one that has an outstanding lead over other producers, it is instructive to examine the factors that have led to this situation. Output data for the leading countries appear in Table 6.1.

(i) *Labour costs*

The introduction of more advanced methods of construction has succeeded in reducing the importance of skilled labour requirements, but because it has not been possible to mass produce a large number of identical ships, the industry has remained labour intensive. Ships, like buildings, are mostly 'one-off' jobs in the sense that they are built to the requirements of individual customers, so the scope for mass production is limited. Such a situation does not favour the high wage economies. In the U.S.A., wages are 44% of the value of the product, compared with 15–20% in Britain. In the mid-1950s shipbuilding wages were estimated to be 75p/$2 per hour in the U.S.A., 30p/80c in Scandinavia, 19p/50c in Great Britain, 15p/40c in West Germany, 12p/33c in Italy and 4p/10c per hour in Japan.[14] It is not surprising that the absence of opportunities for mechanisation and high wage rates combine to make American output quite unimportant. The increasing size of ship has not brought the economies in labour needs that were originally anticipated. For tankers larger than 133 000 tons, labour requirements per ton of vessel actually increase, and it would seem as though these large ships are bigger than the optimum size in labour cost terms. This gives particular advantages to low wage economies for the construction of large tankers.

Sweden and West Germany among the high wage countries have had some success in offsetting labour costs by means of modified flow production techniques. These involve the construction of entirely new berths, such as those at Arendal where vessels are built under cover at the head of the dock and are slowly pushed out of the factory as building progresses. Enormous cranes capable of lifting 900 tons allow assemblies to be fitted to the ship as a unit, thereby saving labour charges. These methods have halved the time taken to complete a vessel compared with the traditional construction from keel to stack in an open dock. However, Japan, apart from being a low wage economy during the 1960s, also uses these methods. Moreover, the Japanese yards enjoy peculiar advantages which further reduce effective labour costs and improve productivity. An unspoken pledge of loyalty exists between the firm and its workpeople. It is the rule for a man to work for one firm for life, in return for which he is never dismissed or laid off, and can participate in a wide variety of fringe benefits such as low cost housing, subsidised food and free medical treatment. Strikes are virtually unknown, and although trade unions exist, they have little power. No such bond between labour and management exists elsewhere, while in the West unions have real power and frequently invoke the strike as a means of forcing wage increases. In Great Britain the number of days lost per 1000 workers per year between 1960 and 1964, as a result of industrial disputes, was 1457 for shipbuilding, compared with 667 for coalmining and 436 in engineering and vehicle production.[15] British unions are not even organised on an industry basis, as in Scandinavia, and each craft has its own representation, leading to involved demarcation disputes. Japanese labour is prepared to work round the clock shifts, further reducing the incidence of labour charges. Western yards have not been able to match these labour costs, and it is only in countries such as Spain, where it is possible to enforce collective wage agreements covering a number of years, that labour costs are being kept in check. As a footloose industry, shipbuilding is becoming oriented to labour on the global scale.

(ii) *Innovation*

The early innovators in iron ship construction were to be found in Britain, but leadership in this field passed to continental yards in the inter-war period, especially in respect of engine design. British shipbuilders tended to perpetuate the coal-fired tradition while builders elsewhere turned to the diesel engine. Between 1927 and 1930, Britain built 65% of the world's steam vessels, but only 41% of diesel ships. These were cheaper to run, they gave a better power to space ratio, and they allowed faster speeds to be maintained. Since 1950 the Japanese have been the great innovators. The Japanese ability to borrow technology from others 'and the ability to modify and blend the old and the new have given the country great flexibility and adaptability, often lacking in other countries'.[16] They pioneered the commercial production of ships by assembly line techniques, employing the methods used in the U.S.A. during the Second World War for the mass production of Liberty ships. They sought to emulate Henry Ford by the large-scale manufacture of diesel and turbine engines. The 'tear drop' bow, which improves speeds by as much as one-third without an increase in engine capacity, originated in Western Europe, but it was the Japanese who adopted it as standard in their tankers. The first vessel to be built with welded plates was launched by Cammell Laird at Birkenhead in 1919, but the welded ship was not wholly accepted as satisfactory in Great Britain until after 1955. Welded plates were employed in the Liberty ships, and the Japanese had no doubts as to their efficacy. By eliminating overlaps, welding allows a 10% saving in the weight of steel used.[17] By reorganising their existing yards and building others specially designed to permit the construction of large vessels by flow production methods, the Japanese have been able to reduce the time required for the completion of a ship to a quite remarkable degree. The relationship of the tonnage launched to the tonnage under construction is known as the turnover rate. A country which can launch a greater tonnage during the course of a year than it has under construction at the end of that year is said to have a high turnover rate. In 1969 Japan had a turnover rate of 200%, that is, the tonnage launched was twice the tonnage under construction at the end of the year. West Germany and Sweden had turnover rates of 120%, but the United Kingdom figure was only 60%. Obviously the faster a vessel can be completed, the more intensively can the building facilities be used, and the lower the price of the ship becomes. The Yokohama yard of Ishikawajima Harima Heavy Industries, completed in 1965 on reclaimed land, is capable of producing one tanker every two months, but the average time taken in Britain is between 10 and 14 months. The *British Admiral*, the subject of Fig. 83, took 12 months to complete.

(iii) *Integration*

We have seen how some British yards were integrated with steel firms. A similar situation exists in other countries, such as West Germany, where A. G. Weser at Bremen is controlled by Krupp. Since the nationalisation of the British steel industry, however, shipbuilding has lost its links with its steel suppliers. British yards have never been integrated with component suppliers, who often have small interest in shipbuilding as a market because of the fluctuating demand from this source. In Japan shipbuilding was one of the first branches of engineering to be established, and it therefore integrated backwards into the production of assemblies for shipbuilding. Diversification into electrical engineering followed. In this way the Tokyo Shibaura Electric Company grew out of the Ishikawajima Shipbuilding firm, and Mitsubishi Electric was established by Kobe Dockyard.[18] Since block building requires much work to be carried out by specialists, there are obvious advantages in integration of this kind. Although not all Japanese yards have their own blast furnaces and steel plants, steel can be obtained at favourable prices because of the close relationships, often financial, between the two industries. Integration in Japan is not limited to diversification into engineering, for shipbuilding itself is frequently one aspect of the many activities of the large trading companies, or zaibatsu. Sumitomo, for example, not only has chemical, glass, cement, electrical and mechanical engineering and iron and steel divisions in addition to shipbuilding, but is also involved in banking, insurance and real estate.

(iv) *Demand*

The realisation by oil refining, iron and steel and other industries in the last fifteen years that transport costs on bulky low-value materials can be greatly reduced by employing large ships, has led to a great upsurge in demand for such vessels. Those countries, such as Japan, that adapted their production lines to this particular specialisation were at a great advantage over countries, such as Britain which were geared to the construction of complex naval vessels and liners. The closure of the Suez canal in 1967, obliging tankers on the Middle East–Western Europe run to take the route round the Cape of Good Hope, has served to emphasise the value of large tankers for very long runs. It has been Japan that has benefited from these political events, although some West European yards are now in a position to build very large tankers. Japanese yards have been further assisted by the strong domestic demand for tankers and bulk carriers consequent upon the need to import a substantial proportion of such materials as coal, oil, iron ore and bauxite. On the other hand the high level of wages in the U.S.A. makes the cost of operating a ship with an American crew virtually prohibitive, resulting in an absence of a domestic market for ships.

(v) *Government support*

Shipbuilding in virtually every country has come to be regarded either as an instrument of national economic development or as a regional planning problem. None of the major building nations feels that the industry should be permitted to compete on the world market without some form of support, and there is no doubt that the map of world shipbuilding would be substantially different were it not for government assistance. It is very likely that there would be no commercial building in the U.S.A. at all in the absence of subsidies, which amount to 40% of the cost of a ship. Even in Japan, for all its efficiency, there is a long history of assistance dating from 1953 when the Japan Development Bank began to subsidise interest rates above 5% on loans by banks to yards. In order to stimulate the industry and encourage economic growth, the government has continued this cheap money policy in one form or another ever since. For example a Japanese shipowner can obtain 80% of the cost of a ship at 4% interest payable over 15 years, with a moratorium for the first three years. These generous terms for sales to the home market ensure that yards are kept fully occupied even if export orders are small. Vessels for export qualify for 8-year loans on 80% of the purchase price at 6% interest. In addition there is a 15% protective tariff on imported ships, making matters even more difficult for builders outside Japan.

The success of the Japanese yards obliged the governments of many competing countries to take retaliatory measures to prevent the closure of yards and to avoid the ensuing problems of localised unemployment. Thus in 1963 the British government introduced the Shipbuilding Credit Scheme under which mortgages of up to 80% of the cost of vessels, repayable over 10 years, were made available to British shipowners ordering in British yards. The government subsequently took a shareholding in Fairfields on Clydeside to allow this unprofitable yard to continue. In 1967 the Shipbuilding Industry Board recommended, and advanced money towards the creation of two large Clydeside groups in an attempt to improve profitability. Upper Clyde Shipbuilders was formed from John Brown at Clydebank, Yarrow at Scotstoun, Connell at Scotstoun, Stephen's at Linthouse and Fairfields at Govan. The Scott–Lithgow group was formed by the amalgamation of two firms by these names with yards at Greenock and Port Glasgow. Between 1966 and 1970, Upper Clyde Shipbuilders have received £20 million in government aid, and in February 1972 a further £35 million was allocated to the firm to prevent total collapse after the workers had taken over the yard and run it themselves. The Belfast yard of Harland and Wolff is an essential part of the regional economy, for it is the largest firm in Northern Ireland, employing 9% of the country's manufacturing labour. The firm received a grant of £8 million in 1970, and despite losses of £9 million in 1969, such is the socio-economic importance of the firm for Belfast that continued assistance seems likely. Cammell Laird at Birkenhead has also been saved from bankruptcy by government intervention. All the major yards in Britain are located in Development Districts and receive the relevant subsidies, which amount to 4% of the cost of a ship. Outside Britain, many of the most efficient yards in Scandinavia continue in existence because they are important employers of labour. The Swedish government has nationalised the Uddevalla yard, and it has been forced to intervene to prevent the collapse of Götaverken's extremely modern yard at Arendal, where 9000 people are employed. The Copenhagen yard of Burmeister and Wain, the largest Danish shipbuilding employer, is also in receipt of emergency credit from the government, although other Danish yards receive no assistance other than the preferential rates of interest recommended by the O.E.C.D.

The Spanish government supports its shipbuilding industry from a desire to promote the economic growth of the country, rather than to avoid the disruption of regional economies. As a result Spain has risen from a position of the world's twelfth largest shipbuilder in 1960 to sixth place in 1970. Shipbuilding is a traditional activity, there is an indigenous iron and steel industry, wages are relatively low, and the domestic demand for ships is considerable, but government action has been largely responsible for growth. Collective wage agreements have been negotiated to remove the possibility of unpredictable wage claims. All orders by Spanish owners must be placed in Spanish yards. Grants of 9% of the value of the ship, providing the engine is manufactured in Spain, the removal of import duties on tools, provided they cannot be supplied by a Spanish firm, and credits on new equipment of up to 70%, all provide very useful support for the yards. Export credits of 80% of the value of the ship at a rate of interest of 6% repayable over 8 years are available. Foreign orders are passed through Costrunaves, a central sales organisation, which then distributes the orders among the appropriate yards. Sometimes orders from developing countries are arranged against purchases of food and raw materials. Yards build each other's standard vessels if this proves necessary, and yet there is much yard specialisation. This has been fostered by the creation in 1969 of a state company, Astilleros Espanoles, involving the amalgamation of three private firms with yards at Cadiz, Seville, Bilbao and Gijon and engineering works at Bilbao, Cadiz, Manises near Valencia and Reinosa near Santander. This company now has two-thirds of Spanish yard capacity. The three Cadiz yards specialise in large tankers and the two yards in Bilbao build medium-sized vessels. However, to allow tankers of up to 400 000 tons to be built, the Cadiz yards are to be replaced by a completely new dock in the vicinity.

The price of a completed vessel is determined by a combination of the five factors we have considered. Thus the Geddes Report, 1966, considered British prices for cargo liners to be comparable with those quoted by European yards, but higher than Japanese prices. Dry cargo vessels were thought to be equal in price to vessels of this kind produced in Europe, but between 7½ and 15% more than the price of similar Japanese ships. In the case of tankers, British tankers were more costly than the Swedish product, and between 15 and 20% more expensive than those built in Japan.[19] It is thus apparent that the level of production is largely a function of a yard's ability to compete on the world market. If prices are too high in one area or yard, there will be contraction, while in other areas there will be expansion and the construction of new docks.

6.3 THE BRITISH RAILWAY ENGINEERING INDUSTRY

The construction of steam locomotives grew out of the production of stationary steam engines. Although the most prolific builders of the latter were Boulton and Watt at the Soho Manufactory in Birmingham, they could be, and were, produced at various locations in coalmining and metalworking districts for use both in these and other areas of the country. The most important producing districts were the industrial areas of Lancashire, the West Riding of Yorkshire and north-east England. It is not surprising that steam locomotive construction was first embarked upon on a large scale in the same areas. By 1840, 21 of the 32 locomotive workshops were to be found in the three regions mentioned.[20] With the exception of the works in London and that at Wolverton, Buckinghamshire, the remaining works were sited on coalfields, the great manufacturing districts of the 19th century. The great upsurge of railway building in Britain and elsewhere caught the railway engineering industry unawares, and the railway companies were forced to enter the industry themselves to ensure a reasonable supply of locomotives. There were other advantages, however, for repairs could be carried out more rapidly than if engines had to be returned to the makers, and company-built locomotives were found to be more reliable than those built 'privately'. Since many railway systems did not run through Lancashire, the West Riding or the North-East, or even through a coalfield at all, and since most of the larger companies had set up their own works by 1860, it follows that some company-owned plants deviated from the established pattern of location. Plants such as those at Wolverton (1838), Crewe (1843), Swindon (1843) and Ashford (1847) represent the establishment of a footloose industrial activity at a very early date in industrial history.

THE DEVELOPMENT OF RAILWAY COMPANY WORKS

Works operated by private firms in the 19th century were material-oriented. They used coal and coke for heating and for their furnaces, and large tonnages of iron and steel were required. By mid-century, locomotives weighed approximately 25 tons, almost wholly iron. These supplies were obtainable at least cost on coalfields. Markets, that is the railway companies, were spread throughout the country, and they also existed overseas, for example, in Belgium, France, the U.S.A., and later in the countries of South America and Africa. In contrast, many railway companies were obliged to bring their coal, iron and steel supplies from the coalfields, and they were equally obliged to offer inducements to skilled craftsmen to leave the established engineering districts for works often set up in rural, dominantly agricultural areas. In spite of these difficulties, the railway companies continued the practice of building most of their own locomotives to the end of the steam era in the early 1960s. We must presume, therefore, that Wolverton, Swindon and Ashford lay within the spatial profitability margins for the locomotive engineering industry in Great Britain. If this had not been the case, the railways would have found it more economic to purchase their engines from the private builders on the coalfields. As passenger and freight traffic developed, the railways also found it profitable to establish their own carriage and wagon works, rather than take deliveries from

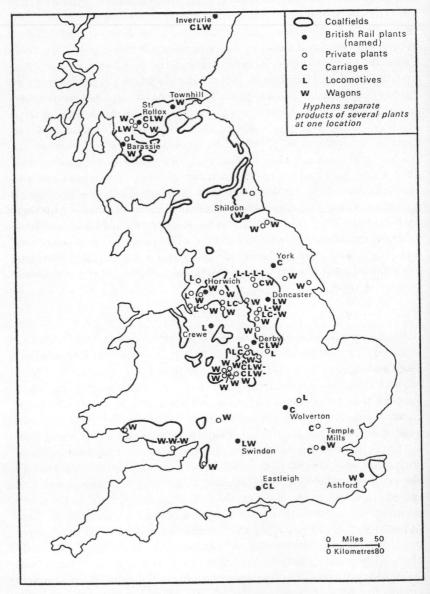

Fig. 84 The British railway engineering industry, 1969

suppliers in the industrial districts. Many carriage and wagon works were set up adjacent to existing locomotive plants, including those in rural districts, so that in this aspect also the railway engineering industry could be termed footloose by mid-19th century.

Footloose industries always allow entrepreneurs a wide range of choice of location. The railway engineering industry was such that it allowed the railways successfully to set up works off the coalfields. Following this, the precise site of the works within each company system was entirely the result of boardroom decisions, or behavioural factors. Different railway companies came to different conclusions as to the best site for their works, and this lack of uniformity is to be expected with such freedom in the choice of location. As the railways developed, small companies were taken over by larger organisations. In 1923 more than 150 different companies were grouped into four systems, and finally in 1948 these four were unified and British Railways created. Only one works, the Townhill steel wagon works (1961), has been built since nationalisation, in part because of the contraction of the system and in part because of geographical inertia, with the consequence that engineering has continued at historic sites. Some works have been closed and those that remain are in strategic positions on the national network, but nevertheless the precise location of the existing works, shown in Fig. 84, can best be understood by considering each works in the context of the system as it existed both at the time of the decision to build, and on the occasion of subsequent mergers. British Rail's (British Railways became British Rail in 1966) workshops can be classified into four groups according to their relationship to the system they served before 1923.

(i) *Works central to the system*

The choice of the most nodal point in the network is an obvious solution, given that the network does not include an important engineering district. Deliveries of materials, finished locomotives and rolling stock, and of vehicles for repair, can be most easily effected, and therefore at least cost, when the works is centrally situated. For a works to continue in existence, however, it was necessary that it should also be central to the network as it expanded, whether this be a result of amalgamations or the laying of new routes. Wolverton was chosen by the London and Birmingham Railway because it was mid-way between the two termini, and it was subsequently retained on similar grounds by the London and Northwestern Railway. Swindon was mid-way between London and Bristol, the main line of the Great Western Railway, and despite the considerable expansion by this company, involving the purchase of more than 40 railway companies, the works retained a focal position within the

P

system. The South Eastern Railway selected Ashford for its works because of its position on the London to Dover route, and under the aegis of the larger South Eastern and Chatham Railway the town became an important junction. York and Inverurie were nodal points on the North Eastern Railway and the Great North of Scotland Railway systems respectively. These works were established in rural areas or in towns with no engineering tradition, and as such they make up the most footloose of the four categories of works.

(ii) *Works marginal to the system*

The powerful influence exerted by London on railways in Britain, causing many companies to have stations and depots in the capital, also resulted in some companies setting up works close to their London termini. Although not on a coalfield, London is an important engineering area not lacking in skilled labour. The works at Stratford was opened in 1847 by the Eastern Counties Railway, and became the main plant of the Great Eastern Railway in 1862, in preference to more central towns such as Norwich and Cambridge. Fortunately the site of the Stratford works in the Lea valley was capable of being expanded, and the plant was used by British Rail until the mid-1960s when operations in London were transferred to the adjacent Temple Mills works. Other marginal works in London were forced to migrate, usually to central locations, because of the difficulty of acquiring adjacent land for expansion. Examples include the shift of locomotive production from Longhedge to Ashford in 1900, and from Nine Elms to Eastleigh in 1888 (rolling stock) and in 1909 (locomotives).

(iii) *Works central to the system with good access to materials*

These works were able to combine the advantages of nodality with the main advantage of the private plants, that is, low cost materials and low cost, skilled labour. At Swindon, Ashford and Eastleigh, for example, the companies were obliged to build houses and other facilities for their workpeople. Derby (1839) was central to the networks of both the Midland Counties and the Midland Railways. It was also an engineering and industrial town of importance. The same holds true for Shildon (1826) on the Stockton and Darlington Railway and later the North Eastern Railway, Horwich (1884) on the Lancashire and Yorkshire Railway and Barassie on the Glasgow and South Western Railway. Crewe (1843) was established in a purely rural area by the London and North Western Railway, and a company settlement created, but it is close to the North Staffordshire coalfield and had very much better access to materials than works in the south of England.

(iv) *Works marginal to the system with good access to materials*

Companies whose network was close to industrial districts at its periphery had to choose between a central and a marginal location for their works. The Great Northern Railway initially preferred a central works at Boston, Lincolnshire, mid-way between its termini at Grimsby and Peterborough. The completion of the London to York route in 1852 rendered Boston unsuitable and made Peterborough the most central site. However, the company decided that the advantages of a marginal works at Doncaster, capable of receiving coal and iron supplies from the nearby West Riding coalfield by means of existing railways, were greater than those of a nodal works at Peterborough. The works was opened in 1853 and craftsmen were brought from Boston. The St Rollox, Glasgow works of the Caledonian Railway on the highly industrialised Lanarkshire coalfield, was also marginal in relation to the network, although the Glasgow district itself generated a great deal of traffic, and the works might alternatively be regarded as central with good access to materials.

Unlike most industries that have been studied, the railway engineering industry is declining. As recently as 1962 British Rail had 30 works compared with 15 in 1969. Therefore, rather than accounting for the location of new plants, it is necessary to seek reasons for the retention of these 15 works in particular. In normal competitive conditions, it could be assumed that the closed works had become unprofitable and had been forced to cease operations. However, in public corporations such as British Rail, cost comparisons are not the only criteria to be used. Just as the British and French governments have been responsible for the dispersal of automobile manufacture as part of regional policy, so British Rail has had to consider the effect of closing works on the local employment situation. Many of the settlements in which works were built have become 'railway towns' in which employment in railway workshops is a very large proportion of the total. In 1962, 58% of the male working population of Horwich was employed in railway workshops; the data for other settlements were: Crewe 34%, Wolverton 30%, Swindon 22% and Darlington 15%. The data for Inverurie are unavailable, but the figure was probably higher than that for Crewe. An additional consideration is alternative employment opportunity. Although one-fifth of male employment in Swindon was in railway engineering, the town is not short of alternative jobs. The same cannot be said of Horwich, Crewe, Wolverton and Inverurie.

A second important factor is the need for works to be strategically dispersed. Most works are now more concerned with repair than construction, and it is important that vehicles spend as short a time as possible moving to and from workshops. Thus while it was necessary to compare the efficiency of two or three works in one area, it was not necessary to compare the efficiency of all works.[21] It was irrelevant that Darlington was more efficient than Swindon, because there could be no question of Swindon's servicing locomotives from the North East. These strategic considerations ruled out the possibility of reaping economies of scale, at least in locomotive building and repair. It is thought that two works would be sufficient for this purpose, and Crewe and Derby would be best suited by virtue of their low operating costs. However, because of the high cost of depreciation on diesel locomotives (£35 per day on a locomotive costing £110 000).[22] locomotive works must be dispersed throughout the system. Fig. 84 indicates that in 1969 they were at Inverurie, St Rollox, Doncaster, Crewe, Derby, Swindon and Eastleigh. Carriage and wagon production and repair could not be carried out in only two plants, but here again strategic factors result in a dispersed distribution pattern. Efficiency and social and strategic influences have, together with historic site factors, created the present-day map of British Rail's engineering workshops. It is interesting to see that Darlington's efficiency was not sufficient to ensure its retention.

THE DEVELOPMENT OF PRIVATE WORKS

In the inter-war period, many private firms began to experiment with diesel and electric traction. The Hunslet Engine Company of Leeds first made a diesel locomotive in 1927 for example. By the time that British Railways made the decision in 1956 to re-equip with these forms of traction, the private builders had had considerable experience in the production of diesel and electric engines for overseas markets. The railways therefore chose to purchase their power units and transmissions from private builders, and in some cases whole classes of assembled locomotives have been bought. Thus the 509 locomotives of class 47/48, with Sulzer engines and Brush transmissions, were assembled by Brush at Loughborough. British Rail is now effectively a locomotive assembler rather than a builder.

The steam locomotive is a simple piece of engineering. Its manufacture is normally effected in one integrated plant. Diesel and electric locomotives are very much more complex pieces of machinery, and like the automobile require a great many specialised parts, usually made by specialist firms. Linkages between plants are important, and there are advantages to be gained from a location within main manufacturing areas. The coalfields have become the principal heavy engineering producers, and it is here that the private railway engineering firms are to be found, although they are not material oriented as were their steam-building predecessors. Only one firm building locomotives is located away from the coalfields, Motor Rail at Bedford. However, many firms purchase engines and transmissions from specialist producers such as Perkins at Peterborough, A.E.C. at Southall, London, and Rolls Royce at Shrewsbury. These specialist firms cannot be regarded as part of railway engineering, since they make engines for a variety of industries, so their location away from coalfields does not imply a dispersal of railway engineering. Other specialists are to be found on, or close to, coalfields; these include English Electric-A.E.I. at Preston, Manchester and Sheffield and Gardner Diesel at Manchester. Only two carriage and diesel multiple unit manufacturers, Park Royal in London and Wickham at Ware, Hertfordshire, are located outside the heavy industrial districts. Of the wagon producers, only three, at Gloucester, Radstock, Somerset, and Hull, are distinctly nonconformist.

Since private plants are not encumbered by social and strategic considerations, we would expect a less dispersed pattern of distribution. Indeed, 44 of the 50 plants are in the heavy engineering districts. The existence of 6 plants outside this area, which might be regarded as the profitable area, suggest the situation envisaged by Pred in his behavioural matrix (Fig. 31). He would argue that in respect of their location the 6 nonconforming firms have poor information and low ability to use that information. However, since the 6 plants are at no great distance from the engineering areas, and they have, in most cases, been established for more than half a century, it can be alternatively argued that all 50 plants lie within the area of profitability and that there are no nonconforming works at all. In the same way it can be assumed that within the context of a public corporation, the 7 railway company works lying outside the coalfield areas are within the area of profitability. Since only 6 of the 50 private plants are located outside the heavy industrial districts, compared with 7 of the 15 railway workshops, we may conclude that the spatial profitability margins of the private plants are more constricted than those of the plants operated by British Rail. Because of social factors and the importance of vehicle repairing to railway workshops, the latter are more footloose than those of private firms.

References

1. Neil P. Hurley, 'The Automotive Industry. A Study in Industrial Location', *Land Economics*, 35, 1959, p. 1.
2. *The World's Automobiles, 1880–1925*, London, 1958.
3. S. B. Saul, 'The Motor Industry in Britain to 1914', *Business History*, V, No. 1, 1962, p. 25.
4. J. B. Rae, *American Automobile Manufacturers*, 1959, p. 60.

5. Graham Turner, *The Car Makers*, Penguin, 1964, p. 22.

6. Michael Beesley, 'Changing Locational Advantages in the British Motor Industry', *Journal of Industrial Economics*, VI, No. 1, October 1957, p. 51.

7. Graham Turner, *op. cit.*, p. 50.

8. *The Observer*, London, 21.1.68.

9. B. P. Birch, 'Locational Trends in the American Car Industry', *Geography*, November 1966, p. 375.

10. Neil P. Hurley, *op. cit.*, p. 9.

11. J. W. Alexander, *Economic Geography*, Prentice Hall, 1963, p. 376.

12. *The Economist*, London, 14.11.70.

13. E. W. Miller, *A Geography of Manufacturing*, Prentice Hall, London, 1962, p. 377.

14. E. B. Alderfer and H. E. Michl, *Economics of American Industry*, 3rd ed., McGraw-Hill, 1957, p. 147.

15. *Report of the Shipbuilding Inquiry Committee, 1965-6*, (Geddes Report), H.M.S.O., 1966, p. 105.

16. R. B. Hall, *Japan: Industrial Power of Asia*, Van Nostrand, 1963, p. 89.

17. A. K. Cairncross and J. R. Parkinson, 'The Shipbuilding Industry' in Duncan Burn (Ed.), *The Structure of British Industry*, Vol II, Cambridge University Press, 1958, p. 115.

18. G. C. Allen, *Japan's Economic Expansion*, Oxford University Press, 1965, p. 40.

19. *Report of the Shipbuilding Inquiry Committee, op. cit.*, p. 27.

20. B. J. Turton, 'The British Railway Engineering Industry: a Study in Economic Geography', *Tijdschrift voor Economische en Sociale Geografie*, 58, 1967, p. 194.

21. P. Lesley Cook, *Railway Workshops: The Problems of Contraction*, University of Cambridge, Department of Applied Economics Occasional Papers No. 2, 1964, p. 51.

22. *Ibid.*, p. 17.

CONCLUSION

There are a number of factors that influence the location of a manufacturing plant, but the extent to which any one of these factors has a bearing on that location depends, for example, upon the nature of the industry, its degree of technological sophistication, the time period in question and upon the political and socio-economic environment. The way in which location factors interact with one another is complex, and this has led to considerable differences in the models advanced by writers on industrial location. Later models are very often refinements of earlier ones, so that Hoover, who stresses the importance of transport, owes much to Weber, whose main concern is to find a least-cost location by minimising transport costs. In the same way an important springboard for the behavioural school is the work of the marginal location school. To some extent the locational schools considered are products of their time. It is no accident that it is the earliest writer, Alfred Weber, who regards the cost of moving weight-losing materials as critical, for this was indeed an important consideration for 19th-century manufacturing. Technological changes and the development of high value-adding industries have allowed entrepreneurs much greater locational flexibility than was once possible. With this freedom to choose a viable location within manufacturing belts has come models which reject the idea of an optimum point—whether it is least cost or maximum profit—and see the precise siting of a factory as dependent upon the decisions made by manufacturers who possess less than perfect knowledge, and who are hardly likely therefore to find the optimum point. Weber considers both materials and markets, although he ignores the price mechanism, while Losch ignores materials and concentrates on markets, the shape of market areas and competition between plants. The marginal location and behavioural schools are less concerned with industries that are clearly located in respect of materials and markets than with providing a rationale of the location of the footloose industries.

One of the most important trends to have occurred in the 20th century has been the diminishing significance of materials upon the location of manufacturing. Changes in the technology of power, transport and processing are the root cause, and the result has been that only a small number of industries are still drawn to the source of their material supplies. Even then developments in processing have frequently allowed the separation of the various stages of manufacture, so that only the initial processing need be carried out close to the source of the material.

The copper and paper and pulp industries are cases in point; both transform low-value materials which lose weight in processing. There are great advantages in avoiding transport costs on material a large part of which is destined to become waste, and copper concentrating mills and pulp mills are therefore material-oriented. Subsequent stages of manufacture have greater locational flexibility, and are frequently, although by no means always, to be found at markets. The importance of movement-minimisation renders the Weberian model of considerable relevance to the explanation of the distribution of material-oriented industries such as these.

Like copper ore and wood, coal is a low-value material, and while it was employed to provide industry with both fuel and power, there were obvious incentives for entrepreneurs to take up a coalfield location. The use of water power was even more restrictive upon location for a riverside site was obligatory. However, the advent of oil, natural gas and electric power has severely reduced the pull of the sources of energy. One method of studying the effect of water and coal upon the distribution of manufacturing is to select an industry whose location has barely changed since the water- and steam-power era. The textile industry is such an example. Possessing great geographical inertia, it has not substantially altered its pattern of distribution since the development of the factory, and the present situation in Western Europe reflects the influence of water and coal as sources of power. Many mills, notably in the upland areas, are at water-power sites, although they now use electricity, and the majority of the remainder are on or adjacent to coalfields. In the U.S.A. the strength of the inertia of the old-established district, New England, has been insufficient to retain the industry at its former level, and modern mills, their location uninfluenced by power considerations, have sprung up in the South.

Just as technological changes in power supplies have endowed textile mills with mobility, so developments in some of the industries which process low-value material—iron and steel and aluminium production for instance—have had the same effect. Additionally the weight lost in initial processing is less and the value of the raw material is greater than in the case of copper manufacture, emphasising the wider scope for location. The result is that the industries mentioned are multi-locational, for in some circumstances they may have plants at the material source, at the origin of electric power, at historic sites, at the market or at a break of bulk point. Transport costs are still important, and in this respect there is similarity to the material-oriented industries. Indeed, the Weberian model may profitably be used to assist in the explanation of the locational pattern. However, distortions of the model occur because of the international basis of these industries; tariffs on semi-finished materials (alumina) may cause imports of the raw material (bauxite) to take place, and political events may both encourage the development of plants (aluminium smelters) and in other places lead to migration (oil refineries from the Middle East).

Transport costs are an important consideration for those industries whose products, rather than materials, are expensive to move. Because these activities frequently sell their output to the final consumer, they exhibit a close correlation with the distribution of population, and are hence known as the residentiary or market-oriented industries. Once again technological change has played an important part in geographical patterns. In both brewing and town gas manufacture plants have become larger and methods of transport more efficient, with the result that there has been a marked reduction in the number of breweries and gasworks. At the same time migration from small towns to medium and large towns has occurred. Losch's model is useful here in that it is possible to contrast his ideas regarding the hexagonal shape of market areas and monopolistic competition with reality. Furniture manufacture is a case of a residentiary industry which is associated with cities and only sporadically with smaller towns. Some market-oriented industries are linked to industrial or intermediate markets; the British textile machinery industry correlates closely with the distribution of the textile industry.

A large number of 20th-century industries are not located in respect of materials or markets, but are distributed throughout broad areas. Typical is automobile manufacture. Their locational criteria are very flexible for they consume a large number of semi-finished materials, they market their products throughout a nation or continent, or often the entire world, and transport costs are not especially significant. Since manufacturers have considerable choice of site, they tend not to seek the least cost or maximum profit location, and are thus satisficers rather than optimisers. The models postulated by Rawstron and Smith concerning the margins of profitability are most helpful in the understanding of the distribution pattern of the increasingly numerous footloose industries. Recourse may be had to Pred's behavioural model for an explanation of the precise site chosen.

APPENDIX

Since the examples in the foregoing chapters are selective, some of the more important manufacturing industries are listed in their appropriate locational categories in the table below. For a definition of these categories, the reader is referred to the appropriate chapter in the text.

Classification of industries according to their locational category

Material-oriented industries	Power-oriented industries	Multi-locational industries*	Market-oriented industries	Footloose industries
Copper manufacture	Hydro-electric power generation	Iron & steel RM, bb, M	Towns gas	Automobiles
Zinc manufacture	Textiles (in developed countries)	Aluminium RM, bb, P	Brewing	Shipbuilding
Cement		Oil refining RM, bb, M	Baking	Railway engineering
Fruit and vegetable canning		Petrochemicals RM, bb, M	Soft drink bottling	Aircraft
Beet sugar refining		Fertilisers RM, bb	Clothing	Instruments
Cane sugar production		Industrial chemicals RM, bb	Furniture	Electronic products
		Carbochemicals RM, bb	Textile machinery	Consumer durables
		Thermal electric power generation RM, bb, M		Man-made fibres
		Meat packing RM, M		Plastics
		Flour milling RM, bb, M		Synthetic rubber
				Textiles (in emergent countries)

* Categories of site at which these industries may occur are shown by means of the following abbreviations: RM, material source. bb, break of bulk point, whether coastal or riverine. M, market. P, source of hydro-electric power.

INDEX